TOFU

TOFU

A CULINARY HISTORY

RUSSELL THOMAS

REAKTION BOOKS

For Joy, who preferred jellied eel

Published by
REAKTION BOOKS LTD
Unit 32, Waterside
44–48 Wharf Road
London N1 7UX, UK
www.reaktionbooks.co.uk

First published 2024

Printed and bound in India by Replika Press Pvt. Ltd

A catalogue record for this book is available from the
British Library

ISBN 978 1 78914 953 1

CONTENTS

INTRODUCTION

Tofu has been, is and probably always will be an integral part of East and Southeast Asian cuisine. It appears in many guises, like the different avatars of one highly nutritious deity. Whether it's fried, fermented, dried or raw, there's no discounting the multitude of uses for this variously textured foodstuff, nor its history in feeding the multitudes, from peasants to the nobility, from Buddhist monks to modern vegetarians. Tofu has been, is and to some extent may remain an alien insertion to Western cuisine, where it is often misunderstood. Whether this is due to its association with vegetarianism and left-leaning politics, or a lack of familiarity with its texture, there is no getting away from its pariah status. In the East, tofu is a treasured ingredient, component of myriad dishes. In the West, it has always been a replacement. It is this adoption and adaptation of tofu, bent to the whim of Western palates, scorned by carnivores, that keeps it somewhat separate from mainstream Western cuisine.

A typical plate of *hiyayakko*. Literally meaning 'cold servant' in Japanese, the name for *hiyayakko* is thought to derive from the square pattern typically seen on the clothing of *yakko* (servants).

Tofu is the poster child of vegetarianism. In the eyes of many in the West it's a meat substitute, but in many Asian cuisines tofu and meat can be found in the same dish. The Japanese staple nikudofu literally means 'meat and tofu' and even the simple hiyayakko (chilled tofu) is topped with katsuobushi (dried bonito flakes). The most famous Korean treatment of tofu, sundubu-jjigae, often contains meat, while wanja-jeon are tofu and minced-beef patties. Over in Indonesia, gulai tambusu (or gulai usus) – a dish in the Minang cuisine of West Sumatra[1] – consists of beef intestine stuffed with tofu and egg, cooked with curry sauce, kind of like a sausage. In China, xiehuang doufu involves tofu cooked in a stew of crab roe.[2] Tofu is a much-loved co-star, soaking up meaty, saucy goodness in its silky smooth, yielding texture for added variation.

WHAT IS TOFU?

According to a composite of definitions of tofu from a slew of notable English-language dictionaries, tofu is a soft, pale, white, bland, flavourless, cheese-like curd made from soybeans (also called soya beans), packed with protein. The emphasis on the flavourlessness of tofu is telling; evidently in the anglophone world, this is something that readers must know. The soybeans are boiled, mashed, coagulated and drained, roughly in that order, before being pressed into a just-solid block. This process is relatively simple, but laborious. First you need to soak the soybeans in water for several hours, then grind them, and filter to remove the dregs. Voila: you have soy (or soya) milk. This resulting liquid should then be boiled, stirring all the while. This is when the temperature is lowered slightly and coagulants are added, much like the cheese-making process. A sixteenth-century Chinese source, the groundbreaking encyclopaedia-meets-medical text

Compendium of Materia Medica written by Li Shizhen (a 'kind of patron saint of Chinese herbal medicine'), lists a variety of tofu-creating coagulants.[3] These include *cu* (vinegar), *yanlu* (bittern salts), *suan jiang* (physalis) and *shigao* (gypsum), but 'probably anything salty, sour, bitter or pungent can be used'.[4] When curds have formed, strain through a cloth and press them. That's how you make tofu, generally speaking. The exact method and what coagulants are used varies, and nowadays it's possible to boil at optimal temperatures and bring the temperature down to add coagulant, but centuries ago making tofu would have been an enterprise of experience.

How best to eat tofu has always been subject to question, illustrated in part by the many varieties of tofu and the countless recipes that feature it. It has also been frequently up for debate, to such an extent that there is a north–south divide in China based on tofu. Salty or sweet *douhua*? The subject blew up on the

Hagino Tofu: a humble shop with two centuries of history nestled in the mountains of Hakone, Japan.

Chinese social network Weibo in the summer of 2011 with a post that began, 'The question of sweet or salty tofu curd jelly is the greatest difference between north and south.' Tens of thousands of comments later, fence-sitters were few and far between, with posts and abuse flying from the two factions: *tian dang* ('sweet party') and *xian dang* ('salty party').[5] Generally, *douhua* in southern China is a dessert, a sweet snack served cold; in the north, it is spicy and decidedly savoury. In 2013, netizens clearly of *tian dang* persuasion took to Barack Obama's *We the People* petitioning initiative on the White House website with a petition of their own: 'We politely request that the U.S. government establish that the official flavour of tofu curd should be sweet, by adding syrup, granulated sugar, brown sugar or other sweeteners.'[6] This example demonstrates that the cultural importance attached to tofu, something explored later in this book, is unmistakable.

THE HEALTH QUESTION

Tofu was hailed as a superfood when it was first properly 'discovered' by the Western world in the early twentieth century and then later in the 1970s. Both waves of tofu inception saw it taking on the role of something that could replace meat – something this book looks at in more detail in Chapter Four. More recent research, however, has superseded this somewhat basic approach to looking at tofu and soy products in general. While it does very well as a meat substitute, thanks to its high protein content, tofu is also cholesterol-free, low in sodium and a good source of calcium, iron and B vitamins. Studies abound that look more deeply into the alleged health benefits of soy and tofu.[7]

Bone health can benefit from bean curd; one study in Singapore that followed 63,257 men and women for more than seven years found that eating more tofu decreased hip fracture

The gift that keeps on giving: tofu production results not just in the bean curd itself, but by-products like *okara* (dregs) and *yuba* (tofu skin). Here *yuba* is served topped with *konbu* (kelp), spring onions and young bean shoots.

risk by 30 per cent in women (though not men).[8] A 2018 study found a significantly lower risk of cerebral haemorrhage in women under 65 who ate tofu regularly.[9] The isoflavones in tofu and soy foods can also lower low-density lipoprotein (LDL) or 'bad' cholesterol, which is the type that clings to the walls of blood vessels and leads to increased risk of heart disease.[10] These isoflavones seem to work: eating a serving of tofu once or more per week, as opposed to once per month, is associated with a decreased risk of coronary heart disease – even more so in young women and post-menopausal women not on hormone replacement therapy.[11] The predominant isoflavone in tofu, genistein, may also inhibit the growth of cancer cells.[12] It turns out it is something of a superfood after all.

WHEN IS TOFU NOT TOFU?

All soybean curd is tofu, but not all tofu is soybean curd, controversial as that may seem. Tofu is more of a visual, textural descriptor, as many foods get the 'tofu' name without involving soybeans or a curdling process. Though not strictly tofu, a curd made from pig's blood is called zyu hung in Cantonese, but is known in Mandarin as xue doufu, literally 'blood tofu'. Less meaty, but still far from vegan, is egg tofu. Called tamago-dōfu in Japanese, it contains neither soybeans nor coagulant, the egg itself (and steaming) providing the necessary solidity. An egg tofu of sorts, actually a composite of both tofu and egg together, is sold in Thailand (also Hong Kong), often in squeezable plastic packs. In Japan there is also goma-dōfu (sesame tofu); annin-dōfu (apricot kernel tofu); edamame tofu, which is made using young green soybeans; kurumi-tōfu (walnuts); and jimami-dōfu (peanuts). Chickpeas are used in to hpu, better known as Burmese tofu, while black soybeans create hei doufu (black tofu) in China. Because of these various raw materials at the root of a spectrum of tofu, anything that resembles tofu can be fairly dubbed so.

Take the Chinese jidou liangfen, for example, which is a gelatinous mixture also made from chickpeas. Historically this was also referred to as 'black tofu', but it belongs to a separate branch of self-coagulating or starch-solidified, rather than curdled, dishes: liangfen (literally 'cold powder') or jelly. There are regional varieties of these in China, but they are equally famous in Korea, where they are called muk. Here they range from dotori-muk (acorn jelly) to memil-muk (buckwheat jelly) and nokdu-muk (mung bean jelly). A similar concoction in Japan is konnyaku, made from the tuberous roots of the konjac plant.

Away from jelly, the process of curdling a liquid other than animal milk has implications that stretch the boundary of what

Piinatsu tōfu, otherwise known as *jiimāmi tōfu* (peanut tofu), is one of many products called 'tofu' not made from soybeans. Hailing from the Ryukyu Islands (present-day Okinawa), peanut tofu was once eaten only on special occasions but is now more readily available.

constitutes 'tofu' way beyond China, Japan and South Korea. In fact, European nobles may once have hankered after similarly textured dishes. Among others in the English cookbook compendium *The Forme of Cury* (c. 1390), compiled by the master cooks of King Richard II, one recipe for 'crème of almaundes' is interesting.

Take Almaundes blaunched, grynde hem and drawe hem up thykke, set hem ouer the fyre & boile hem. set hem adoun and spryng hem wicii Vyneger, cast hem abrode uppon a cloth and cast uppon hem sugur. whan it is colde gadre it togydre and leshe it in dysshes.[13]

These soy milk noodles are equal parts refreshing for a hot day and packed with the fiery kick of *doubanjiang*, topped off with chewy noodles, the crunch of cucumber and the comforting yield of tofu.

That is, almond milk that has been curdled with vinegar, strained through a cloth, chilled, sliced and served, just like a recipe for tofu. It is less an almond crème and more like almond cheese, solid and separable by knife. Had this recipe started 'Take *Soybeans* blaunched . . .' we would have had a fourteenth-century European variant of tofu on our hands. Imported almonds and their milk (a dairy substitute in Lent when milk and cheese, like meat and sex, were forbidden) were the preserve of the rich at this time. Almonds are thought to originate in Central Asia, from where they spread east and west.[14] This English recipe and ones like it in Persia, as well as analogues in Asia, may share a common ancestor. It is hard to believe that similar dishes in the kitchens of the wealthy were isolated incidents along such a crossroads of trade. Coagulation doesn't exist in a vacuum, which sheds light on the as yet unproven but probable non-Han Chinese roots of tofu, however dimly.

To trace the global history of tofu we need to go further back. Much further. This book begins with a chapter dedicated to the birth of tofu, how linguistics and myths may place its origin. Moving on, we take a detour in the next chapter concerning the evolution of tofu regarding its preservation and fermentation, creating valuable members of the bean curd family. In the third chapter, we chart tofu's inevitable spread across East and South-east Asia thanks to maritime trade, and its more modern spread to Central Asia, South America and Africa via immigration, deportation and soft power plays. The fourth chapter dives into the Western world's first contact with tofu, excavating early prejudices that persist to this day. Following that is a look at tofu's cultural impact, from idioms and slang to religious practices and depictions in the media. Lastly, Chapter Six examines tofu as a globalized foodstuff and as an industry both booming and yet in decline, tethered to environmentally unfriendly soybean production and evolving with the world's changing dietary requirements.

The story of this foodstuff, as niche as it is institutional, takes twists and turns through a foodscape littered with intrigue. The journey of tofu begins with a quest for immortality (or was it an attempt to make cheese?), after which the curd becomes the inspiration for courtly poets; is offered to the gods; is eaten by ghosts; is left to rot; transforms into a thousand different dishes; gets mixed up with political intrigue, immigration, racism, war; turns salty; goes sweet; gets past life regression and remembers being born from the brain of an ancient deity; joins hippies; feeds the world; gets delivered by fictional boy racers; fights zombies; and winds up in a supermarket near you. Its twisting, mysterious history is anything but bland.

ONE
LIU AN AND LI QI:
ANCIENT ORIGINS OF TOFU

Once upon a time in China there lived a king. Liu An was his name. He ruled over the kingdom of Huainan. There was nothing Liu An liked more than alchemy, the principal aim of which (or at least one of them) is to find the key to immortality. Liu An was obsessed with this quest. He surrounded himself with a cohort of thinkers and fellow alchemists, and together they searched for the recipe to eternal life, among many other esoteric wanderings of the mind. One day, so the story goes, Liu An soaked beans in water, crushed them, filtered out their juice and cooked the shimmering white liquid with a concoction of secret ingredients, hoping to create an elixir for longevity. As he stirred the mixture, a sour, acrid mist curling in the gloam of early morning, it began to curdle and solidify. Taking a tentative taste of the creamy white potion, he was surprised to find it soft, supple and tasty. It was tofu.

Or something like that. Nobody really knows when or how tofu was first discovered and who made it. Nor are they ever likely to know, probably. The exact story was never written down. In this first chapter charting the global history of tofu, attempts

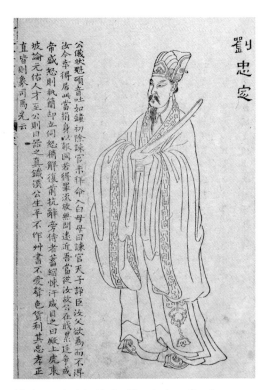

Liu An, as depicted in the *Wanxiaotang Zhuzhuang Huazhuan* (1743), an illustrated biography by Shangguan Zhou (active 1665–c. 1750).

have been made to grasp at the ghosts of the past, taking a trip through tomes of pharmacology, poetry, funeral songs and observations, analysing mythology and archaeological sites, and tracing the linguistic spread of the very word 'tofu' to ascertain when and where it may have been conceived. There are definitely more legends than the one ascribed to Liu An, some attached to figures of times more ancient still, and these have been analysed in their turn.

Liu An (179–122 BC) certainly existed, but his attachment to the invention of tofu is legendary, even mythical. With no solid evidence, the claim that he invented tofu, or that the invention of tofu occurred any time near his reign, is about as truthful as any ancient origin myth from the Maya to the Minoan and everything in between. His court is much peddled as the origin point of tofu, and this dating of two millennia is so common that it has become something of a truth. There are incorrect claims such as, 'the first recorded use of tofu was during the Han dynasty over 2,000 years ago,' or that it is a 'meat alternative that originated 2,000 years ago in China', or that tofu 'originated in China around 2,000 years ago'.[1] The surety of these statements and preambles – hundreds of them littering vegan blogs, tofu company websites, news outlets – ranges from acknowledgement of the story as a legend all the way to factual reportage. Though widely accepted as a tentative truth, it lacks real evidence and so the exploration of this as an actual event, and of the potential of it having happened at all, is necessary.

First, who even was Liu An? He was the grandson of Liu Bang (256–195 BC), founder of the Han dynasty, which ruled large swathes of China from the third century BC to the third century AD. Liu An was an aficionado of Huang-Lao, a politico-philosophical branch of Taoism, and is credited with writing a book about it, the *Huainanzi*.[2] This was 'an early Western Han [202 BC–AD 9] cosmological text, produced at the court of the kingdom of Huainan', more likely a product of various literati in this loose academy than a solo effort.[3] His dabbling in the Tao attracted attention. 'Liu An became very popular and all men of talent resorted to him,' writes scholar and missionary Evan Morgan (1860–1941) in his 1933 treatise on Taoism, referring to Liu's own academic talents.

> He was inclined to Taoism and attracted men of similar tastes. Amongst the latter there were eight famous scholars.

> They gathered together for study and chose the subject of Tao
> and . . . Love and justice, as the theme. This is how the essays
> of Huai Nan Tzû [Huainanzi] came to be written.[4]

These eight scholars are known as the Eight Immortals of Huainan. Today they can be found immortalized in statue form in Bagongshan Park in the modern-day city of Huainan. Alongside them are stone tablets professing Liu An's alleged discovery of tofu.[5]

The earliest reference to Liu An by name as the inventor of tofu can be found in the *Bencao Gangmu*, better known as the *Compendium of Materia Medica*. It was written by herbalist, pharmacologist, physician and all-round naturalist Li Shizhen (1518–1593) in 1578 but not printed until 1596 in Nanjing. The entry for tofu in this pharmacological work mentions the legendary originator: 'The method of tofu began in the Han dynasty with the king of Huainan, Liu An.' It also states that 'in general, black beans, soybeans, white beans, autumn soybeans, peas, mung beans and the like can be used.'[6] Given the lack of specificity here, it seems as though soybeans were not the primary source material for the creation of tofu as recently as the sixteenth century. The first item in the list being black beans is suggestive of a preference for them over soybeans, or perhaps a positioning due to their historical use prior to soybeans. Li Shizhen's masterpiece, which took ten years to compile, may offer these insights into tofu, but it may not offer much in the way of truth. Li was, according to historian of China Carla Nappi, 'a man obsessed' who filled his 52-volume pharmacological tome – the largest in its day – with just about everything he could get his hands on. This meant 'prescriptions for dragon bone, stories of corpse-eating demons and fire-pooping dogs, instructions for using magic mirrors, advice for getting rid of locusts, and recipes for

Li Shizhen on a commemorative stamp
in the 'Ancient Chinese Scientists' series,
issued in 1955 in China.

excellent fish dinners', among other things.[7] There certainly is a touch of the magical about the whole text, despite the dedication to naturalism, which lends mythical implications to the Liu An origin. Li did, however, share some early health benefits of tofu. For those who have drunk too much alcohol, Li suggests: 'thinly slice hot tofu and stick it all over your body, replacing them when cooled, and your sobriety will be restored.'[8] Perhaps a discovery from experience. To this day, according to the classification system of traditional Chinese medicine, tofu is branded a 'cooling' food, used to 'clear fire and detoxify'.[9]

The attribution of the invention of tofu to Liu An in Li's *Compendium* is flimsy evidence, a corroboration made roughly 1,800 years after Liu An's death. Going further back, the Huainan king's status as the inventor of tofu is mentioned in a poem about tofu, one of several 'tofu poems' that comprise a loose canon of works written during the Song dynasty (960–1279) on the subject of bean curd. They can be roughly divided into several categories: 'poems that record tofu delicacies, poems that record tofu names, poems that record the heritage of tofu, and poems that record tofu's origin'.[10] Most impactful among the last is the composition commonly known as 'Tofu', a poem written by Zhu Xi, a Southern

Song (1127–1279) Confucian master, which has been influential in furthering the Huainan theory of origin for tofu:

> Sowing beans, yet the sprouts are sparse;
> Your strength is spent, your heart rotten.
> Long had you known the arts of Huainan,
> Hoping to sit back and reap money.

The 'arts of Huainan' is an allusion to Liu An. Zhu Xi even attaches a note to the poem: 'Legend has it that tofu was originally a technique invented by the King of Huainan.' Other tofu poems are not as kind to this alleged origin, such as this anonymous ditty, 'Huaigu' (Nostalgia), penned during the Northern Song dynasty (960–1127):

> Dogs and chickens still cry in Shouyang,
> The Eight Masters crumble into dust.
> We die with laughter at Huainan's alchemy:
> It makes tofu instead of an elixir for immortality

The 'Eight Masters' are those Taoist philosophers and thinkers with whom Liu An surrounded himself. Their crumbling into dust suggests that the anonymous writer did not have much faith in Taoist alchemy; even their dogs and chickens, thought to follow immortals into heaven, remain. They discovered not immortality, but tofu (accidentally). This is in essence where the trail ends for the Liu An theory.

Liu An aside, these poems were not the first ever Chinese texts to mention tofu. The earliest reference to tofu by its current name, *doufu*, was in the *Qingyilu* (Clear Water Records), a collection of writings on various aspects of life authored during the tenth century by Tao Gu (903–970), a scholar and government official.

In one part titled 'Xiao Zai Yang', Tao recalls the story of Shi Jian, a hardworking deputy minister of the province of Anhui who was 'virtuous . . . and didn't eat meat'. Thankfully for him, 'there was a lot of tofu to be found at the daily market. The common people [there] call it xiao zai yang ['little mutton'].'[11] Xiao zai yang literally means 'little slaughtered sheep', an ironic nickname for a vegetarian foodstuff. This is the first specific mention of tofu in any text, and interestingly makes no reference to Liu An. It is tempting instead to surmise that the invention of tofu can be dated to around the same time. The fact that a specific section of this text has been dedicated to tofu, which has been given a derisive nickname, however regional that may have been, gives it a sense of novelty, the mantle of a new product introduced from elsewhere, perhaps. Given that there was 'a lot of tofu' on sale at the market, however, it may have already been a staple. In fact xiao zai yang was one of the many monikers of tofu in China during this time. Other names included li qi (written two ways with Chinese characters), lai qi, ruzhi (milk fat), yan lao (salt milk), doupu (bean preserve) and, of course, the name that stuck, doufu (rotten beans).[12] It is very possible that these names may have been regional; the myriad nicknames reflect the many origin theories of tofu itself.

Where exactly the word li qi arose is a mystery. It is claimed by the poet and historian Lu You (1125–1210) that the people of Shu Han (present-day Sichuan and Yunnan provinces) referred to tofu as li qi. Though it may have come from the now-extinct Ba-Shu dialect of Sichuan, it could also be a loanword; the characters used to spell li qi are employed for their phonetic value rather than their literal meanings, after all – a signpost towards its non-Han Chinese origins. Given the similarities of tofu and cheese in their processing, looking at neighbouring languages and their words for cheese reveals potential discovery. For example, across the border in Myanmar, which shares several ethnic minorities with China, the word for cheese is *din-hkai*. As languages evolve, the l, d, r and even n sounds can mix up (or change to match the sounds of another language), a process called rhotacization. This could have resulted in the *din* of *din-hkai* morphing over time into the *li* of *li qi*, while the *hkai* transforming into *qi* is easy to imagine. Another candidate for the origin of the word is with the language of the Lisu people, who live in the far north of Myanmar. 'Bean curd' in Lisu is *a no dzi*, which is not dissimilar to *li qi*.[13] It may have arrived in China via the Naxi language, in which the word for tofu is *nvqzzee*, while the Naxi word for lentil ('used to make a gray bean curd') is *liujil*, pronounced almost identically to *li qi*.[14] A connection of *li qi* to cheese may also be found in Thai, whose word for cheese is *noei khaeng*, which is remarkably similar. Furthermore, *dahi*, the word for 'curds' in Hindi, among other languages of India, is not too far removed.

BEAN CURD IN CREATION MYTHS

In 1982 another legendary tale, the *Hei'anzhuan*, was uncovered in the town of Songbai in Shennongjia, Hubei province, by a civil servant named Hu Chongjun who worked at a local culture centre in Shennongjia.[15] Translating to the *Story of Chaos* (also *Epic of Darkness* or *The Legend of Darkness*) in English, it was a dusty, hand-brushed parchment that contained an epic 3,000-line poem charting the mythical, primordial beginnings of the Han people. Anecdotal evidence collected by Hu from local people in the region suggested that the *Hei'anzhuan* was sung by funeral singers as part of folk funerary rites in Hubei known as *sang gu ge* (literally 'mourning drum songs'); some of these funeral singers told him that the sung form of the *Hei'anzhuan* could stretch back to the Tang dynasty (618–907). Hu spent several years searching

the region for more written copies of the *Hei'anzhuan*. Visiting
hundreds of funeral singers and collecting oral narratives as he
went, he found eight old manuscripts in total. It was not until
2002, with a few incomplete versions published before then,
that Hu was able to publish the final collated epic.

One of the main figures of the *Hei'anzhuan* is the mythical
emperor Shennong. When (or if) he is believed to have reigned
or lived is up for debate, but tradition places his life within the
28th century BC.[16] Born with the head of an ox (or a dragon),
Shennong taught people to grow crops, notably the important
Wu Gu (Five Grains) of ancient China, and treat illnesses with
herbs and plants. He also appears in Liu An's tome *Huainanzi*:

> People of old . . . often were sick and poisoned. Then Shen
> Nung [Shennong] appeared and taught them, for the first
> time, the art of sowing and planting cereals . . . he taught
> them to differentiate between the dry and humid, the rich
> and poor, the high and low lands.[17]

Legend has it that Shennong personally tested 365 herbs (he
once ate 70 poisonous plants in one day) for the good of the
people. According to some accounts, the efficacy of his doing so
was thanks to his transparent torso, through which he could see
his organs at work and study the internal effects of various herbs.[18]
Shennong's findings were passed down orally until appearing in
written form sometime during the Eastern Han dynasty (25–220)
as *Shennong Bencaojing* (Classic of Materia Medica), a book on
medicinal plants and the 'first book wholly devoted to the
description of herbs and their medicinal value'.[19] In a section of
the work devoted to soybeans there is the possible appearance
of soy milk, provided that the 'juice' mentioned is indeed soy
milk: 'Raw soybeans can be applied to carbuncles. Boil the juice

Guo Xu (1456–1526), *Shennong, the Divine Farmer*, 1503, ink on paper. Here Shennong is depicted testing one of the many medicinal herbs he sampled throughout his legendary life.

and drink it to kill *gui du* [ghost poison] and relieve pain.' Tofu is absent, even though it would only take the addition of another ingredient in traditional Chinese medicine, *shigao* (gypsum), to curdle the liquid. Even brine or vinegar can curdle soy milk to create tofu. If it were this simple, and if it had already been done around 150 years before by Liu An, or the Taoist philosophers and alchemists at his court, it wouldn't be a stretch to imagine the recipe for making tofu appearing in *Shennong Bencaojing*. Given that Liu An was charged with rebellion and committed suicide in 122 BC before he could be captured, it may be possible that the alleged discovery made at his court faded into obscurity. But as this book will later reveal, the absence of tofu from this and subsequent landmark texts in Chinese thought sheds further doubt on the Liu An legend altogether.

Factors that work in favour of the Liu An story are several geographical quirks that surround stories of tofu, including the 'little mutton' anecdote, which occurred in Anhui province, the location of Huainan. For example, one tract of the recently discovered *Hei'anzhuan*, to which the 'origin' of the Five Grains is traditionally traced, describes the way in which Shennong sought out and cultivated these prized pulses. Unlike Confucius, who counted the Five Grains as broomcorn, foxtail millet, rice, soybeans and wheat, Shennong's granular discoveries numbered more than five, featuring millet, rice, adzuki bean, barley, wheat, sesame seed and soybean, the cultivation of which is described in the epic:

> The soybean was produced on Mount Weishi,
> So it was difficult for Shennong to get its seeds.
> He left one seed of it with a peach tree,
> He planted it five times,
> Then it produced fruit,
> And later tofu was able to be made south of the Huai River.[20]

The mention of tofu in a potentially thousand-year-old mythical epic says much about not only its age, but its status. Geographically speaking, the pinpointing of a locale 'south of the Huai River' is also interesting. This almost certainly refers to Huainan (the name meaning literally 'south of the Huai [River]'), the kingdom over which Liu An presided, perhaps supporting the lore that puts Liu An in the founder's seat. Being taken from a mythical epic, this certainly isn't concrete; for instance, what sort of time period has elapsed between the soybean producing fruit and tofu being made 'later' is vague in the extreme. However, this is still a tantalizing indication towards the birth of bean curd.

A more visceral story can be found in another oral tradition, namely in one of several creation myths of the Dong (also known as Kam) people, who populate several provinces of southern China. One of these myths concerns the tale of Leng Shun. Born as 'a strange baby', his parents, displeased at his appearance, hack him up and leave him on a sandy riverbank. The next day, his dismembered body has undergone a miraculous transformation.

> His nose became a dog, his eyes became a cat, his mouth became an egret, his heart became an eagle, his teeth became mice, his ears became fungi, his brain became tofu, his head a gourd, his gallbladder became wine . . . Thus, everything in the world came into being.[21]

For tofu to be listed as one of the primordial facets of the world, born from a fated creator god, speaks to the importance of tofu, at least for the Dong people. Potentially it also points to the age of tofu, being something so ancient that only myths can explain its existence. Another version of this fable has the 'eccentric' Xing Lang as the originator of a plethora of plants, animals and fish from his corpse; again, 'his brains became tofu.'[22] This is similar to the content of another Dong national epic, in which two siblings, sole survivors of a great flood, bear a child described as a 'meat ball' covered in eyes, noses and mouths. Upset by its appearance, they hack it up. Among its posthumous transform-ations, its blood becomes the Miao people, its flesh the Han. Ultimately, the conclusions of these stories are virtually iden-tical to the myth of Pangu, creator of the universe in not only Han Chinese mythology but that of 'many other ethnic groups', including the Bai, Buyi, Gelao, Miao, Yao, Lisu and Zhuang. After gestating in an egg for 18,000 years, Pangu then lived for another 18,000 and 'his body transformed into the universe after his death,' as was first recorded in the third-century *Wuyun Linianji* (A Chronicle of the Five Circles of Time).[23]

Colourful as they are, these stories are myths. They hint at an integral role played by tofu in some regions of China, but they offer no hard evidence for tofu's true origin. This is where archaeological evidence would come in handy, but due to its propensity to spoil quickly no tofu is likely to have survived the centuries as a specimen. Soybeans, on the other hand, have left behind both a number of mentions in ancient texts and traces of their ancient existence from numerous archaeological sites. One of the earliest references to the cultivation of soybeans can be found in the Chinese text Shijing, known in English as Classic of Poetry, dated between the eleventh and seventh centuries BC. Woven into the text is the tale of Hou Ji, a cultural hero credited with introducing millet, among other crops, during the Xia dynasty (2070–1600 BC). He planted 'large beans' (ren shu, an archaic name for soybeans) which 'grew luxuriantly'.[24] The dates for this pioneering agricultural work, mythical though it may be, lie in the neighbourhood of soybean cultivation according to archaeological evidence. Large caches of soybean seeds have been found in Neolithic settlements in China, Korea and Japan. These discoveries have been made at archaeological sites connected to the Longshan and Yangshao cultures in China (dating to c. 3000–1500 BC and 5000–3000 BC respectively), those associated with the Chulmun culture in Korea (8500–1500 BC) and Japan's Jōmon culture (10,500–300 BC). According to a paper by an international team of researchers, the unearthing of these soybeans, which show a marked difference in size to wild counterparts, points to 'a long history of soybean and human interaction'.[25] The same paper concludes that it is implausible to posit a single place of origin for the soybean, even within China. From this, with multiple regions to harvest the raw material for tofu, there may be tentative truth in an equal multitude of places that could lay claim to being the birthplace of tofu.

INDUSTRY GODS: MORE TOFU MYTHS

The Liu An story is one example of the attribution of ground-breaking or important inventions and innovations to powerful or legendary figures of history. These convenient discovery myths may even be applied to those who are already mythical; the Yellow Emperor, for example, is credited with 'inventing musical instruments, developing the production of silk, instituting law and customs, and the development of medicine and agriculture'.[26] If the myths can be believed, China itself could seem to owe itself to 'a succession of wise emperors who "invented" the elements of a civilization, such as clothing, the preparation of food, marriage, and a state system'.[27] As one article on the difficulties of translating Chinese dishes into English states, 'Chinese food culture attaches much importance' to anecdotes of food, including the invention of dishes, related historical figures and events, all naturally leading to 'old stories about the cuisine itself', tofu included.[28] A 1922 book, *Myths and Legends of China*, notes that there are 'gods, goddesses, patrons, etc.' for everything from 'flowers, theatres, horses' to 'wine, bean-curd, jade', referred to as *hangye shen* (industry gods).[29] In fact, the younger sister of Du Kang, the deified patron of wine and winemaking, features as the inventor of tofu in one legend, but unfortunately she is not named, remaining eternally Du Kang Meimei ('Du Kang's little sister').[30] As far as Liu An is concerned, he is but one of a group of individuals associated with unprovable tales surrounding the origin of tofu.

These discovery myths stretch beyond the boundaries of China, as shown by the story of first-century Vietnamese general Tam Trinh. Born in 22 BC in the village of Dong Son (located in the city of Thanh Hoa today), Tam Trinh is said to have been tall and passionate about martial arts, learning wrestling in his home town. Having become a good wrestler, but with little money, he travelled north to what is now Hanoi, stopping at Co Mai (today's Mai Dong), passing through a famous apricot (mơ in Vietnamese) grove near present-day Thanh Tri district, Hanoi, before building a house along the Kim Nguu River. Here he taught literature and martial arts to the local youngsters. Noticing the hardworking but poor villagers, Tam Trinh also imparted his knowledge of farming, which in addition to agriculture included how to make tofu. The villagers grew to love and respect Tam Trinh. He was later a part of the uprising against the Han dynasty rule of northern Vietnam, in which he raised a 3,000-strong militia, and fought alongside Hai Ba Trung, better known in English as the Trung Sisters, to expel (albeit briefly) the Han Chinese occupiers in AD 40.[31]

Tam Trinh's contributions to wrestling were apparently more noteworthy than his tofu. After his death, the people of Co Mai built a temple and *dinh lang* (communal house), honouring Tam Trinh as the tutelary god of the village as well as the ancestor

The Trung sisters going to battle on war elephants, Đông Hồ-style woodblock print.

of wrestling.[32] Today part of the Ke Mo cultural area of Hanoi (modern-day Hoang Mai District), the village retains links to the tale of Tam Trinh; a wrestling festival is held from the fourth through the sixth day of Tet, recognizing a 2,000-year-old tradition.[33] The area is also renowned for its đậu phụ Mơ (sometimes đậu phụ Kẻ Mo). Literally meaning 'apricot tofu', it references the apricot trees that once grew in the region where the wrestling tofu-master Tam Trinh settled. This style of soft, white tofu, branded 'authentic', is famed in Hanoi and often used in family meals.[34] Its shape lacks the perfect right angles of box-pressed, store-bought varieties today, and exhibits a far more handmade aesthetic, like a brick with rounded edges (resembling rubing, a type of cheese native to Yunnan, China). In one village, Mơ Táo, the anniversary of the tofu-making profession is celebrated on 4 January every year, thus showcasing the recognition, on a very local level, of the legendary contribution of Tam Trinh (and not Liu An) to the development, or at least the introduction, of bean curd.[35]

Dong Son, where Tam Trinh was born, gives its name to the Dong Son Culture, which was active in the Southeast Asia region from the mid- to late first millennium BC.[36] According to French linguist Michel Ferlus, archaeological evidence for the invention of a rice-husking pestle and the subsequent linguistic spread of the word for that tool, as well as everyday words denoting useful objects like 'oar' and 'pan to cook sticky rice', indicates that 'Dongsonian' speakers 'belonged to a culture which encouraged them to innovate'.[37] It is pure speculation to say tofu was one such innovation, or that the connection of Tam Trinh to this culture indicates some reason for his knowledge of tofu-making, but the Tam Trinh legend itself hints at a multiple-origin theory. That tofu may have originated independently in several places at once, including a locale in northern Vietnam, over different time periods, and at the hands of a non-Han Chinese culture, should not be discounted.

Tam Trinh is not the only military man associated with the birth of tofu. At the opposite end of the Chinese sphere of influence, far in the north, there is the story of Yue Yi. Living during the turbulent, by name and nature, Warring States period (453–221 BC), Yue Yi was one of many famous elites of the day who drifted from state to state offering their military expertise, eventually winding up serving Yan.[38] An apocryphal story recounts that Yue Yi was the inventor of tofu. His elderly parents being unable to chew soybeans, Yue gave them soy milk instead. When a doctor prescribed them gypsum (*shigao*, an ingredient of traditional Chinese medicine), Yue took a shortcut and put it into the soy milk, which curdled and became tofu. It was dubbed *doufu zhi yu* ('jade of the blessed bean').[39]

The connection between a martial life and tofu continues with its attribution to Guan Yu, a general under Liu Bei in the Three Kingdoms era (220–280). Guan Yu is revered to this day as a deity but is traditionally given much more humble origins. The story was so widespread that British consular officer and Sinologist Herbert A. Giles (1845–1935) thought to include Guan Yu's origins in his *Chinese–English Dictionary* (1892). 'Originally a seller of bean-curd', the entry for Guan Yu reads. 'Was canonised in the 12th century, and made a god in 1594 by the Emperor Wan Li of the Ming dynasty. Is the tutelary deity of the present [Qing] dynasty.'[40] A different tradition puts Guan Yu behind the introduction of tofu to Shipai, a village in Zhongxiang, Hubei, where the people were suffering from eye diseases; Guan Yu, after consulting a doctor, brought tofu, with its appropriately medicinal properties, to Shipai, whose variety of tofu is famed to this day.[41]

Another story credits Pang Juan (d. 342 BC) and Sun Bin (d. 316 BC), both generals of the Warring States period. While the pair were studying under the renowned philosopher and hermit Guiguzi, the latter pretended to be ill to test the two students. Sun made soy milk for his teacher, but some salt water got into the mixture and curds appeared. Guiguzi praised Sun for the delicious accident; Pang got jealous. He replaced the brine with a mixture of gypsum water, hoping to thwart Sun's next attempt

Yashima Gakutei, *Guan Yu*, early 19th century, woodblock print.

LIU AN AND LI QI: ANCIENT ORIGINS OF TOFU

to create tofu, but apparently the results were even better.[42] If this story or that of Yue Yi contained any kernel of truth, the discovery of tofu would have to be backdated earlier than the inception of the purported Liu An legend.

The mingling of tofu's backstory with military men of yesteryear is compelling. Here there is an intersection of several traditionally desirable qualities befitting a leader in war-fraught ancient China. First there is zhi (wisdom) involved in the knowledge attached to the mystical origins of tofu, the know-how of the alchemical process involved in its creation and in tofu's link to medicine. Second there is modesty, qian in Chinese; being so closely attached to food either as its maker or seller displays humble origins and humility (as opposed to that of a courtier concerned only with eating food). As one traditional Chinese saying goes, 'There are three sufferings in this world: punting a boat, forging iron and making tofu.'[43] The last has been seen, and rightly so, as a labour-intensive process for as long as tofu has existed, suggesting that a general or other military leader who has made it (or sold it) has paid their dues or can empathize with the lower classes. Even xiao, or filial piety, appears as a moral in these tofu discovery stories: Yue Yi cares for his parents; Sun Bin tends to Guiguzi, his elder. Putting great figures in the midst of such stories bestows upon them valuable merit in a merit-driven society: they deserve to be great – just look at their tofu-tinged pasts. But like the much-touted Liu An legend and the creation myths, these fictive accounts of virtuous sons and soldiers don't do justice to the interesting possibilities involved in a possibly more factual lineage of tofu.

CHEESY BEGINNINGS: THE SIMILARITIES
OF DAIRY PRODUCTS AND BEAN CURD

The method of heating and curdling to create tofu is essentially the same as that for making cheese. With this in mind it is not far-fetched to conclude that tofu arose as a result of approximation of the cheese-making process, rather than by alchemical experimentation or medicinal meddlings. The comparison of cheese with tofu is not a new thing: it was noted in a poem by the prolific Chinese poet Lu You (1125–1210), in which he professes that tofu and *su* (cheese or butter) are equally matched.[44] Putting both these foodstuffs in the same poem and pitting them against each other in a hypothetical battle hints at a link between the two which may have been more commonly known in the twelfth century. Indeed, cheese itself has a far older heritage within China than is commonly believed. The earliest evidence for dairying within modern China is a 3,800-year-old piece of kefir cheese that was found at the Bronze Age Xiaohe cemetery in Xinjiang.[45] However, the discovery of dairy fats in jars excavated in Zhanqi, eastern Gansu province, provides evidence for a more easterly tradition within the Siwa culture, which flourished between 3,350 and 2,650 years ago.[46] A tradition of 'milk consumption by Chinese elites' has also been noted as far back as the *Qimin Yaoshu*, an important agricultural work written by the Northern Wei dynasty official and agronomist Jia Sixie in 544, which includes 'yoghurts and goat cheeses' in its pages.[47] At the time this text was compiled northern China was ruled by the Tuoba, a clan of the nomadic Xianbei people, suggesting a cultural culinary exchange at least among the elite level of both Xianbei and Han society.

The tradition of milk- and cheese-making among nomadic tribes has long been known in China. One such people were the

Xiongnu, a nomadic confederation and the Han dynasty's biggest enemy, with whom there was on-and-off war and a shaky marriage-based alliance (heqin). It was a complicated relationship. Historian Sima Qian (c. 145–86 BC) relates in his *Records of the Grand Historian* that Zhonghang Yue, a Han defector and an advisor to the Xiongnu, told his new paymasters, '[When you] receive the Han consumables discard them all and this shows that they are not as fitting and delicious as milk and cheese.'[48] He also suggested riding around in gifts of delicate silk, bound to show wear and tear quickly, to demonstrate their unsuitability for the Xiongnu's rough-and-tough lifestyle. Clearly there was a divide between what constituted Han food on one hand, and the 'milk and cheese' of the Xiongnu on the other; a divide that, it seems, was not easy to bridge. For the cheese-making skills of a hostile culture to be applied so readily to soybeans, or beans of any variety, seems unrealistic during this earlier, conflict-strewn period of Chinese history. This was the food of barbarians.

Nonetheless, Osamu Shinoda (1899–1978), the 'uncontested pioneer' of research in the field of East Asian foodways,[49] believed that the nomadic Hu people (a grouping of barbarians including the Xiongnu), passed the tradition of cheese-making to China around the turbulent Northern and Southern Dynasties period (420–589), when the Hu flooded south, collectively rising up against Han Chinese rule. Shinoda also proposed that the variously spelled other words for tofu, li qi and lai qi among them, indicated phonetic equivalents for a foreign word.[50] But finding an analogue is tricky. Proto-Turkic, which can be associated with the Xiongnu, has a few examples.[51] There is ayran, a kind of salty yoghurt, and dorak, a kind of cheese or quark; but nothing promising.[52] In Manchu, a language descended from the older Jurchen language, turi miyehu (bean crust) is the word for tofu, which provides no etymological connection.[53] This potential route for tofu's ancestral introduction to China has its predecessor arriving via the north and west, from Turkic and Tungusic peoples, but Shinoda also believed that tofu may have taken a southerly route into China. Specifically, he theorized, it may have been directly inspired by the very tofu-like *rubing* (or milk cake) of the Miao people.[54] It is easy to see the similarity between *rubing*, a non-aged cheese not dissimilar to mozzarella, and tofu. For example, when travelling in Yunnan, food writer Fuchsia Dunlop was 'struck by how similar the snack is to tofu, which is made in almost exactly the same way'.[55] Authors of the past have recounted 'a Miao myth placing their origin thousands of years ago in some snowy land in the North',[56] a myth that could lend some credence to Shinoda's theory – provided that it were true and that nomadic Miao ancestors brought cheese-making techniques with them, dropping off the necessary process for making tofu along the way. The name of *rubing* in the language of the Bai, another people of Yunnan, is *youdbap*. The name of another cheese product in this region, which is known as *rushan* (fan cheese) in Chinese, is *nvxseiz* in Bai, also *yenx seip*, which sounds as though it may be related to *li qi* via the Lisu word for tofu, *a no dzi*, and Naxi *nvqzzee*.[57] The geographical and lexical connections and similarities of these words for cheese and tofu could prove instrumental in more concretely proving tofu's evolution from cheese both practically and linguistically. Taking into consideration the location of these cheeses and languages, it is likely instead that they either evolved by themselves or came from a southerly direction, indicating a possible southern placing for the birth of tofu. Whether or not these words were an approximation of Hindi *dahi*, or its Sanskrit ancestor *dadhi*, is difficult to tell, but its probable evolution to *datshi* in Dzongkha, referring to widely used Bhutanese cheese, suggests a midway en route from dh to qi of li qi.[58] The utilization in Naxi of a word for tofu that is very similar to a Bai word for cheese highlights their pivotal position along the Tea Horse Road, a route which facilitated trade and cultural exchange between China, Tibet and India for centuries.[59] This does not necessarily explain tofu's origins per se, but it does explain that people in this region at least thought that tofu, perhaps an import from the north, was similar to cheese.

While archaeological artefacts relating to cheese have been found, and the linguistic evidence for a southerly sojourn of cheese may provide insight into the genealogy of tofu, actual proof for tofu is hard to come by. The closest thing to archaeological evidence of tofu in ancient China is a particular mural, one of several that adorned the walls at the Dahuting Han tombs, Henan, which were discovered in the mid-twentieth century. These murals piqued the interest of scholars with regard to the pre-Tang dynasty existence of tofu because, according to archaeologist Chen Wenhua, they are 'drawings of tofu processing' and

A banquet scene painted as a mural on the walls of the Dahuting Tombs, a Han dynasty monument in Xinmi, Henan.

The procedure for making tofu, which some scholars suggest is depicted
on the walls of the 1st-century Dahuting Han Tombs, near Xinmi, Henan:
1) soaking soybeans, 2) grinding soybeans, 3) filtering the soymilk,
4) adding brine and 5) pressing for solidification and dewatering.

depict the endeavour in detail: milling the beans, filtering and
cooking soy milk, stirring in coagulant and pressing to drain off
excess water.[60] Some scholars are more sceptical. There are several
problems with accepting this as historical evidence for a Han
dynasty (or earlier) origin of tofu, namely in the likelihood that
'subjective conjecture was added in the process of copying the
picture carved on the stone', and overlooking that it could depict
some other culinary process instead, for example liquor-making.[61]
It also comes with the assumption that the tofu production was
then as it is now; as no other contemporary pictorial evidence
exists, there is nothing to compare to whatever culinary process
was carved on those stones. With the alleged illustration time-
worn and comprising nothing more complex than silhouettes,
the details being later additions, the implements and people
depicted in this mural may well have been employed in soup-
making. Who knows: they may have even been making cheese.

FOOD FOR THE MASSES

That just one person was behind the origin of tofu is about as believable as the mythic tale of bean curd birthed from the brains of a dead god. Ultimately the origin of tofu could lie in necessity. French Sinologist Jacques Gernet argued that poverty was the root of 'the highly developed Chinese food culture' that makes 'full use of potential edible vegetables and insects', citing long-term drought and famine as factors.[62] On the other hand, as argued by archaeologist Kwang-Chih Chang, 'creativity' in cuisine may simply derive from the importance of 'food and ways of eating [as] cores of Chinese lifestyle and a component of Chinese ethos'; poverty, that is, a 'scarcity of resources', could explain a favourable condition, rather than a cause, for this inventiveness, which may have included the creation of tofu.[63] It is often believed that 'in place of animal fats and meats [Chinese peasants] consumed plant oils, vegetables and beancurd', potentially putting tofu in the peasant diet for centuries.[64] However, social stratification may have had a large part to play in the development of tofu, especially in terms of its provenance as a meat substitute. According to the Shujing (Book of Documents), compiled around the third century BC, and the Guanzi (Writings of Master Guan), dated to the seventh century BC, diets were to be assigned via status in society. Meat-eaters were in one class – the emperor and courtly individuals – while commoners were, not only by necessity but by societal designation, vegetarians. Commoners could eat meat, but only after the age of seventy.[65]

Further compounding these ancient rules, Philip Huang, professor emeritus of history at UCLA, writes that 'Chinese peasants have long been vegetarians, not by choice, but by the dictates of the Chinese agrarian system.' Away from those living and working on the land, for the wealthy mystics or urban

populations of China, vegetarianism was 'a choice, not a necessity'.[66] Even into the Qing dynasty (1636–1912), the advocacy of
vegetarianism and 'preaching on non-killing' was the remit of
the elite. One pamphlet of the day, known as 'morality books',
that polemicized such a view was actually published during the
White Lotus rebellion (1794–1804), triggered by rural poverty
and carried out largely by people described as 'millenarian' (that
is, peasant spiritualist) vegetarians, and who were denounced
as belonging to Buddhist 'sects'.[67] We can take that to mean that
the poverty experienced by large swathes of the rural Chinese
population, people who were most likely vegetarians by necessity, was being co-opted as a virtue by the upper-classes of Qing
society, the same group who demonized the uprising. Therefore
any Taoist–Buddhist associations with tofu and its virtues – even
tofu itself – may have been borrowed from the lower classes,
much like the morality associated with being a humble tofu-
seller like Guan Yu. Deputy governor Shi Jian's purported dislike
of meat may have been a way to convey a man-of-the-people
image more than it was a moral dietary choice. Liu An's attribution was probably no more than a rumour that served to enhance
his own wisdom and mystical connections. The spread of myths
such as this, as well as the ordered, diligent control of the land
as suggested by scholarly grain-growing and tofu-making as
opposed to hunting and animal slaughter, might have furthered
the depiction of 'a civilized society of settled farmers and literati-
officials surrounded by nomadic and belligerent hunter-gatherer
tribes'.[68] During the Song dynasty an 'aversion to eating beef' may
have arisen not only owing to religious reasons but as a result
of pragmatism, as there was an 'increasing predominance of
small family farms, where draught animals were considered part
of the family'.[69] Chronologically this coincides approximately
with the prevalence of 'tofu poems' mentioned earlier in this

chapter, which though somewhat correlative may simply be a coincidence.

In summary, nobody knows where tofu came from exactly or who 'invented' it. Though this might not be the most sound logic, this probably says much about its age and its stature – in the same way that nobody knows who invented bread, nor who first made cheese, or beer. The chances are it was not one singular person. Because it seems like such a specialist product, one almost like a dish in itself, it is easy to ascribe its creation to one place and time and be done with it. But tofu isn't a Waldorf salad. It has been a staple part of Chinese and wider East Asian food culture since at least the tenth century and probably for much longer. In all actuality, there is a chance it has existed for as long as the knowledge for making soy milk has been available, something potentially mentioned in the Shennong Bencaojing around 2,000 years ago. Given the simplicity with which soy milk is curdled, and if the 'juice' in the Shennong Bencaojing were soy milk (though this could just as well be aquafaba), the origin of tofu could be placed reasonably sometime within the Han dynasty.

On the other hand, the lack of actual appearances of the word 'tofu' in any text prior to the tenth century doesn't lend much credence to this more ancient inception, especially given the tendency of various Chinese compendia to cite the properties of myriad miscellany; soybean curds would surely have made the cut of any number of texts. There is a very slight possibility that the appearance of tofu in the Hei'anzhuan could point to a Tang dynasty (or earlier) origin, if the anecdotal evidence of its oral tradition is to be believed. The intent with which the Han dynasty origin of tofu is pursued and reported in various Chinese media may also be an attempt to align its invention neatly with

Han Chinese people, the majority population of China, rather than with nomadic northerners, ethnic minorities of the mountainous southwest, or India. Evidence for this is usually presented by utilizing the Dahuting murals with added details, or simply by parroting the Liu An legend.

One thing is almost certain, however, which is tofu's similarity to cheese. Cheese being a more ancient foodstuff puts it as an ancestor of tofu. Tofu may not be an animal product, but the way in which it is made, practically the same as for making cheese, plus a selection of linguistic links between tofu and cheese in southwest China, puts the two with some surety in the same family tree. Extrapolating further from this, given the essential nature of dairy products in the Tibetan Plateau, it may be that the process found its way to enterprising farmers in milder climes via the Tea Horse Road, who tried it out with their crop of soybeans instead of goats and yaks.[70] It is this same necessity-meets-trial-and-error approach to food that likely heralded the preservation of tofu, the subject of the next chapter.

TWO
WHAT'S THAT SMELL? PRESERVING TOFU AND ITS BY-PRODUCTS

On the chopsticks, the creamy mass is slippery
In the pan, the white jade is fragrant

P resumably it was the distinct lack of a strong smell that inspired Chinese poet and gastronome Su Shi (1037–1101) to pen those lines on tofu, comparing it to precious *ruan yu* (white jade).[1] In its usual guise, the one most people know, tofu has a delicate scent, but the aroma of tofu in its fermented form is anything but subtle. Fermented tofu has long formed a part of Chinese cuisine, and given that it is not a dish as such but a successor to tofu itself (think of it as tofu in its afterlife), it deserves a chapter of its own. Different methods of preserving tofu and its by-products have been dreamt up over the years, all of them generally separable into either fermentation or drying.

As with its non-fermented form, the origins of the fermented variety are obscured by thick plumes of centuries gone by. It goes by many names in China, *furu* (literally 'preserved milk') and *sufu* included. Since the eighteenth century fermented tofu has often been referred to by the term *rufu*, which was once used exclusively for dairy milk curds between the Sui (581–618) and Ming (1368–1644) dynasties.[2] Herbert A. Giles defines *rufu*

Poet Su Shi
appearing on
the cover art for
his *Former Ode
on the Red Cliffs*
by calligrapher
and scholar
Zhao Mengfu
(1254–1322).

in A Chinese–English Dictionary as 'stinking bean-curd; noxious'.[3] Generally fermented tofu is created by introducing a mould to fresh tofu, creating a pehtze (pizi) or semi-finished product, then fermenting in brine and ripening until ready. According to different processes involved, this can be further separated into several types. These involve pre-salting before mould introduction, or salting afterwards; some require only kōji to do the job enzymatically.[4] The brine involved in the fermentation process can be composed of a variety of substances, including (but not limited to) rice wine or sorghum liquor, into which peppercorns, star anise and other flavour-packed herbs and spices can be added.[5] The result is not dissimilar to cheese, giving fermented tofu the occasional nickname 'vegetarian cheese', but as food writer Cathy Erway describes, it is more like a condiment in its use.[6] As with cheese, there is plenty of variety. The raw materials involved, resulting in variously hued end products – usually red, greenish or yellow – showcases the typical ingredients of regional cuisine. For example, Shaoxing wine, hailing from the city of the same name, is used to create shaoxing furu, a venerable version of the fermented speciality that won an award at the Nanyang Industrial Exposition in 1910, China's first 'landmark' world's fair.[7] Fermented tofu is far from an oddity in China, where it wins accolades and earns regionally protected status in much the same way cheese or wine does in Europe. Yet, as this chapter later describes, it has not travelled well.

Though some may assert that 'the introduction of Buddhism to the Northeast Asian region from the third to fourth centuries AD contributed to the development of fermented food,' this is based on an assumption that vegetarianism did not exist in the region prior to this.[8] Taoist beliefs of purifying oneself through both meditation and zhai (vegetarian meals) persisted centuries before the Graeco-Buddhist monks from Kushan came trundling through Chinese realms. Religion notwithstanding, a simple combination of 'cooked soybeans, saltwater, and pottery could have resulted in the birth of fermented soybean products', which were a good 'supplementary source of protein'.[9] This is definitely the case with things like *doenjang*, Korean fermented soybean paste. But exactly when this happened with regard to tofu is not precisely recorded at this ancient stage of history, which indicates that it either did not exist or was such a remote and locally made foodstuff as not to have made it into the pages of any important tracts of writing.

The likelihood is that fermented tofu is fairly old, with some claims placing its origin in the Three Kingdoms period (220–280).[10] A fifth-century text from the Northern Wei dynasty (386–535) purportedly states, 'dried tofu is salted and matured to become *furu*'.[11] The trail from here, even what alleged text this was or who wrote it, leads to a dead end; the provenance of the text cannot be established beyond the essay in which the quotation appears. It would not be until the Ming dynasty that fermented tofu was first described reliably. This description appeared in the *Penglong Yehua*, which was written by Li Rihua (1565–1635).[12] However, as a bureaucrat, artist, critic and serial art collector, Li's passing mention that the people of Yixian in Anhui province like to ferment bean curd in summer and autumn (noting that 'it stinks') is not overly reliable for dating fermented tofu.[13] We can only wonder if he would have looked into the matter further than this one observation. Anhui serving as the location for his anecdote is interesting, however, given that both Liu An and the 'little mutton' story also find their homes in Anhui, potentially marking the province out as something of a tofu heartland.

One reason for the difficulty in pinpointing the origin of tofu may have to do with the very general way in which it is made. Aside from a variation in coagulants, the end, raw product is unlikely to have strayed too much from the conceptual ideal that is bean curd, give or take the size, shape or consistency. However, when it comes to fermented tofu, there are regional variations aplenty. So, in a different way, discovering the single origin point of fermented tofu is difficult because each variety is a type in itself, probably an isolated discovery, and traced back only to its founding legend or the inception of a particular company. One of these tales is that of Wang Zhihe. Legend has it that in 1699 Wang took himself off to Beijing to try out in the civil service examinations. He didn't make the cut, but decided to stay in the capital and open up a tofu shop. One day, wondering what to do with surplus product, he cut it up and put it in a jar to save it. Later looking in the jar, Wang was hit by a waft of something entirely new as he saw that the tofu chunks had turned grey. Sampling one, he found to his surprise that the result was delicious. And so fermented tofu was born. Today the Wangzhihe brand bears his name, part of the Beijing Capital Agribusiness & Foods Group, whose corporate website claims that its product was indeed founded in the eighth year of the Kangxi Emperor, 1699.[14] It is a popular story that finds its way into the historical preambles of several articles relating to both furu and the slightly different (but also fermented) chou doufu, also known as stinky tofu.

There are also dozens of varieties of furu occupying a spicy spectrum of hues from grey to yellow and red – too many for space to allow. One particularly visually arresting type is dubbed mao doufu (hairy tofu) because of the wispy, hairlike mould that grows all over it. Though a speciality of Anhui, it can be found elsewhere. According to conversations between travel writer Brent Crane and producers of hairy tofu in Kunming, this variety of fermented tofu was once the preserve of the imperial family in Beijing.[15] Another fermented variety from Shandong, Lingqing Jinqing Rufu ('Lingqing Entering-the-capital Fermented Tofu'),

Two of the many types of Wangzhihe brand *furu* (fermented tofu) available.

made by Jimei Sauce Garden, purportedly dates to the founding
of the company in 1792; by 1822 it was being offered to the Qing
court as an imperial tribute.[16] Elite connections abound. Empress
Dowager Cixi (1835–1908), on her way back to the capital having
fled westward in the wake of the invasion by the Eight-Nation
Alliance in 1900, came across one type of furu native to Lankao,
Henan, which she liked so much that it became part of the palace's
culinary repertoire. This apparently four-hundred-or-more-year-
old variety, qiu you furu (autumn oil furu), is named for the soybeans and sesame, fresh from their autumn harvests, of which
it is made.[17]

Cixi is not the only leader to have been seduced by the tang
of fermented tofu. A legend that appears in 'Doufu', an essay by
writer Wang Zengqi (1920–1997), has it that Mao Zedong (1893–
1976) was a great fan of the stinky tofu in Changsha, Hunan

大清國慈禧皇太后

Katharine Carl (1865–1938), *The Empress Dowager, Tze Hsi, of China*, 1903, oil on canvas. Carl was the first artist to paint a portrait of Cixi.

province, not far from his home town of Shaoshan.[18] Changsha
stinky tofu, locally called chou ganzi (stinky jerky), with its black
outer crust making it look like craggy cubes of volcanic rock, is
a prized treasure of hot-and-sour Hunan cuisine.[19] When he
was young Mao frequented Huogongdian (Fire Palace), a historic
Changsha restaurant, to eat their speciality stinky tofu. Years
later, in 1958 according to a 1993 article by Fan Minghui in China
Food News, he returned to Changsha, once again visiting Huogongdian to sample their signature dish.[20] 'The stinky tofu at Huogongdian is still delicious,' Mao declared. A statue of the man himself
stands proudly at the entrance to the restaurant. This anecdote
serves as a further illustration of the difference in describing food
culture in China compared to that of the West, persisting into
the modern day. Though interesting, this type of legendary doc-
umentation has a tendency to obfuscate food research as much
as ignite a drive for it.

Furu likely originated somewhere on the Chinese mainland, but
there is a very similar dish in Okinawa called tōfuyō. It is believed
to derive from Fujian's red-hued hongfuru (red fermented tofu),
also called nanru (southern milk). In Okinawa it is made using
shimadōfu. Literally 'island tofu' in Japanese, this differs both in
the manufacturing process and in the finished result. In the
usual Japanese method, the moisture is squeezed out of the
soybeans after they have been boiled; the method of making
Okinawan shimadōfu involves draining the moisture from the
raw, ground soybeans prior to boiling. Tōfuyō is fermented in a
mixture of kōji, benikōji (red yeast rice) and awamori, a rice-based
distilled alcoholic beverage.[21] The use of the red yeast rice, which
is the result of Monascus purpureus mould cultivated on rice, gives
tōfuyō its striking carmine colour. British naval officer Basil Hall

(1788–1844), during a voyage around the west coast of the Korean peninsula and the Ryukyu Islands (Okinawa being one of these), describes what is assumed to be tōfuyō: 'There was something like cheese given us after the cakes, but we cannot form a probable conjecture of what it was made.'[22] Modern-day analysis of three-month aged tōfuyō demonstrated that its 'viscoelasticity' was 'similar to that of commercial cream cheese or soft-type processed cheese':the scientific proof of tōfuyō's cheese-adjacent credentials.[23] Hall ate this at a feast of the 'Chief' during his 1816 visit to Okinawa, a setting that may corroborate present-day assertions that tōfuyō was the enjoyment of the king and nobility alike, as seems to have been the case in Qing China.[24] But in the popular mindset, Okinawa is an outlier in the stinky-tofu world. Instead it is Taiwan that is best known for stinky tofu, though it can also

Shimatofu-ya, a venerable tofu eatery on the island of Amami Oshima, Kagoshima Prefecture, serves *shimadōfu* and tofu products in a century-old building.

be found across mainland China and in Hong Kong (among other places), where it is considered to have been taken by Shanghainese immigrants in the 1930s.[25]

In terms of how fermented tofu made its way to the Ryukyu Kingdom, the archipelago's central location between Taiwan, China, Korea, Japan and the Philippines has endowed it with centuries of trade and maritime significance. As early as the eighth century the main island of Okinawa acted as a convenient stop-over for envoys travelling from Japan to Tang dynasty China and vice versa.[26] It was during the Ming dynasty that a newly unified Ryukyu Kingdom took advantage of its special trade position, flourishing while paying tribute to the Ming court.[27] This close contact elicits a strong possibility that fermented tofu made its

The Ryukyu Kingdom, represented in this 19th-century folding screen by the ship in the centre flying the flag ('returning to Japan'), was instrumental in facilitating trade between China, Japan and Southeast Asia.

way to the Ryukyu Islands during this period, though it is claimed that this was not until the eighteenth century, when *hongfuru* arrived from Fujian.[28] It is also not impossible to assume that the Ryukyu Kingdom, mercantile as it was, helped facilitate the spread of Chinese culture around maritime Southeast Asia. After the 1932 surfacing of the *Rekidai Hōan* (Precious Documents of Successive Generations), which charts the Ryukyu Kingdom's trade relationships with China, Japan and Southeast Asia over the course of four hundred years or so (between the fifteenth and nineteenth centuries), pre-eminent Japanese studies professor

Shunzo Sakamaki called them 'an invaluable source of primary information for the study of East and Southeast Asia in medieval and early modern time[s]'.[29] Such is the historical significance of the seafaring kingdom. Beginning in 1372, the Ryukyu Kingdom embarked on what would be a 'vast and generally very profitable' trade, with expeditions to Annam (Vietnam), Malacca (Malaysia), Luzon (the Philippines), Sumatra and Java in Indonesia, and Siam (Thailand). But these islands' connections to the rest of Asia probably began much earlier. Yonaguni, one of Okinawa's Yaeyama Islands and the westernmost inhabited island of Japan, lies 111 kilometres (just under 69 miles) from the shores of Taiwan. Their proximity, and the likelihood that ancient humans would have been able to make the journey between Taiwan and Yonaguni thanks to the Kuroshio Current despite primitive tools,[30] hints that cultural contact between the two islands, even as long as 30,000 years ago, may have been a reality of both their developments.

THE HOUSE OF STINK

Taiwan's stinky tofu is infamous. While rufu and tōfuyō are preserved over many months (and presumably longer once purchased and added to your larder), chou doufu, aka stinky tofu like the Changsha variety, is a different beast. This stuff isn't made to keep: it is made to be served fresh. More often than not the process is expedited with a shorter fermentation period, from 'several days to a week' in a concoction consisting of 'anything from Chinese cabbage and tea leaves to meat, shrimp or milk' – it is difficult to be certain as its purveyors are 'fiercely protective' of their recipes.[31] Taiwan's stinky tofu can be simply described as a 'fermented bean curd that came via immigrants from mainland China'.[32] But the truth is likely more political in nature. It was

Taiwan is famed for its snack-packed night markets, like Raohe Street Night Market in Taipei.

Chiang Kai-Shek's retreat to the island of Taiwan in 1949, after his army's defeat at the hands of Mao's Communist forces in the Chinese Civil War (1927–49), that prompted some 2 million people to relocate by his example.[33] It is generally believed that stinky tofu arrived with this mass movement.

Stinky tofu is often found at Taiwan's famed night markets, where it is sold as a *xiaochi* (small snack). No place on the island is more famous for tofu than Daxi Laojie, better known as Shenkeng Old Street, located in New Taipei City. This is the veritable capital of tofu in Taiwan.[34] It is not just regular stinky tofu on sale; the fried variety is sold here, too, as well as a cavalcade of other tofu products, from dessert tofu to tofu beverages and tofu ice cream, which has a roasted quality to it.[35] Back in Taipei, the craft and popularity of stinky tofu are evidenced in one of the city's most celebrated establishments: the House of Stink. Known by its full name, The Dai Family House of Unique Stink in Taipei, the restaurant was established in 1989, though the production method involved is based on a sixty-year-old family recipe.[36] The 'stink' in question is used positively. It is such a focus of the experience that each menu item features a corresponding 'stink score'.[37] Myriad odours in the scoring are compared to 'decaying garbage, rotten meat and smelly feet'.[38]

According to a paper published in 2012, there are a total of 39 volatile compounds that contribute to the aroma of stinky tofu.[39] Because of its strong odour but palatable taste, stinky tofu is sometimes referred to as 'Chinese cheese', but Chinese cheese already exists. There was a widespread culture of cheese in China from at least the Tang dynasty, with ample cookbooks attesting to the existence of a surprising range of dairy products. There were strained yoghurts (lulao) and dried yoghurts (ganlao); there was clotted cream (suyou) and ghee (tihu); not to mention the cheese traditions of Tibetans, Mongolians and the Bai and Miao people; Uyghurs have been making cheese called askuru 'for centuries'.[40] There were even cheesy mock meats, for example 'fried bones' (zha gutou) made from milk balls (rutuan) of semi-hardened yoghurt. The sheer scale of it all points to what historian of Chinese food Miranda Brown calls 'a long-forgotten cheesemaking tradition'.[41]

Cheese aside, one of the main culprits for the intense smell of stinky tofu is a chemical compound called indole, which occurs naturally in coal tar and faeces. Although 'at low concentrations

Stinky tofu, Taiwan.

indole has a floral odour . . . at higher concentrations it smells putrid'.[42] Despite this it is not just smelly, but important: 'The normal smell of human faeces is largely due to indole, one of the major metabolites. Recent studies indicate that this foul-smelling substance is also of utmost importance for our health'; for example, it is possible that the production of gut microbes is promoted by indole, which in general has 'a beneficial effect on the host's intestinal function'.[43] Favourable compounds notwithstanding, the aroma of stinky tofu is certainly powerful. In 2016 Japan's *Mainichi Shimbun* reported that train services on the JR Kansai Line were disrupted when a bin emanating a pungent odour on a train from Yokkaichi to Nagoya, Aichi Prefecture, was found to contain the remnants of stinky tofu.[44] The fame of stinky tofu looms large in Taiwanese cuisine; however, it is important to remember that this is not the only thing on the menu. 'Beef noodle soup, stinky tofu – people know these dishes. But in Taiwan, we're not eating those every single day,' said Taichung-born chef Tony Tung, founder of Good To Eat Dumplings in Emeryville, California, in a *New York Times* interview.[45]

The frequency with which this foodstuff courts attention in the media is a testament perhaps to its singular fame in Taiwan, but also to a persistent othering of Asian food. Stinky tofu frequently appears on lists of 'gross' or 'weird' foods, little being said of its health benefits and much of its smell.[46] It can be found at the Disgusting Food Museum in Malmö, Sweden, where journalist Jiayang Fan 'felt like one of the exhibits'. As she wrote, 'seeing stinky tofu, century eggs, and other staples of my childhood branded as "disgusting" stung me with self-consciousness. Those foods were in my fridge at that very moment.'[47] The museum's website includes stinky tofu on a list of what can only be presumed highlights, alongside durian and cuy (roasted guinea pig) from Peru. However, though not publicized as highly (if at all), Jell-O, Twinkies, Pop Tarts and other totems of North American 'junk food' also feature in the museum, perhaps in an effort to appear balanced. One of the more recent articles on their website listing the 'Most disgusting' foods boasts that '108 vomits have occurred in the Disgusting Food Museum'.[48] Their logo features a beautifully designed cursive 'Yuck!' on an illustrated bowl. These aspects, among others, lend the whole venture the atmosphere of a side show, something that belongs in the Victorian age. Stinky tofu branded as 'disgusting' echoes many initial, and some present-day, Western reactions to unfermented tofu in general, illustrating a continued ignorance among Westerners of Asian, particularly Chinese, cuisine. While the museum's director urges that the name is tongue-in-cheek, and that disgust is 'highly individual' and an 'effect of our upbringing', there is something distastefully contradictory about the use of 'museum' in the name.[49] This suggests some level of authority, implying that everything within its doors is objectively disgusting. A more neutral approach, for example 'International Food Museum', would have been just as interesting, but the focus on disgust, however jovial, is deliberately provocative and serves to create a negative cultural space where entire cultures and their cuisines are prodded for entertainment. It is tempting to agree that the entire museum 'could have been a buzzfeed article', as one Google review put it.

Tastes, of course, can and do vary. Food writer Fuchsia Dunlop, for example, writes of 'a comparative tasting of fermented tofu and Stilton, to highlight the distinction made by some Chinese friends of mine between what they found the clean, rapidly-dispersing stinkiness of fermented tofu, and the greasy, clingy, mouth-coating stinkiness of cheese'.[50] Across the South China Sea, Indonesia's most famous fermented soybean product, tempeh, does not smell strongly by comparison to furu or stinky tofu. It has more of an earthy aroma. The same cannot be said of oncom (or oncom tahu), a lesser-known fermented product from Indonesia. This is created using food by-products, chiefly the dregs or pulp left over from tofu production, better known by their Japanese name, okara (also called soy pulp). Other raw materials for its creation include peanut press cake (bungkil kacang tanah) and the remnants of cassava and coconuts once their respective starch, oil and milk have been extracted. The bacteria responsible for the fermentation of oncom is Neurospora intermedia.[51] Broadly speaking, there are two main varieties, oncom hitam (orange) and oncom merah (black), but the fermented foodstuff can be made in a number of different ways.[52] For example, a variety from the city of Bandung is created with peanut press cake, tapioca flour and soybean curd in a ratio of 15:5:1.[53] Oncom hitam made with tofu dregs is relatively low in fat and protein, but is relatively high in vitamin B$_{12}$ and iron.[54] Nobody is quite sure how oncom got its name, but according to food historian Fadly Rahman it seems to have originated in the seventeenth century in West Java.[55]

DRIED TOFU AS A METHOD OF PRESERVATION

Fermentation is not the only way to preserve tofu. It can also be dried, with various processes involved in creating it. One of the most used items in this clan is tofu skin. As with *okara*, this is not strictly tofu but rather a by-product of the tofu-making process. The process of making tofu described in Li Shizhen's late sixteenth-century *Compendium of Materia Medica* is believed to contain the first mention of *doufu pi* (tofu skin): 'A skin will form on the surface, peel it off and air-dry it. This is called tofu skin, which is also very good to use as food,' he writes.[56] This is not a process unique to tofu, but had already been seen in the ancient dairy product *so*, a hard, brown cheese-adjacent foodstuff created by lifting off the skin of heated milk, layering and pressing it. Arguably, the look, feel and behaviour of soy milk when compared to milk from cows, sheep and goats lends further credence to the idea of tofu's general lineage as a distant kin of cheese.

Tofu skin may also be better known by the name *fuzhu* (meaning 'preserved bamboo') or *dou bian* (bean strips). Also called *fu pi* (preserved skins) when fresh or rehydrated, in Chinese cuisine these have long been used to create mock meat known as *su ji* (vegetarian chicken). This is created by sandwiching a filling of mushrooms and vegetables simmered in soy sauce between multiple layers of tofu skin; this multi-level sandwich is then tightly rolled, sliced into chunks and further fried. A similar recipe appears as *su shao'e* (roasted vegetarian goose) and is included in *Recipes from the Garden of Contentment*, the 1792 treatise on culinary delights written by poet and painter Yuan Mei (1716–1798).[57] In the section of the book in which this recipe appears, 'Miscellaneous Vegetable Dishes', Yuan prefaces it with the claim that 'privileged and wealthy [people] indulge themselves more on vegetable dishes than they do on meat-based dishes.'[58] This hints at the elite status

Some *fuzhu* (dried bean curd sticks) on sale at a supermarket.

given to elective (or selective) rather than necessary vegetarian cuisine at the time, despite the use of meat and fish to flavour many dishes, especially considering that this section of Yuan's work contains some rather 'elegantly wasteful and refined court dishes'.[59]

Another form of dried tofu, *dougan*, plays a role in vegetarian cuisine. This dry-ish variety of tofu, made with added calcium sulphate and aromatized with spices including licorice, star anise and cinnamon, is made by dehydrating the tofu and pressing it until extra firm. This brown-coloured tofu features a fibrous texture that is ideal for use as a meat substitute. Describing it in his essay 'Doufu', musing on the many forms taken by bean curd in China, Wang writes that *dougan* can be further pressed and rolled out into sheets, *doufupian* (tofu slices); when further thinly sliced it is called *bai ye* (hundred pages), or *qian zhang* (thousand sheets)

Creamy *yuba* (tofu skin) fresh from the *tōfu-ya* (tofu shop) complete with soy sauce accompaniment.

in the south.[60] Though often dried and rehydrated, tofu skin is sometimes served fresh, for example in Japan, where it is called *yuba*.

Tofu itself, and not only the by-products, is frequently dried in Japan. Its development is intrinsically linked with Buddhism, of whose cuisine tofu forms an 'essential part' in Japan.[61] Widely available across the country is *kōya-dōfu* (also called *shimi-dōfu*), dried tofu possibly originating from the *ichiya-gōri* (literally 'frozen overnight') technique of food preservation, after which it is rehydrated for use in soups, among other dishes.[62] It gets its common name from Mount Koya, whose monks are believed to have developed the technique during the Kamakura period (1192–1333). The introduction of this preserved tofu has also been ascribed to Kukai (774–835), founder of the temple complex at

Mount Koya; he is also widely held to be behind the introduction of hiragana, a syllabic script for writing Japanese. Less well known is the preserved rokujō-dōfu, a variety of salted and sun-dried tofu in Japan.[63] A speciality of the mountainous Yamagata Prefecture, rokujō-dōfu was supposedly introduced to the region by a monk from Rokujo in Kyoto who was visiting the three holy mountains of Dewa Sanzan, hence the name. Used by shaving thin slices of it in soups, this extra-hard, long-lasting form of tofu is also called shōjin-bushi (roughly 'devotion flakes'), a portmanteau of katsuo-bushi (dried bonito flakes) and shōjin-ryōri, Japanese Buddhist vegetarian cuisine.[64]

By virtue of its versatility, dried tofu has long had an association with Buddhist cuisine in Japan. There's also kona-dōfu (powdered tofu), which is made from pieces of kōya-dōfu that have cracked or crumbled during production, and which is widely used today especially in creating okazu (side dishes) and elements of bento lunchboxes.[65] This is mainly in the form of kona-dōfu no iri-ni, which sees powdered tofu become a scrambled-egg-esque vehicle for sweet-and-savoury sliced vegetables. Iri-ni refers to a kind of braising technique in which ingredients are first cooked using sesame oil to condense their umami flavours, then simmered in dashi and soy sauce, with sugar, sake and mirin added.[66] Elsewhere in Buddhist cuisine kona-dōfu is utilized in kona-dōfu jiru, or powdered tofu soup. As well as a part of vegetarian temple food, this dish is used as an offering during higan-e, dual festivals observed during the autumn and spring equinoxes. Literally 'distant shore', higan is 'a Chinese rendering of the Sanskrit word pâramitâ, meaning to cross over from this shore of suffering to the other shore of nirvana, the realm where suffering ceases'. In Japan higan-e services are held to aid all sentient beings in passing from suffering to nirvana and 'Japanese families observe the festival period by visiting family graves, cleaning them, and making offerings of flowers, water, and festival foods in honor of deceased family members.'[67] *Kona-dōfu* was once known as something of a *maboroshi no ippin* (literally 'phantom dish'), something so rare that you can only find it in one place, owing to its production chiefly being in Nagano Prefecture.[68]

Another good example of dried tofu from Japan is *hoshi-age* or *hoshi-abura-age* (dried fried tofu), one variety of which is named *Matsuyama-age* after the city it hails from. Created by Hodono Shoten Ltd, it takes the drying process to an impressive stage of preservation. 'Ordinary *abura-age* only lasts for about seven days when stored in the refrigerator,' the website claims. 'Matsuyama-age can be stored at room temperature for about 90 days.'[69] From its spiritual founding in 1882, Hodono Shoten has passed through a variety of hands, and currently it is the sole producer of *hoshi-abura-age* in Matsuyama.[70] Its products are used for various purposes, including at military schools, and while Hodono Shoto

Strips of *dougan* for sale in Taiwan, a meaty addition to any meal.

Tofu powder, known in Japan as *kona-dōfu*, gives a grainy yet scrambled-egg texture to salad dishes, and is also added to soups.

is an industrial operation, in pursuing methods of preservation it nevertheless shares motivations behind many traditional forms of drying and fermentation. There is a similar necessity at work behind the longer shelf-life afforded by *hoshi-age*, generally taken from its usefulness as a *hijō-shoku* (emergency food) in Japan. Long-lasting foods such as this, either easy to eat or simple to rehydrate, can be stockpiled for use after natural disasters when food and water supplies may be cut short.

Just as tofu itself plausibly arose from a mingling of fortuitous discovery and ingenuity in the face of necessity, its various off-shoots, the fermented varieties and tofu by-products, likely find

A salad made with *okara* (tofu dregs) at Shimatofu-ya, Japan. Across the country, and across Asia, even the 'waste' products of the tofu-making process are put to good use.

their origins in a similar realm. Fermentation and drying have, from the earliest alcoholic beverages, cheeses and pickled vegetables, allowed for otherwise fresh, perishable items of food to be kept for longer periods of time. Philosophies of preventing food waste, making the most of every ingredient, such as the much popularized Japanese term *mottainai* (roughly 'waste not, want not'), may be a more modern way of looking at it. But for everyday people of centuries past beset with droughts, wars, famines, floods and other disasters, preservation was essential not only to food culture but for survival. As far as tofu is concerned, it resulted in a wealth of food items – solid, rehydratable cubes, meat-textured skins, soft chunks like strong cheese, all of which defy the popular conception of what can be done with bean curd. More than simply showcase the malleability of tofu and tofu products, these processes foreshadow later inventions in the world of vegan and vegetarian cuisine that drive cutting-edge meat alternatives today. But for these various innovations to flourish the way they have done, tofu would first have to travel the world.

Deep-fried tofu appears in many Vietnamese dishes, including *bún chay* (vegetarian noodles), a salad-type meal.

THREE
SPREADING THE CURD: HOW TOFU
TRAVELLED THE WORLD

As important to the story of tofu as its origins, and its subsequent manipulation by further processing the curd and its by-products, is how it spread from China across Asia (and, later, to continents beyond). Chinese influence in the region cannot be overstated.[1] Culture – from language and philosophy to food, and more besides – links East Asia together with China as the common denominator. For example, literary Chinese was once used to write in Korea, Vietnam and Japan; Japanese is still written using a mix of Chinese characters and native syllabic characters. These countries also use chopsticks, a Chinese invention, as standard. Confucian values have made their mark, especially in Korea.[2] In short, many aspects of language, religion and food in these nations can be traced to China, similar to the spread of ancient Rome's conglomerate culture throughout Europe. Though Southeast Asia owes much of its earlier cultural development to India (particularly in terms of religion and the Brahmic scripts used to write Thai, Lao, Khmer and other languages), many if not all of its former and present-day kingdoms and countries have at some point been tributary

Momen (firm) tofu as purchased from the venerable Shimatofu-ya on Amami Oshima, Kagoshima Prefecture, Japan.

states of China. Here Chinese trade and migration have existed for many centuries, with Chinese communities long embedded and sometimes, as is the case of Malacca in the fifteenth century, helping to 'grow' settlements for trading potential. Naturally these communities took culinary traditions with them.

Evidence for tofu's spread from China lies not only in the present-day culinary landscapes of various East and Southeast Asian nations, but in the very languages of this region themselves. This suggests a 'migration-related' spread of both foodstuffs and the spoken, as well as the written, word. For example, the Hokkien Chinese word for tofu, *tahu*, appears in a tenth-century Old Javanese inscription, making it the 'region's earliest Hokkien loanword'.[3] Dated to 902, placing its origin at the tail end of the Tang dynasty, this carved inscription provides the earliest concrete archaeological evidence for the presence of tofu somewhere other than China.[4] Scholar of Old Javanese inscriptions Antoinette M. Barrett Jones highlights 'mention of tahu eaten at a feast' in the Watakura A inscription of Central Java, which 'points to a Chinese influence'. Jones explains further that the process of making tofu could have been learned from Chinese people, 'either resident or visiting'; tofu must have been made in Java, she theorizes, 'as it does not carry'.[5]

Import and export between the Indonesian archipelago and China had been ongoing for centuries at the time of this inscription. The earliest known trade between the two occurred in 640 when the Javanese state of Ho-ling (also known as Kalingga) sent its first mission to China, beginning a fruitful venture for both nations.[6] It is believed that as many Chinese merchants headed there as they did to Srivajaya, a contemporary maritime empire centred at Sumatra.[7] This continued into the eighth and ninth centuries, evidenced by 'moderate quantities of Chinese stoneware present at most if not all of the temple sites in Central Java'.[8] Some forms of tofu in Indonesia didn't arrive until much later. One example is the turmeric-infused, yellow-hued tahu takwa (a speciality of Kediri), which arrived with Chinese immigrants in the early 1900s. Kediri, affectionately dubbed Kota Tahu ('Tofu City'), 'is believed to be the place of entry for tofu to Indonesia'.[9] One of these early Chinese immigrants to Kediri was Lauw Soen Hok, who started tahu takwa production here in 1912; the outfit he founded continues to trade under the name Bahkacung.[10] Another variety of deep-fried tofu, tahu sumedang, was invented in 1917 by a Chinese immigrant named Ong Kino;[11] crispy on the outside, smooth and melty on the inside, it resembles baojiang doufu ('patina tofu') from southwestern China. This nugget-esque tofu treat has an additional step of being soaked in sodium bicarbonate to soften up the curd before deep frying for that soft-centred finish.

Depiction of a man from
Kalingqa in the *Gujin Tushu
Jicheng* (Complete Classics
Collection of Ancient China),
1700–1725.

Across the Java Sea in Singapore, a Chinese community has
long been present. The island was mentioned in *Dao Yi Zhi Lüe*
(A Brief Account of Island Barbarians), a travelogue by navigator
Wang Dayuan, completed in 1349, in which he describes 'both
male and female Chinese people' inhabiting Singapore, then
called Danmaxi (Temasek in Malay). Wang's account describes
a rather inhospitable place: 'Fields barren. Little rice. Climate
is hot, with profuse rain in April and May,' he writes.[12] Whether
or not this fourteenth-century Chinese community brought
with them tofu-making expertise or even soybeans is unknown.
Several hundred years later, by the twentieth century tofu was
widespread in Singapore. There was a so-called Tofu Street (offi-
cially Upper Chin Chew Street), known for its association with

not only bean curd but the Samsui women, immigrants from Guangdong 'remembered for their can-do attitudes and willingness to work hard', and who are often credited as the 'key driving force through which Singapore managed to achieve its meteoric economic success'.[13] Such was its fame that 'Tofu Street' even inspired a drama series of the same name in 1996. Its association with hard-working, lower-class communities is a constant theme of tofu. It is cheap and relatively straightforward to make, but in order to do so there is a certain amount of elbow grease involved not befitting, at least historically, the middle classes.

A LACK OF TOFU IN SOUTHEAST ASIA

Southeast Asia is not exactly a heartland for tofu. But in various forms it is still an ingredient in popular dishes in the Philippines (most famously tokwa't baboy), Malaysia, Singapore and Thailand, most commonly in two guises: tofu puffs, and the chilled dessert tofu pudding, both of which have various local names. Soybeans prefer to grow in warm climates too, somewhere between 20 and 30°C (68–86°F), making much of Southeast Asia ideal for their cultivation.[14] Despite all this, tofu simply does not have the same breadth of variation or depth of cultural impact that it enjoys in China and Japan. Considering the probable origin of the soybean in this less tropical end of the world, the lack of its prevalence is not too mysterious. Well-established indigenous cuisines, and the region's stronger historical connection with ancient India than with ancient China, probably resulted in an indifferent initial reaction to soybeans, and tofu.

Nevertheless, throughout Southeast Asia, Chinese languages appear heavily in the realm of cuisine, accounting for 21 per cent of Chinese loanwords in Khmer, while Chinese loanwords in Thai 'often [relate] to ... food and beverage'.[15] Today there are around

7 million people who identify as Chinese in Thailand.[16] This number represents up to 10–12 per cent of the population.[17] But this connection with China did not equate to a wide-scale adoption of tofu, not in the same way as Japan, for example, even if it can be found in the cuisines of Thailand and Southeast Asia today. In the case of Thailand, Ernest Young (1869–1952), a fellow of the Royal Geographical Society, noticed the large Chinese population in Thailand during his 'several years' residing there in the late nineteenth century. 'As far as the casual observer can judge . . . in the streets nearly every workman is Chinese. There are nearly as many Chinese in the country as there are Siamese.'[18] Young doesn't appear to have seen, or cared to mention, tofu, but he does note Chinese hawkers with 'great pails of slimy, black jelly having the consistency and colour of blacking, but said to be extremely palatable with coarse brown sugar'.[19] This is most likely *chaokuai* (grass jelly, from the Teochew word *caoguo*) which shares a similar though unrelated manufacturing process to tofu, it being the result of the leaves and stalks of Chinese mesona (a member of the mint family), boiled and jellified.[20] Evidently foodstuffs of Chinese origin were present historically in Thailand. Actual black tofu (*tao hu dam*) does exist in Thailand. It is made by boiling pre-made tofu on a medium heat across three or four days in a mixture of five-spice powder, sugar, sea salt, cinnamon and star anise.[21] Arriving in Bangkok after travelling that way overland from Cambodia, French naturalist Henri Mouhot wrote, 'throughout my wanderings my only food had been rice or dried fish,'[22] which he confirmed in a letter to his brother dated 13 October 1860: 'My food is the same as that of the natives, dried fish and rice.'[23] As is the case with Young, had tofu been a staple foodstuff of either Cambodia or Thailand, chances are Mouhot would have at the very least encountered and, possibly, eaten it. Though the reliability of his testimony is not rock solid, and his

take on things skewed through a lens of superiority, Mouhot's observations are detailed enough to warrant a description of tofu had it been readily available or even in view. It seems that tofu never made such pointed inroads to the heart of Khmer cuisine as it did elsewhere in Asia.

Though 'very little' is known regarding 'the daily lives of Cambodians in prehistoric times . . . their diet, like that of Cambodians today, included a good deal of fish'.[24] It was the Tonle Sap (lake), 'the most densely populated fishbowl in the world', that provided 'generations of Cambodians with much of the protein for their diet'.[25] Indeed, 'mainstay supplements . . . fish, roots, locally grown spices . . . have changed very little from one century to the next'.[26] Mouhot also notes the significance of fish ('most plentiful') in the Cambodian diet, particularly the fact that dried fish both 'furnish food for the whole year, and are also exported in large quantities'.[27] Only recently has this changed. Today, alongside rice, cassava, corn and palm sugar, soybeans are cultivated in Cambodia,[28] and production there has been 'growing steadily since 1980'.[29] However, in 2018 it was announced that Cambodia, alongside Myanmar, would be receiving shipments of 'U.S. food-grade soybeans' for the production of soy milk and tofu, representing 'significant opportunities for U.S. soy to meet their growing demand for high-quality soybeans'.[30] More recently in Cambodia, a growing market for a plant-based diet due to awareness of its health benefits, and a renewed consideration of the meat industry's impact on the environment, may be fuelling a move towards tofu as a protein, though a flagging fish population in the Tonle Sap could, in theory, play a part.[31] The same is the case elsewhere in Southeast Asia. During his travels to present-day Myanmar, English artist Robert Talbot Kelly (1861–1934) observed that 'rice and vegetable curries, bananas, jack-fruit, papaya, and other fruits, form their staple

food, and, forbidden by their religion to take life, fish is practically the only variant to their vegetable diet'.[32] Kelly apparently
didn't see or notice the most famous tofu product of the country,
to hpu (known as 'Burmese tofu'). Usually associated with the
northern Shan region, this variant is not made with soybeans
but with chickpeas, which are ground, boiled with water, turmeric and salt, and then left to set, no coagulant needed.[33]

These three countries, Myanmar, Thailand and Cambodia,
are notable for the powerful status of Buddhism and Buddhist
monks within them. In Myanmar, where the number of Buddhist
monks is thought to be around half a million, there is a 'deeply-
rooted historical role of Buddhism in legitimising rulers'.[34] Min
Aung Hlaing, the leader of the 2021 Myanmar coup, has styled
himself as a protector of Theravada Buddhism.[35] Similarly, the
'Thai state strongly supports a conservative, orthodox and auth-
oritarian mode of Buddhism'.[36] Meanwhile in Cambodia, where
Buddhism was outlawed during the years of the Khmer Rouge
regime only to be re-established as the state religion in 1993, Buddhist monks are 'well respected by members of [their] community' and are 'endowed with importance in Cambodia's society'.[37]
Therefore it seems strange that tofu, given its vegetarian-friendly
credentials, would be overlooked historically, and consequently
there must be a reason for the lack of a widespread adoption of
tofu. First of all, and most obviously, these nations lay outside
what is considered the Sinosphere, and so such ready adoption
of tofu, vegetarian though it may be, should not be expected,
despite their historical trade entrepôts and Chinese communities. Second, in countries where Theravada Buddhism is practised
vegetarianism is commended but not enforced, and monks generally must accept whatever food is offered to them by laypeople;
not doing so 'would deprive the donor of good karma'.[38] Lastly,
using Thailand as an example, a strict vegetarian or vegan diet

has, for many young Thai people, often been associated with conservatism, and therefore avoided due to these ties.[39] Though this conclusion is speculative, it may be worth considering the point that vegetarianism and related foodstuffs, including tofu, could be construed as belonging to a separate, more politically aligned group of people.

At the very least vegetarianism is one of the aspirational '"tokens" of middle-class life . . . based on Sino-Thai ethics' in Thailand,[40] where the concept of *chay* or *jay* (veganism) is a tenet not only of Buddhist but Taoist beliefs, shown most vividly in the country's so-called Vegetarian Festival. With alleged roots in the miraculous recovery of a travelling Chinese opera troupe during a jaunt to Phuket in 1825, the festival sees people switching meat and fish for vegetables, tofu and other meat replacements over its nine-day period, among other expressions of 'Chinese religiosity'.[41] Though extreme aspects of the festival (for example, cheek piercing, tongue cutting, walking over hot coals and climbing bladed ladders) are 'regarded with . . . ambiguity and distrust', its vegetarian element is something that has been more widely accepted by middle-class Thai society.[42] In fact 'now even fast food chains like Burger King and Chester's Grill [provide] special vegetarian dishes' throughout the festival; abstinence from animal products is more easily reconciled with Theravada Buddhism, 'still one of the primary markers of Thai-ness'.[43] As part of a more modern trend participated in by urban Thai society, vegetarianism on this level works. This is not the first time that a foreign, that is, Chinese, concept has been repackaged with a veneer of Thai-ness. One of the nation's most recognizable dishes, pad thai, arose during a nationalistic campaign led by Prime Minister Phibunsongkran in the 1940s, in an effort to create 'a symbolic "Thai" national dish to counter the cultural influence of Thailand's Chinese population'.[44] For outsiders, a multicultural fusion of Chinese-style stir-fried noodles and 'Thai' flavours; in reality, power. And in among the hubbub of it all, the politics and the festivities, tofu is conceptually jostled around in a blazing wok of religion, migration and nation-building.

Some light can be shed on the presence of tofu in Southeast Asia by examining the practicality of tofu-making based on where soy was and was not grown or found growing wild. In his 1883 tome *Origin of Cultivated Plants*, French-Swiss botanist Alphonse de Candolle (1806–1893) maps this out in brief. He marks out the 'Malay Archipelago' as a cultivator of soybeans, as opposed to India, where 'there are no common Indian names' for soy, and the Pacific islands, which didn't grow them 'at the time of Cook's voyages'.[45] Its cultivation in China and Japan, he says, stems 'from remote antiquity', something the botanist himself gathers from 'the many uses of the soybean and from the immense number of varieties'.[46] Ultimately, de Candolle determines through 'known facts and historical and philological probabilities' that soy was distributed 'wild' in a triangulation between Cochin-China (roughly southern Vietnam), the south of Japan and Java. He theorizes that the existence of an indigenous Javanese word for soy, *kedelai*, points to an equally 'indigenous character' for soy, something that may help to explain the ancient Watakura inscription.[47] Though that was written as *tahu*, this was merely a loaned cooking technique rather than a loaned crop altogether. This heritage may also explain the prevalence of Indonesian tofu-makers (in their tens of thousands, as described later in Chapter Six) and fermented soy products including *oncom* and *tempeh*. The tofu-block-shaped spotlight, however, is not fixed on Java; instead, in the estimation of de Candolle and many modern-day onlookers, it is trained squarely on Japan.

TOFU ARRIVES IN JAPAN

Like Taoism and tofu in China, the first mention of tofu in Japan is tied to religion. In 1183 tofu was left as an offering at Kasuga shrine in Nara Prefecture, as recorded in the diary of the shrine's head priest.[48] The priest spelled out 'tofu' using Chinese characters that referred to the Tang dynasty, with which Japan constantly traded at the time, suggesting its borrowed origins during this dynasty.[49] According to the historic pronunciation of Chinese characters in Japanese, it could have been more like *daufu* or *taufu*. The ties of tofu to religion at this stage of its foray into Japan could mean one of two things (or both). First, that tofu as an imported product from their esteemed neighbour held a certain prestige, and was reserved for and enjoyed by the elite of the day. Second, that tofu had been used for similar religious offerings in Tang dynasty China, and Japan was following suit. Either way the production of tofu as far as this morsel of evidence can be trusted suggests that it was not enjoyed by lower-class citizens. Initially it is likely that tofu comprised an element of *shōjin ryōri* (Buddhist cuisine) in Japan and spread from there, first to the upper (samurai) classes. In 1350 there is mention of tofu in 'court documents', apparently in the form of *miso dengaku*: sliced, skewered tofu, grilled and slathered in miso paste.[50] These are named for their resemblance to the stilt-wearing *taka-ashi* (long-legged) or *sagi-ashi* (heron-legged) dancers present at certain iterations of rice-planting festivities called *dengaku*. Another theory maintains the first appearance of *dengaku* in relation to tofu was in 1427, found in *Inryoken Nichiroku*, the daily records of a monastic dormitory of Rokuon-in temple (a sub-temple of Shokuko-ji in Kyoto).[51] Kyoto, likely due to its proliferation of important religious (Shinto and Buddhist) complexes, became a centre of tofu-selling and eating, thus giving rise to *tōfu chaya* (tofu teahouses).

Triptych that depicts women preparing tofu and various fish dishes on an *engawa* (veranda), *c.* 1809, by Utagawa Toyokuni (1769–1825).

Primarily found near the gates to Shinto shrines in Kyoto, their proliferation was noted by various visitors to the city.[52] Nakamuraro, which dates back to the Muromachi period (1338–1573) is one famous example of such *chaya*. Famed for its tofu *dengaku*, it remains to this day located just outside the gates to Yasaka-jinja shrine.[53]

Though tofu is commonplace in Japan today, its status as an easy-to-come-by staple for the masses wasn't always secure. In his *Food and Fantasy in Early Modern Japan*, authority on Japanese food history Eric Rath discusses the limitations on peasants' diets. Shogun Tokugawa Iemitsu – grandson of the famed unifier of Japan, Tokugawa Ieyasu – issued an edict in 1642, reiterated in 1649, that restricted rice to 'tribute payments', limiting commoners to brown rice, barley and millet. There were additional restrictions on everyday fare. Peasants were forbidden from brewing alcohol, or travelling to towns and cities to purchase it; they were also banned from making or buying wheat noodles and tofu.[54] The act had a twofold effect, according to Rath: lower classes were thus compelled to pay taxes in the rice they were forbidden to eat themselves, and it emphasized a 'distinction between class structures in society'.⁵⁵ The context of the edict puts a darker spin on proceedings, given that these restrictions on food were put in place as a reaction to the Kan'ei Great Famine (1640–43), in which tens of thousands of people perished. Despite the mundane nature of tofu in Japan today, its appearance on this ban of foods suggests that the authorities deemed it something that peasants could do without, as if it were something of a luxury. Whether or not the daimyo or regional rulers of the day still enjoyed a select supply of bean curd themselves is unknown; they certainly had access to choice foodstuffs reserved for their class (sea cucumbers and abalone included).

It was only in the later years of the Edo period (1603–1868) that tofu firmly gained its place on tables throughout Japan. Tofu dishes began to appear on *mitate banzuke*. These lists were based on sumo *banzuke*: rankings for upcoming sumo tournaments originally painted on wood but later printed on paper and still produced today. *Mitate banzuke* ranked all sorts of things, from the size and scale of natural disasters to comedians.⁵⁶ As Eric Rath noted in 2013, food was also included, with one particularly unusual listing being concerned chiefly with cheap eats: *Nichiyō kenyaku ryōri shikata sumō banzuke* (Sumo Banzuke for Daily Frugal Cooking).⁵⁷ Dated to the 1830s, the gastronomic *banzuke* features rankings for various types of food, including vegetarian. In this plant-based section six out of ten dishes feature tofu. These are *hachihaidōfu* (simmered eight-cup tofu), *kobu abura-age* (fried tofu and kelp), *yakidōfu suishitaji* (grilled tofu simmered in soy sauce soup), *hijiki shiroai* (tofu with hijiki seaweed), *imogara abura-age* (simmered taro stems and fried tofu) and *abura-age tsukeyaki* (fried tofu marinated in soy sauce and grilled). Tofu's status as a low-cost morsel is further exemplified by other literature of the day, as in *Ukiyoburo* (Bathhouse of the Floating World) by Shikitei Sanba

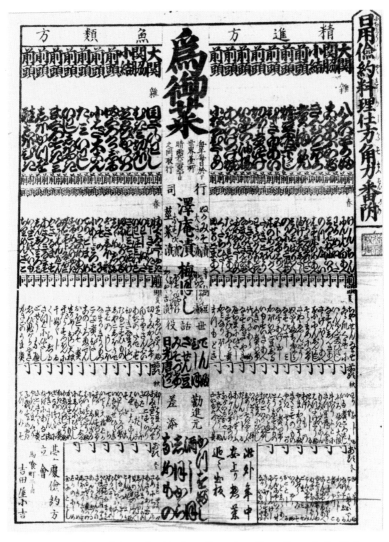

The various rankings of cheap food in the 19th-century *Sumo Banzuke for Daily Frugal Cooking*.

(1776–1822). Published between 1809 and 1813, the *kokkeibon* (comic novel) tells the everyday lives of various bath-goers. One character named Cheap Hyōe declares his love for tofu; thanks to the ubiquitous eateries in the city, he can easily satisfy his appetite by purchasing a portion of grilled tofu. He is one of Edo's 'lower-class diners ... who strove to eat tofu all the time'. Understandable, given the price: 'Small servings of grilled and fried tofu cost just five coppers,' writes Rath.[58]

Nothing quite demonstrates the definitive spread of tofu among the masses, not to mention its versatility as an ingredient, more than *Tofu Hyakuchin*. Published in 1782, this recipe book reflects the transition of tofu from an easily procurable street food to something so everyday that everybody can cook at least one thing with it. Translating roughly to *A Hundred Tricks with Tofu*, this volume quite literally deals with one hundred recipes for

Left to right: *abura-age* (fried tofu), *yakidōfu* (grilled tofu) and *momendōfu* (firm tofu) in Takahashi Yuichi, *Tōfu*, 1877, oil on canvas. Takahashi Yuichi was a pioneer of *yōga* or Western-style painting.

tofu. Here tofu moves from the streets to the kitchens of the emerging middle classes. It begins with kinome dengaku – grilled tofu on skewers slathered with kinome miso, made with the addition of citrusy sanshō (Japanese pepper) – and ends with shin-no-udon tōfu, which involves tofu cut into thick strips (like udon noodles) using a tool called a tokoro-ten tsuki and served in a broth of soy, sake and dashi, garnished with grated daikon, diced root of a spring onion, mikan (satsuma) peel, Asakusa nori seaweed and chilli powder.[59] The book was so popular that not just one but two follow-ups came after: Tōfu Hyakuchin Zokuhen (Sequel to a Hundred Tricks with Tofu) and Tōfu Hyakuchin Yōroku (A Hundred More Tricks with Tofu).[60] One delicious-sounding recipe does not make the cut of the original book: awayuki-dōfu (snowflake tofu). Originally sold along the riverside at Ryogoku, Tokyo, this

Agedashidōfu consists of deep-fried silken tofu steeped in dashi (broth) with toppings such as spring onions, a staple at many izakaya (Japanese pubs). Though it doesn't appear in Tofu Hyakuchin, a recipe for something similar, shaka tōfu, does.

dessert tofu is extremely soft; it was a speciality of Bizen-ya, a confectionary store in Okazaki, Aichi Prefecture, dating back to 1782.[61] This obviously leaves out recent iterations like *karashi tōfu*, a bowl-shaped variety with a mustard centre, served with powdered nori and soy sauce. The list could go on and on. The sheer proliferation of tofu recipes in Japan, numbering in their hundreds according to the *Hyakuchin* series (not to mention the regional varieties and recipes like *awayuki-dōfu* that weren't included), shows that tofu has long been a cornerstone of Japanese cuisine.

TOFU IN THE AMERICAS: IMMIGRANT COMMUNITIES

Japanese tofu didn't stay in Japan. Emigration from the country helped to spread culinary techniques and ingredients well beyond the bounds of Asia. In the case of Brazil, home to the world's largest part of the Japanese diaspora, this began on 8 June 1908, when the steamship *Kasato Maru* brought the first group to work on coffee plantations in São Paulo.[62] Emigration stopped after the arrival of the *Buenosu Airesu Maru* at Santos, Brazil, on 13 August 1941, with Japan's entry into the Second World War imminent.[63] In the intervening 33 years, a total of 188,209 Japanese citizens had made their way to Brazil.[64] Those unfamiliar with agricultural work quickly moved to urban centres, either small to medium-sized cities of the interior or the capital itself, São Paolo. Japanese men and women were 'fought over' by rich Brazilians looking for butlers, drivers and governesses; Japanese men worked as cabinetmakers; some learned new trades, becoming barbers, or photographers. Others filled 'niches directed more towards the other Japanese [people], such as the production of Japanese products – tofu and shoyu (soy sauce), or sake'.[65] Tofu in the setting of Brazil exists surely due to its importance to the many thousands

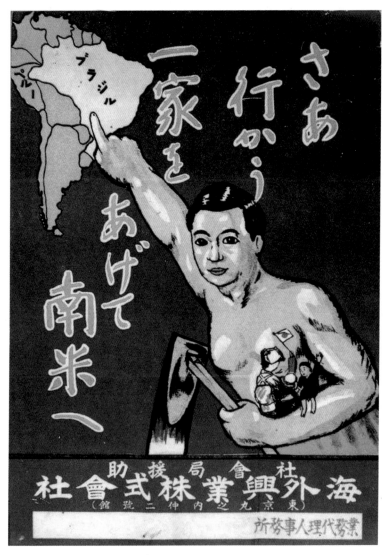

Poster advertising emigration to Japanese people, *c.* 1907. The caption reads, 'Let's go! Take your family to South America.'

of expatriated Japanese people arriving on South American shores. They had not just their skills to offer, but their culinary culture.

Similarly the value ascribed to tofu by Chinese immigrant communities in Latin America cannot be understated. However, without the know-how or raw ingredients for making tofu to hand, substitutions had to be made. This can be seen in Nicaragua. The nation's Chinese community is relatively small today, comprising around 3,000 people according to the Nicaraguan Chinese Association, but the population may be higher (possibly closer to 14,000).[66] An interview in a 2016 paper with one Nicaraguan of Chinese descent related how, though 'some . . . traditions may have been lost', food brought many closer to their identity. Considering Nicaragua's climate, 'proper ingredients' were hard to come by and approximations were often made by immigrants who moved there in the early nineteenth century: 'Chinese Nicaraguans would make their own soy sauce, using beans found [there] instead of the traditional red beans. For tofu, they would substitute almost similar foods like cheese.'[67] Maintaining tofu as part of the diet, even in this edited or reimagined form, was integral to the continuation of culture. While tofu itself didn't spread in this particular case, its physicality was sought after enough for approximations to flourish for the sake of familiarity.

Such communities in other Central and South American countries vary in terms of their size and impact on local cuisine. In Mexico, large-scale Chinese immigration began in the late nineteenth century, but in the wake of growing anti-Chinese sentiment the 1930s saw deportations and expulsions of Chinese Mexicans. In present-day Mexico City, the unofficial Chinatown is in Viaducto, home to 'the city's newest Chinese immigrants'. Here 'small, unmarked groceries with shelves of rice and teas, and petite bakeries selling Chinese pastries' dot the streets, providing much-needed home comforts to recently arrived immigrants. One of the neighbourhood's best-known restaurants, Ka Won Seng, serves 'cold tofu in chile sauce', among other dishes, reflecting the taste for tofu in a recognizable dish.[68] Elsewhere Chinese cuisine has become more readily integrated with national cuisine, as in Peru's 'fusion' cuisine *chifa*. There are thousands of *chifa* restaurants in Lima alone. Some Peruvian dishes reflect not only Chinese but Japanese influence, as in *tiradito Lima-Sichuan*. *Tiradito* primarily involves *sashimi*-like cuts of raw fish (Japanese immigrants arrived in Peru over a century ago on the *Sakura Maru*), yet in this case there is a Sichuan-style twist of spicy sauce, sometimes studded with tofu akin to the Sichuan speciality of *mapo* tofu.[69]

Wherever there is a Chinese or Japanese community, it is likely that tofu also exists there – and in some cases has for generations. In Hawaii tofu was 'definitely made on the plantations by Japanese and probably Chinese immigrants' and spread from there.[70] One local resident, Howard Kodama, recalled in an interview on Hawaii Public Radio: 'They used to have what they called the yasai [grocery] man, he used to come with the truck peddlers, house to house. The tofu was floating in the water and you bring your own bowl.'[71] The *yasai* man may not be around any more, but neighbourhood tofu shops still exist in Hawaii. One is Aloha Tofu, Honolulu, which began in 1950 when husband-and-wife team Kamesaburo and Tsuruko Uyehara took over a pre-existing tofu factory. Rather than simply getting by in terms of tofu production, or opting for an approximation, the heritage of its production in Hawaii illustrates that instead tofu thrived for many years. Also worth considering is the occupation of many early immigrants to Hawaii, who were often destined for plantation work and therefore may have had some level of agricultural know-how, no matter how small. It is a simple equation in this case: the larger the community accustomed to eating tofu, the greater the demand for tofu.

TOFU IN CENTRAL ASIA: THE KOREAN DIASPORA

Hawaii and its plenty in terms of tofu and tofu production is worlds away from the experience of the Korean population of Russia and Central Asia. Integration and making do played their part in a similar way, but while tofu became an everyday item in Hawaii, it is more of a treasure for ethnic Koreans scattered across the steppe, a result of scarcity and the nature of their arrival in the region. Korean migration to Russia began in earnest at the tail end of the Joseon era (1392–1897), with waves of Koreans leaving due to drought (in 1863) and famine (1869–70), among other reasons. This was not to last. In 1937 the Koreans of the Russian Far East were deported and spread out in Soviet Central Asia, leading to the 'near-complete wiping out of the Korean presence in the Far Eastern provinces'.[72] In total around 180,000 ethnic Koreans were forcibly relocated to rural areas of Kazakhstan and Uzbekistan.[73]

One of the lasting impacts of the Koryo-saram (as Central Asian Koreans refer to themselves) population of Russia and Central Asia is their cuisine, not least in the form of carrot salad, one of many *koreyskie salaty* (Korean salads) available in Central Asia and Russia. Called *morkovcha* – from Russian *morkov*, meaning carrot, and *cha* (a transliteration of *chae*, a salad-type *banchan* or side dish in Korean cuisine) – it is ubiquitous. According to a thesis written by Jayoung Francesca-Maria Shin on the subject of Koryo-saram identity in Almaty, Kazakhstan, 'Korean "carrot salad" is a common feature at a bazaar.'[74] Another common *koreyskie salat* is *sparzha*. The name of this salad literally means 'asparagus' in Russian, perhaps coming from the misconception of its main ingredient as stewed asparagus, rather than the dried tofu skins that comprise its true identity.[75] Another more recent misinterpretation appeared on the food-focused Central Asian Facebook group Vegetaristan. Here it was misidentified as 'dried bamboo', presumably in recognition of the literal meaning of the Chinese characters on packets of fuzhu.[76] The dish has older roots than the modern use of dried tofu skins sold in plastic packaging suggests; it was originally most likely born of necessity, preserving this by-product of tofu production through the cold winters of Central Asia, thus providing a lifeline to Korean gastronomic heritage.[77]

In its fresh form, tofu, which takes time and effort to prepare, is imbued with care and respect in Koryo-saram communities. Tofu (dubu in Korean) is thought to have been present in Korea from around the late Goryeo period (918–1392), when it was afforded an elevated status as both temple fare and an element of royal cuisine. Its first mention in Korean literature was by the writer and poet Yi Saek (1328–1396), also known by his pen name Mogeun, who wrote in the Mokeunjip (The Collected Works of Mogeun) that he ate tofu after the gwageo (civil service examination) in 1365, suggesting a ceremonial or symbolic status for bean curd.[78] This hypothesis can be further evidenced by the existence of specialized temples called joposa (literally 'bubble-making temples') dedicated to making tofu for sacrificial rites. The philosopher and agronomist Jeong Yak-yong (1762–1836) mentioned them in 1819: 'Each [Joseon dynasty royal tomb] has a temple. This temple supplies tofu and is called joposa.'[79] Guards placed at Buddhist temples ensured tofu was not being used carelessly, forming a further composite image of its considered place in Korean society.[80]

There seems to be a special status afforded to tofu in Korea, something symbolic and closer to religion than its humble, earthy status in China. In the case of the Korean diaspora in Central Asia, tofu takes on a central role; more than just a hard-to-come-by ingredient, it connects to the effort involved in its creation. 'All markers of festivity, respect, hospitality and prestige in the form of bean curd and rice cake are potent symbols of delayed gratification, a triumphant manipulation of time over nature,' Shin writes.[81] She describes the 'nourishing and emotive aspect' of Korean cuisine in the form of stew, often including dried vegetables and tofu; it is 'perceived as "proper" and gratifying comfort food'. The 'trouble' of sourcing ingredients for stew and the time taken in its cooking carry 'an emotional note of care, indulgence and treats, if not strictly respect'.[82] Most telling of all regarding tofu's role and stature in Koryo-saram cuisine, or identity itself, is Shin's description of 'a gift of a chunk of bean curd, the local Korean delicacy made by . . . elderly parents', almost as if it were a chunk of Korean-ness itself.[83] The use of the word 'delicacy' says it all.

TOFU ON THE AFRICAN CONTINENT: GLOCALIZATION IN MOTION

Tofu can likewise represent a chunk of Chinese-ness for those who find themselves far from their homes. It is an important element in the inventory of workers in Chinese state-owned enterprises (SOE). Before the civil war broke out in Libya in the 2010s, though there were numerous Chinese labourers and white-collar migrants, private entrepreneurs were 'few in number' and catered to SOE workers. These included four Chinese restaurants in Tripoli (all on the same street), a quarry, a steel factory, and one Chinese food workshop that produced tofu and imported Chinese ingredients for Chinese labourers and employees.[84] The wholesale business began as an underground enterprise, but once it started earning stable profits, Zhao, its owner, brought his father, brother and brother's wife to Libya, 'where they began producing tofu and other soya bean-derived products' for Chinese employees of SOEs in Tripoli.[85] Workplaces isolated from the Libyan populace and culture were orchestrated to be 'as Chinese an environment as possible'; gaps left by any lifestyle elements not provided for by contractors were filled by 'astute Chinese business men' who operated services as disparate as Chinese-style barbering and tofu delivery.[86] Here tofu represents a difference between Chinese people and the new country in which they found themselves, a symbolic link to back-home cuisine and culture, and an important aspect of Chinese gastronomy given the foundational level at which tofu-making appears. It also represents a divide between the enclave of expatriates and the local community from which it is cloistered.

In Zambia, Chinese workers live similarly sequestered in settlements locally known as 'Chinese camps', where Zambians cannot enter without permission from the Zambian guard on the gate. Largely isolated, Chinese foremen 'heavily rely on their employers' provision to make a living in Zambia.' For example, living pigs, fresh vegetables and tofu are regularly transported to the Chinese camp from Lusaka, the capital city.'[87] Such provisions are not made in Ethiopia, where tofu and other basic processed products are made locally by Chinese entrepreneurs. The focus of activity is at Rwanda Market in central Addis Ababa, 'the only open-air market in the city that sells Chinese vegetables' – a trade interestingly 'dominated by local vendors'.[88] One of these salespeople described

> homemade food items we receive from the Chinese to sell,
> such as Doya [bean sprouts], Tofu, and homemade noodles.
> There is one woman who makes Doya and Tofu at her home,

and drives here to deliver to us . . . And this Chinese guy also brings us the pasta we sell.[89]

As recorded by a 2019 study into Rwanda Market, there are also non-local vendors, such as Ms Tang, who is originally from Dalian, in the northeastern province of Liaoning. 'Business is brisk, as is clear from the trucks constantly pulling up outside to buy her vegetables, tofu and pork . . . "There are more and more Chinese here," she says, "so business is good."'[90] Tofu is the only non-traditional commodity in Ethiopia that is monopolized by Chinese producers, filling a predominantly Chinese market. It is generally not available in supermarkets, but can be found in speciality shops, only a couple of which exist. As the study goes on to explain, one of these small shops is run by a Mr Bekele. It is 'one tiny undecorated room with plain white walls. A large refrigerator, a table and a couple of chairs are the only furnishings.' The only products sold are fresh tofu 'in large blocks' and 'large squares of *dougan* [firm, spiced tofu] and sheets of *doupi* [thin, dried tofu skin]'. Mr Bekele runs the shop with a Chinese business partner who has also taught him how to make tofu. The other shop selling tofu is that operated by Ms Tang. Though it is mainly purchased by Chinese, as well as a few Korean and Japanese, residents of Addis Ababa, it seems tofu is catching on in Ethiopia even though it is a 'new food'. Mr Bekele himself reported, 'I eat it every day in the morning, with some oil, tomato and spice, just like egg.' Elsewhere in Ethiopia, tofu is gaining traction as a fasting food. Rather than local cuisine assimilating that of the incoming Chinese expatriates, a Chinese ingredient, tofu, has made its way from the more protected, cloistered Chinese community into the lives of Ethiopian people.

Culinary connections with China and any skills in specialized cooking are valued: 'An example of [this is] the tofu producers in Ethiopia, who have cornered the market on a specialty item.'[91]

At the other end of the spectrum is the island nation of Mauritius, which features a long-standing Chinese community and its own idiosyncratic tofu: *teokon*. Presumably this is taken from the Hakka pronunciation of *dougan*. Alongside Madagascar, the island of Réunion and South Africa, Mauritius hosts one of Africa's 'four oldest and largest Chinese communities'.[92] The first wave of settlers arrived in the nineteenth century and later Chinese immigrants arrived from the 1990s onward (the 'second wave').[93] Hakka-inflected cuisine abounds in Mauritius; the French-named *boulettes*, also known by their Hakka name *niouk yen*, are a type of meatball common throughout the island.[94] Elsewhere, reminiscent of *yong tao foo* (Hakka stuffed tofu), *teokon farci* are tofu skins filled with fish paste, *farci* being the French word for 'stuffed'. Time, over a hundred years of it, has allowed for Chinese cuisine to integrate in the case of Mauritius, suggesting that this contemporary adoption of tofu in Ethiopia may yield similar results for the nation's future dinnerplates. If Mr Bekele's breakfast routine is anything to go by, it is already happening.

In West Africa there is a very different relationship between the local populace and tofu. *Wara* is a milk curd product that originates from the historically nomadic Fulani people, who refer to it as *warankashi*.[95] It can be found in Nigeria, Togo, Ghana, Benin, Niger and Algeria, all under similar names. The creation of the curd follows the general process of making cheese: in this case, boiling cow's milk and adding *Calotropis procera* leaves to make it curdle, after which the whey is decanted and the resulting 'soft mass' is cut into small sizes and served raw or fried.[96] What is most interesting about *wara* is how in recent decades the milk used to make it has been swapped out for soybeans instead. The result is soy *wara*, also *awara*, often dubbed 'Nigerian tofu'.

Soybeans, the 'Malayan' variety, were introduced in 1908 to Nigeria, where they were first cultivated for export in small-holdings or in citrus orchards, representing 'a long history of soybean production by indigenous farmers'.[97] Hypothetically, this historical soybean cultivation in Nigeria, combined with an indigenous cheese with nomadic roots, may lend credence to the theorized adoption of soybeans over animal milk for tofu production in ancient China. However, while there is a missing link between cheese and bean curd regarding the exact origins of tofu in China, the story of *awara* in Nigeria has a named agent: food technologist and tofu expert Osamu Nakayama.

Having travelled to Nigeria with the Japan International Cooperation Agency (JICA) in 1989, once there he 'developed a procedure for making tofu', leading to the creation of soy *wara* and its consequential spread around West Africa.[98] Today, 'soy wara is a common ready-to-eat food' in Nigeria and, according to research carried out by cultural anthropologist Hirokazu Nakamura, 'one of the most popular foods amongst Nigerians'.[99] Yet more names exist for the soybean version of *wara*, including *beeske* (or *beske*), seemingly from English 'beans cake', and *k'waidak'wai*, perhaps 'comparing it to the whites of eggs'.[100] *Awara* is the principal moniker of soybean curd in both Nigeria and Niger, and can be 'inferred as the oldest local name for soya bean curd because of its extensively geographical distribution'.[101] Nakayama authored a recipe book with Nigerian education, food, nutrition and agriculture expert Sidi Osho, the purpose of which was 'to enhance the nutritional value and taste of traditional Nigerian dishes, without increasing the time or cost of preparing them'.[102]

Projects abound throughout the African continent regarding the promotion of soybeans, but it is from Nigeria that *awara* has emerged as a rising star of the soybean world. Here it represents a naturalization of tofu as opposed to an unfamiliar product.

Soy has come a long way from its first introduction by Chinese traders to sub-Saharan Africa (SSA) in the nineteenth century, and its subsequent cultivation as an 'economic crop as early as 1903 in South Africa'.[103] Today, according to one 2018 article, Nigeria is 'the best example in SSA for promoting utilization of soy-based food products in rural and urban areas'.[104] The paper suggests that, much like traditional, small-scale operations in East and Southeast Asia, the high esteem for soy-based foodstuffs in Nigeria may be due to the 'development of home-level and small-scale processing technologies'. It involves training people, from 'local farmers and village leaders' to hands-on technical staff, but it also enjoys 'support from the public and private sectors'.[105] This is an example of successful 'glocalization', whereby a globalized product (in this case, soybeans) is adjusted to fit or meet local standards or needs (through the vessel of *wara*). The spread of tofu in this instance could be attributed to the spread of Japanese soft power, while the longevity and popularity of the product relies partially on monetary incentive. In Kenya, for example, JICA representative Tomoko Yakushigawa taught smallholders about growing soybeans and cooking them for home consumption. Yakushigawa also explained, in a video for China Global Television Network (CGTN) Africa, that 'tofu . . . can be sold at a much higher price' (more than double) compared to soybeans for animal feed.[106] This can be traced back to a simple piece of Song dynasty wisdom: acquaint yourself with the arts of Huainan, sit back and reap money.

From the graven stone of Java which told the world that tofu had been eaten in the kingdom of Watakura, to its more recent glocalized spread, the journey of tofu has been a long and varied one. While the lack of integration in some cases does not allow tofu to be enjoyed beyond close-knit immigrant communities, as in Zambia, for example, much of the time tofu, tofu skin and *okara* have been developed for local cuisines and by indigenous traditions. Mauritian, Peruvian, even Russian cuisines have been enriched by the presence of Chinese, Japanese and Korean communities, adding to the perceived repertoire of national dishes, tofu appearing among it all. In many cases in East and Southeast Asia, tofu is deeply embedded. It is without a thought that we consider *taho, tau foo fah* and *douhua* (all names for tofu pudding) a commonplace snack of Filipino, Malaysian, Indonesian and (southern) Chinese cuisine irrespective of ethnicity. It is doubtful that you would consider a *taho* vendor in Manila a purveyor of Chinese snacks. In Japan tofu has developed further into a culinary realm of its own, spawning eight-hundred-year-old bean-curd-based meat substitutes, native preservation techniques and hundreds of other 'tricks with tofu'. Throughout this chapter, one vast swathe of the world has remained absent: the wild, bread-eating West. The scientific study, advocacy, adoption, confusion, co-option, revulsion and rejection of tofu by Westerners, whose general culture engaged in centuries of colonialism and facilitated the spread of peoples (and their tofu) across the world, deserves a chapter of its own – and it's not pretty.

Natef? It's hard to say. This is a savoury-sweet analogue of *douhua* (tofu pudding) as served in Japan.

FOUR
TOFU'S JOURNEY TO THE WEST

Tofu's probable birth in China, a historical heavyweight in East and Southeast Asia, allowed for it to spread with relative ease in the region. Owing to the origin of the soybean in the general area, local populations could produce their own varieties of tofu using their own methods; fresh tofu doesn't travel well, especially without refrigeration, and this early, spontaneous glocalization allowed for tofu to make its mark. Wherever it caught on, it flourished and took on local flavours. Later in the twentieth century, this same introduction of tofu-making processes and skills through immigration by Chinese, Japanese, Korean and other Asian peoples empowered non-Asian soy-growing nations and communities to make good use of soybeans, a crop otherwise destined for animal feed. This provided an innovative source of protein for populations new to bean curd.

Despite its spread across the vast lands of China and the archipelagos and peninsular coastlines beyond, it would take a long time for the Western world to take note of tofu. In the early modern period of European exploration, trade and colonialism, when local habits of Asian countries were documented by variously enterprising and marauding explorers and their retinues and religions, tofu rarely figured among descriptions of a local diet. This may be due to a lack of contact with commoners (by this point tofu had possibly shed its elite connections), meat and other delicacies being the preserve of the upper classes with whom these explorers had dealings. It may also be due to a difficulty in recognizing foodstuffs beyond preconceived notions of what local people ate in whatever given region. It could also be assumed that there was simply no interest in describing foods. Writers concerned with military prowess or trade capabilities, for example, are not likely to have been peering over people's shoulders to see what was on their dinner plates, nor asking questions about it.

NATEF, OR THE WORLD'S FIRST DESCRIPTION OF TOFU

Trade with East and Southeast Asia from a westerly direction, rather than with 'the West', began much earlier than Catholic missionaries or the activities of Europe's various East India Companies. The role of the Middle East in facilitating cultural and mercantile trade with the East, and spreading Islam to Indonesia and the Philippines as early as the seventh century, via the so-called Maritime Silk Road, could serve to explain an early western route of tofu, or even a potential journey to the east of a similar dish. This theory begins with a twelfth-century Arabic manuscript known in English as *Accounts of China and India*. The manuscript, copied from an earlier original, discovered in seventeenth-century Paris, translated by Eusèbe Renaudot (1646–1720) and published in 1718, details in two parts the travels of possibly two Arabic traders during a visit to China. It is attributed to Abu Zayd al-Sirafi, a tenth-century seafarer who wrote what is chiefly a commentary in the second section of the work, and who dated the first, anonymous section to 851. In a tantalizing description of food in China, the narrator describes 'a kind of comfit, like that called *Natef* by the Arabs and some others'.[1] Also referred to as soapwort meringue, *natef* is made using the roots of soapwort (*Saponaria officinalis*) called *shirsh el-halaweh* in Arabic.[2] These roots are boiled until the water becomes brown; strained, the murky water is whipped up, eventually and miraculously forming a thick, white substance with a smooth, sometimes marshmallowy consistency.[3] Given the fairly limited range of matching, white-coloured dessert dishes in ninth-century China, it is plausible that the 'kind of comfit' like *natef* was tofu in some form, maybe *douhua*, or at least a tofu-adjacent product. If so, this would be the oldest known non-Chinese reference to tofu. The original French word used in the text, *confiture*, describes a preserve or jelly; to add extra intrigue to this potential mention of bean curd, an early French term for tofu was *confiture de soya*.

If it wasn't tofu as we know it, made from soybeans, this 'comfit' may have been *xingren doufu* (annin tofu), which is made by jellifying crushed and boiled apricot kernels. Today referred to as almond tofu, given the glint of marzipan in taste, *xingren doufu* wasn't always as solid as it is on modern menus, and also existed in the form of *xingren lao* (apricot kernel curds), a yoghurty version of the dessert. This was traditionally served during the Cold Food Festival (*Hanshi Jie*), a Chinese spring festival marking the death of Jie Zhitui, a nobleman who died in a fire in the seventh century BC, celebrated on the 105th or 106th day after the Lunar New Year. It is characterized by a reverent avoidance of fire.[4] *Xingren lao* seems to be synonymous with *li lao* (sweet curds), a yoghurt-esque porridge made using apricot kernels and maltose, which was popular up until the Sui and Tang dynasties. A recipe for it appears in the sixth-century *Qimin Yaoshu*: 'The people mourned for [Jie] on the anniversary of the death, avoiding fire and eating *li lao*, called "cold food", the day before the Qingming Festival.'⁵ There is an entire section of the *Qimin Yaoshu* dedicated to soybeans that makes no mention of tofu, which, if it were a staple or even if it had been discovered by this stage, seems strange.

Outside China, desserts in this general family also have a long history. According to legend, the traditional Arabic dessert *muhallebi* (or *muhallabiyya*) was first made with almond milk in the sixth century by a Persian cook for an Arabic general. Another similar gelatinous dessert is the Aleppan *heytaliyye*, which may have made its way to Syria from China along the Silk Road, or vice versa; it's also eaten in porcelain bowls with a porcelain spoon resembling a *tangchi* (known as a 'Chinese spoon'). Even blancmange is believed to have roots in Arabic trade. Rather than as an approximation of the cheese-making process, tofu may have arisen as a kind of imitation of dishes like this – whether invented

The marzipan lilt of annin tofu comprises part of the first course of the *kaiseki* dining experience at Amami Resort Hotel Thida Moon, Amami Oshima, Japan.

TOFU'S JOURNEY TO THE WEST

in China or Persia – which required more effort, were much more seasonal and, in many cases, were destined for courtly stomachs only. Soybeans being easier to grow and process, not to mention simple to sweeten with additional ingredients, could have popularized tofu as a substitute for these potentially older almond-based sweet treats. That these desserts, and not cheese, are an ancestor of tofu would perhaps explain its non-appearance in Chinese literature until the Song dynasty. It may also represent the first journey west for tofu desserts like this. Chinese prisoners of war following the Battle of Talus, fought between Tang dynasty China and the Abbasid caliphate in 751, are believed to be responsible for introducing papermaking to the Arab world; Chinese painters and silk weavers were also described as part of Abbasid society.[6] Whether or not they also brought culinary know-how with them is unknown, but their counterparts, more willing Islamic immigrants to China, do seem to have brought consumables along for the ride. Chinese sources from the time document merchants from Persia and Central Asia in Chang'an, the Tang capital, and the 'strong cultural influence of their flourishing activities on the lives of Chinese [people] including foreign fashions, music, and foods'; this was particularly concentrated in the western portion of the city, where Chinese people went 'for wine and foreign foods'.[7] This early contact between two great empires of the day almost certainly resulted in cross-cultural, if not cross-culinary, exchanges, bringing tofu or tofu-adjacent foods from one sphere of the globe to the other.

TOFU IN THE AGE OF DISCOVERY

There are indications that later Western observers were familiar with tofu. Several instances detailing the recognition of bean curd were recorded in the seventeenth century before knowledge of tofu spread further. The earliest mention of tofu by a European was in the 1603 *Vocabulario da Lingoa de Iapam*, a Japanese–Portuguese dictionary compiled by Jesuit missionaries in Nagasaki. These missionaries most likely had some sort of contact with everyday people as they worked to evangelize in local populations, actively employing Japanese lay converts as *dōjuku* (acolytes) in these efforts, and evidently tofu was on the menu. The dictionary lists 'Tŏfu' as 'a certain kind of food that is made from ground grains in the manner of fresh cheeses'. It even mentions 'Tŏfuya', describing it as a 'House where they make, or sell, that manner of soft cheese from milled beans'.[8] Its inclusion in a dictionary hints at tofu's essential status in Japanese food culture by this time; the addition of an entry for tōfu-ya (tofu maker) highlights a universal making and selling of tofu, at least in such urban centres as Nagasaki.

Several years later we have a likely mention of tofu in a journal kept by Captain John Saris, who headed up the first English trade voyage to Japan in 1611. Saris's journal details his time spent on Japanese shores during 1613, in which he mentions that every town and village has 'cooks-shops and victualling houses', and that the most used foodstuff is 'rice of different qualities'.[9] He also writes that 'they have plenty of cheese, but have no butter, and use no milk, because they consider it to be of the nature of blood.'[10] It is a common misconception, as is the case with China, that cheese or dairy products never existed in Japan. Cow's milk was hailed as medicinal by Emperor Kōtoku (596–654), and in the Heian period (794–1185) the manufacture of dairy products was enshrined in a specific imperial agency called the Nyūgyūin (Cow's Milk Section). Taxation based on a brown, cheese-like product called *so*, made from the skin of boiled milk pressed in layers, persisted until the end of the Heian period. Dairy fell into decline, though it showed some 'resurgence' in the eighteenth century with the development of *hakugyūraku* (white cow's milk), which was used medicinally.[11] That said, due to the probable disappearance of any imperial dairy agency by the time of Saris's arrival, what he describes as cheese is very plausibly tofu. *The Diary of Richard Cocks* is another work by a seventeenth-century European that makes mention of cheese in Japan. It was written by the head of the English East India Company's trading post in Hirado, Japan, from 1613 to 1623, when he left because the factory closed down. For example, in the entry for 13 August 1615, Cocks writes: 'And after nowne the capten and masters of the 2 Duch shipps came to the English howse and brought me a present of 2 baricas of Spanish wine, 3 Hollands cheeses, 2 small potts of butter, and a bundell of stockfish.'[12] Prefaced with 'Hollands', it seems the cheeses Cocks is sending, receiving and devouring throughout both volumes of his diary are dairy, and have been brought from far afield for Europeans stationed in Japan. As can be assumed by this need for creature comforts, interaction with local cuisine was limited and tofu did not make its way back to merry old England. This contrasts with the culinary knowledge that had been accumulated a decade prior to this diary entry by the Portuguese missionaries in Nagasaki. That Portuguese foodstuffs, today's tempura and *kasutera* (a type of sponge cake) among others, made their mark on Japanese cuisine indicates a more intimate relationship beyond trade and proselytism.

A more detailed description of tofu, referring to it by name, comes later in the seventeenth century, and comes again from a source with religious interests in mind. This was recorded by Domingo Fernández Navarrete (1610–1689), a Dominican missionary active in China from around 1657 to 1673. Navarrete left China ahead of a dip in popularity for Christianity in the early Qing dynasty, which, though punctuated by the Kangxi Emperor's edict of toleration in 1692, culminated in 1724 with

the proscription of Roman Catholicism altogether until 1858.[13]
His account of tofu, including what it looks like, its vegetarian
credentials, who eats it and how it can be served, appears in a
book published in 1676.

> It was called Teu Fu, that is, bean dough. [Although] I didn't
> see the way it's made, they take the milk from the beans,
> and make curds like cheeses . . . five or six fingers thick.
> The whole mass is white as snow itself . . . It is eaten raw,
> but ordinarily is cooked, and stewed with vegetables, fish,
> and other things. By itself it is bland, but as described it is
> good, and very excellent fried with butter from cows. They
> also make it dry, and smoked, in which they mix caraway
> [seeds] . . . The Chinese who has Teu Fu, vegetables, and rice,
> will not need another bounty for their toil, nor do I think
> there is any who cannot afford it, because it can be found
> everywhere for a *quarto* [former Spanish unit of currency]
> per twenty-ounce pound . . . It is this Teu Fu, one of the
> most famous things in China, for which many will abandon
> chicken [meat]; and if I'm not mistaken, the Chinese from
> Manila do it too, but I don't know if any European eats it,
> which may be for not having come across it, nor in eating
> *buñuelos* [fritters], made with sesame oil, which the Chinese
> make in that City, by which they deprive themselves of a
> delightful snack.[14]

So far, these early historical sources constitute mere touches from
a distance, a window into cultures not necessarily interacted with.
It is only later that soybeans, tofu and the associated process to
turn the one into the other are viewed through a more scientific
lens and auditioned for possible adoption in Western cuisine.
But first there came the travelogues and sociological tomes on

Eastern civilizations published during the era of New Imperialism, when the Western world scrambled to assert its dominance over Asia and Africa.

EARLY NEGATIVE WESTERN PERCEPTIONS OF TOFU

'No question in Japan is so solemn as that of food.'[15] Words from the Italian minister in Japan to British travel writer Isabella Bird in 1878. Bird travelled that same year from Tokyo to Hokkaido, relating her story via letters to her sister which would be published in 1880 as *Unbeaten Tracks in Japan*. She was one of many foreign visitors, travellers and residents in East and Southeast Asia who couldn't quite get over the food situation. Tofu, where it was noticed or consumed, didn't escape unscathed. For example, Ernest Satow, a British diplomat who resided in Japan from 1862 to 1882, was apparently none too impressed with tofu. When landing for lunch at 'Suido-mura, a small village . . . about four miles above Ozaka [sic] . . . There was nothing to be had but rice and bean-curd, which did not constitute a very palatable meal. But à la guerre comme à la guerre,' he quips.[16] Though not published until almost forty years after he left his post, Satow's brush with 'bean-curd' represents an early tendency by Westerners to discount tofu. There is a glut of works written on Japan around this time: travel diaries, fantasies and fictions, tomes of history. Romanticism pervades much of it, though at the same time this fascination with recently opened Japan (it was forced to open for trade in 1853) did lend itself to some eyewitness accounts of everyday life. In 1891 the American travel photographer, writer and all-round Japanophile Eliza Ruhamah Scidmore described tofu in her *Jinrikisha Days in Japan*: 'some child ran down to a provision-shop for a square slab of bean-curd, which, with many cups of tea, a little rice, and shreds of pickled fish, composed . . .

breakfast'.[17] Globetrotters of the day also included descriptions of how tofu was sold, like this one written thirty years later by Julian Street in his travelogue *Mysterious Japan* (1921): 'I saw the bean-curd man jogging along the street with a long rod over his shoulder, at each end of which was suspended a box of tofu, which he announced at intervals by a blast on a little brass horn: "Ta–ta: teeya; *tee-e-e-ta!*"'[18]

Rarely was a work written about Japan and Japanese life by an actual Japanese person, in English, for a Western audience. Jukichi Inouye (1862–1929) in his *Home Life in Tokyo* was the first. Or at least he was the first to 'deign to touch upon . . . homely matters', previous efforts of his countrymen, he writes, being

A tofu vendor depicted in the 1860s *Morisada mankō* (Morisada's Sketches) by Kitagawa Morisada. The illustration compares the *oke* (pails) of vendors in the Edo area (left) with those in the Kyoto area (right).

concerned with 'abstruse subjects'. Considering the 'occidental point of view' with which Europeans and Americans had so far observed and written about Japan, 'it occurred to [Inouye] that notwithstanding the superabundance of books on Japan, a description of Japanese life by a native of the country might not be without interest.'[19] On a gastronomic level such 'occidental' works often mention rice, soy sauce, raw fish, tea and sake, as well as the yōshoku (recently introduced Japanized Western cuisine) served at hotels and the residences of European expatriates. Tofu is seldom mentioned, maybe not because it wasn't visible (it certainly would have been) but because it didn't fit with what Westerners expected to find, nor could visitors recognize something unknown to them. However, Inouye spells out the significance of tofu in the domestic setting for his Western audience:

> Though cooking is mostly done at home, no small quantity
> of prepared food is bought for the meals. The most important
> of such food is the bean-curd . . . This curd is cut into small
> slices and put into soup in the morning; it is sometimes
> thrown into hot water, and as soon as it is warmed, dipped
> into a mixture of soy and mirin and eaten. It is also fried.
> Indeed, the bean-curd shares with the tai [red seabream] the
> distinction of having a special treatise dealing with a hundred
> ways of dressing it.[20]

This importance did not reach Isabella Bird, who had multiple negative encounters with tofu. In one chapter she describes 'villages . . . full of shops' with 'scarcely a house that does not sell something'. Many of these, she says, are 'eatables', before reeling off a list of what she sees, including 'a white jelly made from beans'.[21] Later, presumably now aware of what that 'white jelly' was, she describes a lunch on the road as 'a wretched meal of a tasteless white curd made from beans, with some condensed milk added to it'.[22] The addition of condensed milk does not sound appealing. But continuing onward, she encounters more food woes: 'I made a miserable meal of rice and bean curd, feeling somewhat starved, as the condensed milk I bought at Yamagata had to be thrown away.'[23] While travelling in the mountains she mentions that while she had sake, tea, rice and 'very good' black beans, her guide 'dined on seven dishes of horrors'.[24] It is this perception of Japanese cuisine that manifests itself into what Bird calls 'The Food Question', explaining to her readers that 'fishy and vegetable abominations known as "Japanese food" can only be swallowed and digested by a few, and that after long practice.'[25] Frances Little, who lived and worked in Hiroshima as a teacher

A 19th-century engraving of Isabella Bird, based on a photograph. As of 2015, Bird has been the subject of an ongoing Japanese manga, *Fushigi no Kuni no Bādo* (known in English as *Isabella Bird in Wonderland*).

from 1902 to 1907, joked in her semi-autobiographical novel, *The Lady of Decoration*, 'I've gotten so "acclamitized" I think I could eat a gum shoe!'[26] This humblebrag acts as a confirmation for the unpalatability of Japanese food, an implicit 'I'll-eat-anything' attitude that undermines Japanese fare as far as to suggest what Little has been eating could be considered, by some (perhaps herself included), as on par with an inedible item of footwear.

Length of time spent subsisting on Japanese food seems to have had little bearing on the efforts of Lafcadio Hearn, the scholar, translator and English teacher who styled himself as Koizumi Yakumo during his fourteen years in Japan. In a letter of June 1892 to Page M. Baker, Hearn boasts having survived 'one year exclusively on Japanese food, which Europeans . . . consider almost impossible', but, he admits, 'it broke me down. After twelve months I could not eat at all.'[27] He continues to describe the Japanese diet: 'You know Japanese food is raw fish and fresh fish, rice, beancurds (they look like custard), seaweed, dried cuttle-fish,– rarely chicken or eggs. In short, of five hundred Japanese dishes, the basis is rice, fish, beans, lotus, various vegetables, including bamboo shoots, and seaweed.'[28] Hearn's intolerance of Japanese food is confirmed by scientist and author Marie Stopes, who spent a year and several months in Japan. Stopes wrote in her *Journal from Japan* that, according to his wife, Setsuko Koizumi, 'Japanese food upset [Hearn], and he always had foreign food.'[29]

As shown so far by Bird, Satow and even Navarrete, who also mentioned that tofu is 'used by those who travel from one province to another',[30] tofu by this time is on par with a survival food: something cheap, nutritious and easily procurable on the road. This utilitarian aspect can extend to the use of tofu as food for prisoners. Tofu appears to have been served to the navigator Vasily Golovnin (1776–1831) and other Russians following their capture in the Kuril Islands in 1811. Among other things, prison

Lafcadio Hearn lived for over a decade in Japan, where he studied Japanese folklore and took his Japanese name from Setsuko Koizumi, his Japanese wife; however, he could not stand the food.

food for Golovnin in Hakodate consisted of 'puddings of bean-meal and rancid fish-oil'.[31] This may refer to tofu or its dregs (*okara*) and possibly *gyoshō*, a fermented fish sauce, of which there are several regional varieties in Japan. Things had evidently changed by the time of the Russo-Japanese War (1904–5), when contemporary Western observers noted 'the considerate treatment of the Russian prisoners', with more than 70,000 distributed across 29 camps in Japan.[32] Frances Little comments on the 'good time' Russian prisoners seemed to be having in Hiroshima: 'Japanese officials are entertaining them violently with concerts, picnics, etc.' This may have extended to their dietary requirements, as Little notes a cook was sent for from Vladivostok 'so that they may have Russian food'.[33] Though a good public relations move on one hand, on the other it represents an early national awareness of the Western aversion to Japanese food. On the other side of the coin, monopolies on selling tofu were given to families of soldiers serving in the war, reportedly in Osaka and Hyogo Prefectures, showcasing not only the everyday importance and ubiquity of the foodstuff, but the role that tofu as a vital industry played in rewarding loyalty or sacrifice and upholding morale in imperial Japan.[34]

A late nineteenth-century account by the Scottish diplomat Alexander Hosie further illustrates the travel ration status of tofu during a journey in China: 'My men, who for the last few days had been unable to procure rice, and had subsisted for the most part on bean-curd, rejoiced to find themselves in a valley of their own province ... where silk was being reeled and tea-plantations abounded.'[35] Likewise, observations by the Australian journalist and political advisor to the Republic of China George Ernest Morrison suggest that tofu is equated with poverty-driven necessity. 'We were entering a district of great poverty,' he writes. 'The tea is inferior, and we had to be content with maize meal, bean

curds, rice roasted in sugar, and sweet gelatinous cakes.'[36] The
language used implies reluctance, calling to mind the make-do
attitude and maintaining a stiff upper lip as described by Satow.
Given these appearances of tofu in only relatively dire straits for
adventuring Westerners, who would rather not eat it, there are
two things we can learn at this time: that tofu is a food among
commoners, and that many travel writers of the time would not
have been interacting closely with them, let alone eating their
food. Belfast-born missionary John MacGowan (1835–1922) associates tofu with menial workers in China, writing that a 'coolie,
for example . . . comes to you from an inland country where
poverty is the prevailing characteristic of the whole population.
Sweet potatoes are the staple food three times a day, year in, year
out, helped down perhaps by salted turnip, bean curds and pickled beans.'[37] A later description by MacGowan puts tofu in a positive light, but from his perspective the dish is destined for his
'perspiring chair-bearers' rather than himself: 'nicely browned
strips of fried bean curds to act as appetizer to the rice, and to
arouse [their] flagging appetite'.[38] Similarly in Japan, readers are
told by the journalist and author J. W. Robertson Scott (1866–
1962) that the average person 'lives on rice, bean products (tofu,
bean jelly and miso, soft bean cheese), pickles, vegetables, tea, a
little fish and sometimes eggs'.[39] Despite the chance to try such
dishes during their sojourns in China and Japan, alleged explorers and adventurers of this era actively refuse to do without home
comforts. One of these, the American explorer and curator of
the American Natural History Museum Roy Chapman Andrews
(1884–1960), lists supplies for his travels through China as consisting 'largely of flour, butter, sugar, coffee, milk, bacon, and marmalade'.[40] This description appears in a book he wrote with Yvette
Borup Andrews, his wife, detailing the 'Asiatic Zoölogical Expedition of the American Museum of Natural History to China

in 1916–17'. Later, they describe their cook leaving the party. 'The loss of a cook is a serious matter to a large expedition . . . In Yün-nan natives who can cook foreign food are by no means easy to come by,' but they were 'fortunate in obtaining an exceedingly competent man' to take the place of their recently departed chef.[41] Explorers nominally, but only in the geographical sense: still they must have Christmas dinner, furnished with freshly hunted wild-life. Far-flung Westerners whom the couple come across during their travels are pitied for their having to subsist entirely on Chinese food; they describe one Swiss botanist's over-enjoyment of their Western treats as 'almost pathetic'.[42]

However, A Wayfarer in China (1913), a travelogue written by the American academic Elizabeth Kendall, is slightly different to the norm. Written through 'the lenses of gender and criticism of imperialism', Kendall was sympathetic and enthusiastic about her travels, including the food she saw, which 'on the whole . . . looked attractive', and sampled along the way.[43] Kendall even notes the tofu-making process itself, showing the crucial status it holds alongside rice in the homes of ordinary people: 'In one pot bean-cake was being made, a long, complicated process; in another, cakes were frying in oil; in another, rice was boiling.'[44] Further descriptions highlight that beans were integral to part of a meal, the 'pièce de résistance' of which was a 'good bowl of rice':

> Beans in some shape were an important part of every menu. You could get a basin of fresh beans for ten cash, dried bean-cake for five, beans cooked and strained to a stiff batter for making soup for seven cash the ounce, while a large square of white bean-cake was sold for one copper cent.[45]

At the time of her writing, one copper cent was equivalent to ten cash, which was worth around half an American cent.[46] Even within China, and certainly from the perspective of a Western traveller, tofu was affordable in the extreme. This status of afford-ability with which tofu was endowed, and its natural associations with lower-class citizens, contrasted greatly with the economic class of people who could afford a trip to East Asia from Europe or the United States. From 1872 travel to Japan was made more possible by its inclusion as a stop on Thomas Cook's inaugural round-the-world cruise.[47] Despite this the average person in Britain and other Western nations would not have been able to afford it. The cruise cost 200 guineas (£210), which, adjusted for inflation, would cost the equivalent of £19,154 today.[48] For any-body but diplomats, the relatively wealthy and sponsored bot-anists, travel to Japan would have been out of the question. With this in mind this first package holiday to Japan probably made the country that much more unattainable and intriguing. The only way to experience it, for many, would have been through literature. For tofu to be described as 'wretched' and 'unpalat-able' in providing the picture of what constitutes Japanese food and lifestyle to readers back home does not add to its reputation. It is likely that, despite efforts made later to adopt soybeans and their curd as foodstuffs in the West, tofu was already laden with the distaste of late nineteenth- and early twentieth-century travellers to Japan and China. That these commentators were privileged individuals, laden with as much whiteness as wealth, signals their sense of superiority towards Japan and other Asian nations; tofu and other elements of Asian cuisines were evidently far from measuring up. It is ironic to note how Japanese food in particular was so feared by many European travellers at this stage, when today it is a globalized cuisine afforded a level of status in terms of cost and quality; many ingredients, from miso to vari-eties of mushroom (called by their Japanese names *shiitake*, *maitake* and so on), find their way into the repertoire of many a Western chef, or become a whole new food trend. This does not mean that tofu has travelled well, or ridden the coat-tails of Japanese cuisine into the hearts and minds of Europe, far from it, but there have been efforts made for well over a century to introduce it into the Western diet.

HOW TOFU BECAME A HOUSEHOLD NAME IN THE WEST

The story of tofu in the USA begins with a legendary figure. While Benjamin Franklin (1706–1790) definitely existed, the stock put in his introduction of tofu to this part of the world relies heavily on his status as a heroic polymath, and one letter, rather than the truth. A Smithsonian Magazine article published in 2018, 'Ben Franklin May Be Responsible for Bringing Tofu to America', ushered in plenty of blogposts and Reddit threads that discuss the possibilities. This letter, dated to 1770, was sent from London by Franklin to the American botanist John Bartram (1699–1777), founder of what is considered America's first botanic garden. Franklin expresses an interest in both soybeans and tofu, informed by the description of tofu by Navarrete a century before.

> I send . . . some Chinese Garavances, with Father Navaretta's [sic] account of the universal use of a cheese made of them, in China . . . some runnings of salt (I suppose runnet) is put into water when the meal is in it, to turn it to curds. I think we have Garavances with us; but I know not whether they are same with these, which actually came from China, and are what the Tau-fu is made of.[49]

'Garavances' is an approximation of garbanzo (Spanish for 'chickpea'); presumably 'Chinese Garavances' refers to soybeans. With no tofu appearing in the USA for another century, it is doubtful

that the letter ever went beyond an Age of Enlightenment equivalent of sharing an Instagram post. Even so, in 2011 PETA peti-
tioned Pennsylvania, lacking a 'state food', to adopt tofu as the
dish that best represents the state.[50] The nonprofit organization
wrote to then Pennsylvania governor Tom Corbett, suggesting
that the move would 'help to quell the state's obesity epidemic
and honor his predecessor in the governor's seat by getting
Pennsylvanians to eat more tofu and less meat'.[51] The popularity
of this romanticized version of events reflects an eagerness to
ascribe yet further talents to an already famous man, much like
the industry gods of Chinese culture. This Franklin myth also
omits the work of an entrepreneur named Samuel Bowen. In 1765,
following his 1758 voyage to Canton (today's Guangzhou) with
the British East India Company, Bowen gave some soybeans to
surveyor Henry Yonge to plant and cultivate in Savannah, Georgia.
Evidently impressed with the beans' potential, Yonge wrote that
the beans, here called 'Luk-Taw' and 'Chinese Vetches', could be
of 'great utility and advantage to this, and his majesty's other
southern American provinces'.[52] They were: soybeans grown at
Savannah were used to make soy sauce and soybean vermicelli,
which were then exported to England.[53] But not tofu.

Instead tofu first arrived in the United States not with
curious colonialists but with Chinese immigrants during the
California Gold Rush (1848–55), and with labourers working on
the Central Pacific Railroad in the 1860s.[54] Quong Hop was
established in 1906 as 'the first tofu shop in America' by Sing
Hau Lee, who originally sold it from the storefront of a small
grocery.[55] Once one of the biggest tofu makers in California, one
that helped popularize tofu outside the Asian American market,
production halted at Quong Hop in July 2010 when food inspec-
tors found the pathogenic bacteria *Listeria monocytogenes* in its
warehouse.[56] The company had previously recalled products in

David Martin (1737–1797), *Benjamin Franklin*, 1767, oil on canvas. Franklin was one of the first Westerners to take an interest in tofu.

2007 due to the presence of *Listeria*.[57] Another claimant to the first tofu shop in America is Wo Sing & Co., which opened its doors in 1878, but it no longer exists.[58] With both these Chinese-run enterprises out of business, that leaves Japanese-run Ota Tofu as the oldest extant tofu maker in the United States. Ota Tofu was opened in 1911 by wife-and-husband team Shina and Saizo Ota, who had previously immigrated to Portland from Okayama in Japan. It was for decades one of numerous tofu factories frequented by the Japanese and Chinese American population of East Portland, and comprised one of 42 tofu shops nationwide as of 1910 (not including Hawaii).[59] In 1941 Saizo and Shina were forced into an internment camp in Idaho, two of some 120,000 Japanese Americans imprisoned during the Second World War. Many Japanese-owned businesses were seized, looted or sold off during this time. Saizo died a year after arriving. Now alone, Shina returned to Portland in 1945; thankfully her shop and its equipment remained intact. Today Ota Tofu produces around 1,360 kilograms (3,000 lb) of tofu daily, all handmade, providing 150 businesses in Portland with tofu and soy milk.[60]

While Asian communities in the United States were manufacturing tofu in factories and small-scale enterprises, the same food was being studied under a microscope as far as their Western contemporaries were concerned. By the early twentieth century the soybean had been grown in European botanical gardens for around a hundred years, and in 'Austria, Hungary, and France especially, attempts [had] been made on a large scale' to grow it because, according to botanist Alphonse de Candolle, 'more extensive information about China and Japan excited [in the 1890s] a lively desire to introduce it into [European] countries.'[61] Soybeans generated the same sort of interest on the other side of the Atlantic Ocean. A 1914 leaflet entitled *Let's Use Soybeans* issued by the University of Illinois Department of Home Economics advocates the bean's use at a time 'when the rationing of many of the protein-rich foods of animal origin has made [Americans] aware of the possibility of insufficient protein in our dietaries'.[62] The pamphlet shares recipes, but the closest it gets to one for tofu is one for 'Baked Soybeans Croquettes' that uses soybean pulp.

In 1919, at the tenth Annual Nut Growers Association, the nutritionist John Harvey Kellogg (1852–1943) gave a speech on the subject of soybeans. Kellogg, a Seventh-Day Adventist, was an avid advocate of soybeans, which he called 'the beefsteak of China and Japan'. In that speech he described tofu and how it was made:

> In China the soy bean is very little used as we use beans. They do not cook the bean and eat it as we do; but instead they make it into a cheese which they call tofu, and this cheese is made by soaking the beans, grinding them into a pulp, then boiling for ten or fifteen minutes with about five volumes of water; then the milky mass is precipitated with sulphate of magnesia or citric acid, a very small amount because they use it as a curd.[63]

Kellogg then produced a sample and passed it around. He continues, probably describing types of fermented tofu like *mao doufu* and *furu*: 'The soy bean curd is stored on wooden trays in a dark room. It is also stored in large earthen jars. They cure it and make cheese out of it which very closely resembles our American milk cheese.'[64] Far from being on the dinner tables of Americans, however, tofu remained firmly in the petri dish, an Asian oddity that needed to undergo thorough, clinical study to be deemed fitting.

This is perhaps unsurprising given the reception that Chinese cuisine had so far enjoyed in the United States and globally. An 1892 guide book, *King's Handbook of New York City*, details Manhattan's Mott, Pell and Doyer streets as 'given over to the Chinese', calling it 'a veritable "Chinatown," with all the filth, immorality and picturesque foreignness which that name implies'.[65] Later, restaurants in the district are deemed 'dirty, foul-smelling and cheaply furnished', selling 'viands of a mysterious character';[66] these were visited by those who went 'slumming', a kind of tour taken for entertainment by the middle classes into ethnically diverse, low-income neighbourhoods. Countless instances of prejudice towards Chinese people and their food can be found in various travelogues to the country itself. The Qing dynasty diplomat and scholar Jitong (1851–1907) wrote in 1895 that 'many dreadful things have been said about Chinese cooking,' referring to 'certain prejudiced travellers'.[67] But it wasn't just travellers. Thomas Taylor Meadows (1815–1868), a renowned British Sinologist, proclaimed the 'unscrupulous stomach' of Chinese people.[68] Writing in 1913, British journalist and humourist Nathaniel Gubbins (1893–1976) listed 'pigeons eggs in bean curd' among various Chinese dishes, before ending with an ironical question: 'Can it be wondered at that this nation should have been brought to its knees by gallant little Japan?'[69] This implies that Chinese food culture itself contributed to China's defeat by Japan in the first Sino-Japanese War. Logic at the time, even science, dictated that diets perceived as inferior to those of Western nations (of which Japan, at the time, was an honorary member) could rationally explain the successes of colonialism.

The first real effort to bridge the tofu gap between Asian Americans and European Americans was made by Kin Yamei (1864–1934). Born in Ningpo, China, Kin spent five years operating a health clinic in Kobe, travelled to California in 1897, then returned to China ten years later as the director of the Imperial Peiyang Women's Medical School and Hospital in Tianjin, travelling between China and the United States. By now something of a celebrity, in 1917 Kin toured China to study soybeans for the U.S. government. Food scarcities in the First World War – notably in red meat – had prompted the search for protein-rich alternatives.

Kin Yamei's work in studying and introducing tofu may not have stuck, but her efforts represent an early attempt to get Americans to eat soy.

She brought her soy-based findings back to the United States in 1918, showcasing them at a laboratory of the U.S. Department of Agriculture Bureau of Chemistry. Despite the warm reception Kin's experiments garnered from fellow chemists, it came too late: the war ended that November.[70] She was not alone in her efforts. The Chinese revolutionary Sun Yat-sen (1866–1925) claimed that the soybean 'has been used as a meat substitute for many thousand years' and has been 'proved by modern chemists to be richer than any kind of meat'.[71] Once more the task falls to 'modern chemists', that is, Western science, to first deem these foreign meat substitutes fit for human consumption. Sun proposed the introduction of 'artificial meat, milk, butter and cheese to Europe and America, by establishing a system of soya bean factories in all the large cities of those countries'.[72] Before Sun wrote these words in 1922 another Chinese revolutionary had tried just that. In Paris, 1908, the political activist and educator Li Shizeng (1881–1973) opened L'Usine de la Caséo-Sojaïne, Europe's first tofu factory.[73] It actively employed fellow Chinese students as part of the Mouvement travail-études, a quasi-exchange programme that saw labour traded for study in French political and economic education. Students on this programme included Zhou Enlai (1898–1976), first premier of the People's Republic of China, and Deng Xiaoping (1904–1997), the country's leader from

Sun Yat-sen in Canton, 1924.

1978 to 1989. Inadvertently tofu had become part of the primordial soup fomenting socialist revolution.

Amid a turn-of-the-century flurry of experimentation and discovery in the fields of chemistry and physics, scientists in Japan were fully involved in the field of nutrition. In 1908 monosodium glutamate (MSG) was first isolated by Kikunae Ikeda (1864–1936), who also identified umami as a distinct flavour the same year. Umetaro Suzuki (1874–1943) extracted micronutrients from rice bran in 1910 and called it aberic acid, now known as thiamine (vitamin B_1). In 1922, J. W. Robertson Scott met and spoke with a 'Professor Morimoto' of Sapporo University, who believed that Japanese people needed meat and bread added to their diet. Scott disagreed: 'As far as meat is concerned he did not convince me,' he wrote, adding: 'Let me quote [the professor] on the soy bean: "It is a remarkably good substitute for meat. It is very low in price but its nutritive value is very high. The essential element of miso, tofu and shoyu is soy bean."'[74]

It was a promising time for tofu. But the efforts to introduce soy and its various products to Western diets were, despite the rationale and good intentions, in vain. Apart from a well-received cookbook by health food pioneer Mildred Lager (1900–1960) called The Useful Soybean (1945), which included a recipe for 'tofu sandwich spread', Western interest in soybeans and tofu waned.[75] As one reviewer of Lager's book said, '[the soybean] has come into its rightful place in our economy only during the past 25 years, and then only as a result of the impact of two world wars.'[76] With no world wars and no resultant protein shortages to necessitate it, in the 1950s tofu was evidently still mystifying North America. Its inclusion in the 1955 cookbook The Complete Book of Cheese is a giveaway: 'Bean Cake, Tao-foo, or Tofu', described as 'Soy bean cheese imported from Shanghai and other oriental ports, and also imitated in every Chinatown around the world. Made from the milk of beans and curdled with its own vegetable rennet.'[77] That sort of description may as well have been written half a century earlier.

Three years later, however, Boys Market in Los Angeles became the first American supermarket to stock tofu.[78] And then in the 1960s, with soaring soy production and the rise of counter-culture-inspired vegetarianism, conditions were ideal for tofu to make its foray into the world.[79] This 1960s counterculture 'embraced Japanese cuisine', and saw a macrobiotic diet as a healthy alternative to 'mainstream American food'.[80] Because of this, 'miso, bean curd, soy sauce, and other Japanese foods started to become widely available in the United States, first in health food stores . . . then in supermarkets.'[81] The general acceptance of Japanese food was also aided by favourable reviews, such as those written by the pioneering food critic Craig Claiborne, who 'alerted readers to the rise of Japanese restaurants'.[82] This cocktail of conditions carried on into the 1970s. Just as books spread the news of tofu and its strange appearance and taste to Westerners of the late nineteenth century, books played an important role in tofu's mainstream debut in the West. In *Diet for a Small Planet* (1971), American researcher Frances Moore Lappé expounded the benefits of a vegetarian diet. According to the *Vegetarian Times* it 'broke the news that raising animals for food was a grossly inefficient way to feed the world's people'.[83] In a one-two punch of vegetarian-minded tomes came Akiko Aoyagi and William Shurtleff's influential *The Book of Tofu* in 1975, which inspired people to make their own tofu, actively instructing them how to do so and how to use it in vegetarian cuisine.[84] According to a *New York Times* article published in 1978 titled 'What Is This Thing Called Tofu?' a 'combination of events awakened the West to the wonders of tofu', one of them being the publication of Aoyagi and Shurtleff's book, which it describes as a 'cookbook and resource manual that caught on quickly with natural food followers'.[85] Their research continues via their SoyInfo Center website, which represents a vast swathe of research into all things soy, from tofu to tempeh.

Another instrumental factor was the existence of The Farm, a community in Tennessee founded in 1971. Among other things the alternative inhabitants of this settlement 'were trying to figure out how to feed themselves on a vegan diet. They grew soybeans and set up a soy dairy, making soymilk and tofu.'[86] An article in a 1990 issue of *Vegetarian Times* (which still called tofu 'a bland, white custard') reported that *The Farm Vegetarian Cookbook*, published in 1975, 'became a staple in vegetarian kitchens across the country'.[87] It was written by The Farm member Louise Hagler, also the author of *Tofu Cookery* (1982) and *Tofu Quick and Easy* (1986). The same article claims, 'if you know what to do with tofu . . . you can thank The Farm.' When members of UNICEF caught wind of a community all subsisting on a vegan diet, they sent nutritionists to study the results; they found that by replacing meat with soy, the community had kept their daily protein requirements at a good level.[88] Tofu was a superfood after all. All it took was its 'discovery' by white, European America, much like in the earlier portion of the twentieth century, when Dr Kellogg passed around a block of tofu at the Annual Nut Growers Association meeting. Its association with liberalism and left-wing politics is something this book will discuss in the next chapter, but it is this connection that has led to an erasure of its Asian roots. In her 2021 book *How the Other Half Eats*, discussing food inequality, sociologist Priya Fielding-Singh lists tofu among 'foods that are culturally white', which are 'paraded as healthy and sophisticated'.[89] For tofu to be branded 'culturally white' denies its heritage, ties it instead to a half-century of Western vegetarianism, erases the experience of Asian Americans and ignores a very real stigma that quite clearly surrounded its gradual adoption as a mainstream ingredient. As this next section will uncover, nothing could be further from the truth. The only thing white about tofu is its colour.

THE ROLE OF THE MEDIA IN SHAPING
THE REPUTATION OF TOFU

For the past few decades journalists writing about tofu have felt it culturally distant enough to discuss it in tones that range from adulation to confusion and disgust. Media may have put tofu on a pedestal, but media constantly tears it down. From the latter end of the twentieth century to the present day there are numerous articles, blogposts, forum posts and comments, too many to list, that make a point of negatively portraying the look, texture and taste of tofu, no matter the general crux of the piece of writing itself. The gist may be positive, or it may be a simple news story charting an increase in tofu sales – it doesn't seem to matter. In discussing the global history of tofu, at least some of what has been written about it in recent years should make an appearance. This glut of literature represents a continuing dislike of tofu among Western anglophone audiences, despite its availability and the availability of cookbooks dedicated solely to tofu, not to mention recipes written in publications with global reach and shared on social media such as TikTok.

And it isn't just the written word. The 1966 novel *Make Room! Make Room!* by Harry Harrison (1925–2012) is lesser known than its iconic celluloid treatment, *Soylent Green* (1975). Without spoiling the book or film's big reveal, synthetic food in this instance puts the word 'soy' itself in a realm of dystopian horror.

There is still a stigma towards tofu around the world, not only in Europe and North America. One Malaysian magazine article from 2008 begins: 'It is said that only the Japanese and

Chinese can truly appreciate tofu. White as chalk and tasting almost as bland, it is a wonder tofu has managed to get this far as a major food ingredient.'[90] Another non-Western publication, the Indian edition of *Reader's Digest*, features a similar opening gambit in a 2020 article: 'Until a few years ago, most Indian kitchens would look down upon tofu as the poor, bland cousin of paneer or cottage cheese, only meant for lactose-intolerant people.'[91] Publications held in high esteem have published and continue to publish pieces in which tofu is isolated and mocked. In 1988, the *New York Times* published a piece about Berkeley, California, and its co-operative stores:

> In the 1980s, while Berkeley became one of the most influential and obsessed centers of new American cuisine, many people felt the co-op acted as though everyone still lived in a commune and bought brown rice in 50-pound sacks. The co-ops continued to stock six kinds of sprouts and a nasty looking substance called 'tofu puffs,' but not raddichio [sic].[92]

For the most part, a lot of this late twentieth-century disparagement appears to stem from confusion. It seems that people despaired of what to do with tofu as an ingredient. Cookbooks with titles like *This Can't Be Tofu!* (2000) sum up that sentiment. A 1998 story in the *Los Angeles Times* makes several references to tofu 'dressed up' in flavours like barbecue and with oregano and parsley added; an interviewee suggests using tofu to make a chocolate mousse pie to 'break down the psychological barrier against tofu'.[93] Similar confusion regarding how to approach tofu had already arisen in a 1983 *Washington Post* article, which asks, 'Why would anyone want it?' before suggesting readers 'do anything to avoid confronting the substance in its natural state: boring'.[94]

Seventeen years later, in 2000, the same newspaper declared 'for many Americans, soy-based foods like tofu are too unappealing to swallow in any form.'[95] Writing for the *New York Times* the same year, food columnist Jonathan Reynolds jokingly puts tofu between sea urchin and okra on the list of 'Most Despised Foods on the Planet'.[96] How an allegedly 'culturally white' food can have so little hold over a majority-white population speaks to the ignorance with which even well-intentioned sociologists approach tofu, a foodstuff that even at the beginning of the twenty-first century was still clearly seen not as a 'white' food but as a new one. Still more recently, in 2010 *Guardian* writer Oliver Thring (now an editor at the *Daily Mail*) called tofu 'vile on its own' in a detailed, damning description of the foodstuff: 'without the zip and shimmy of ginger, garlic and Cantonese whatnot, it tastes of mulched loo roll or a slime of dead skin, with a texture both firm and somehow unpleasantly brittle. Bean curd, whatever else you can say for it, is best mixed with other ingredients.'[97] In defence of tofu, many things are 'best mixed with other ingredients'. It's called cooking. Though this may be open to interpretation, almost every single cuisine in the world not only consists of ingredients 'best mixed with other ingredients', but more essentially is ingredients mixed with other ingredients. Many simple, everyday items, 'culturally white' food such as plain bread and Weetabix among them, are very bland by themselves. The problem is not its blandness, but rather its difference. The dismissive 'Cantonese whatnot' to which Thring refers signals racist undertones, or ignorance at the very least, that may still bubble around some opinions of bean curd and Chinese food. His gonzo-esque approach to the article, which involves him describing a plate of tofu in front of him, like prodding something underneath a bell jar, suggests that it is still an alien food to be tried, examined and ridiculed, and that he is brave to have done so.

Writers still prelude even positive articles about tofu with statements regarding its apparent societal unpalatability. To acknowledge its perceived repulsiveness, and perhaps its connection to vegetarianism, before mentioning health benefits and versatility, seems to be structurally inherent to many pieces of writing on the subject of tofu. One example article by food writer Fuchsia Dunlop comes from the *Financial Times* in 2022, whose very title, 'Tofu Is a Cornucopia of Taste. No Really', suggests a radical statement. Being the headline, this wording would have been an editorial decision, an attempt to echo and pre-empt readers' disbelief in mentally processing the first part of the statement. The article begins: 'A dried yellow soyabean is hardly promising.'[98] The apologist rhetoric displayed in this and many articles like it demonstrates an assumed collective dislike or mistrust of tofu in the Western world. In 2020, as part of a *Bloomberg* article heralding the increasing sales of tofu during the COVID-19 pandemic, Michele Simon, then executive director of the Plant Based Foods Association, was quoted as saying that tofu 'has a funny name' as well as 'a reputation of being a tasteless food that people don't understand'.[99] Nothing seems to suggest any cultural whiteness that is inherent to tofu.

Tofu's journey to the West has been an arduous one. Observed by travellers but, for the most part, left well alone until the nineteenth century, when adventurers in Asia had their first taste of bean curd, it remained firmly within East Asia until Chinese and Japanese immigrants and students began to move to the USA and Europe. This was only part of its journey. Once there the recognition of its potential as a meat substitute fizzed and popped during the First and Second World Wars. It would not be until the 1960s, very recently considering its ancient origin, that tofu had any sort of standing within the West, in this case the USA. The spread of tofu in the West took off following a perfect storm of conditions: the popularity of Japanese cuisine, the fledgling health food scene and vegetarianism. Towards the end of the twentieth century, tofu had been assimilated, but only partly. Meat alternatives like Tofurky arrived, quite literally invented by the company's founder, Seth Tibbot. 'We would spend long days in a cramped kitchen, mixing 25-pound batches of the dough – a blend of tofu, wheat gluten, soy sauce, and spices – then bake it,' he recalled in an article for Inc.[100]

On arriving in the West, tofu split and exists in two forms. One is this assimilated guise: Tofurky, a meat replacement, vegan food, niche, extra-hard crumbly tofu, flavoured for consumers' convenience, a state of existence that imbues it with mistaken cultural whiteness. The other, as an import: its original form, soft, supple, but diverse, and still somewhat locked away from mainstream society in Korean, Japanese and Chinese food stores and restaurants, still very much Asian. In being thus simultaneously tolerated and assimilated, tofu remains an experiment, as if its destiny in the West was already written a century ago by Kellogg and Kin Yamei. But 'what many view as an alternative, foreign, or new food' has a very long history as an ingredient all of its own, something that, so far, this book has made efforts to examine.[101] Its age, universality and significance have resulted in an emblematic status for tofu across China and Asia and beyond. As the next chapter will discuss, these range from idioms and political insults to funeral practices and appearances in video games, from the British parliament to Buddhist temples in Japan.

FIVE
`EATING TOFU` AND
ITS PLACE IN CULTURE

Tofu is more than just a food. Over the years it has proven itself a cultural touchstone. It may not have structural integrity, but as with its culinary versatility tofu boasts the power to stand up in a range of figurative and real-life settings, inserting itself into language and aspects of culture, both popular and traditional, across the world. In China alone 'tofu provides not only protein, but also a set of social and linguistic symbols ranging from humbleness and integrity to instability and corruption,' and something similar could also be said of Japan.[1] Naturally, in charting the global history of tofu, it would be reasonable to see how it symbolically slots into the societies that birthed and developed it, and examine its place in the world beyond its use in various cuisines. In particular the influence of tofu on language today reaches far beyond the countries that are most associated with it, joining the already jostling ranks of slang in the English language, in which it is used to denigrate vegetarians and 'liberal', left-leaning individuals and allege effeminacy on the part of males who eat it. In this context tofu is used negatively with guilty-by-association logic, but tofu has long had deeper and

Miso soup.

more visceral connections with two facets of humanity, those being sex and death.

For example: can you hit your head on the corner of tofu and die? According to one Japanese idiom, yes, you can. In Japanese, '*tōfu no kado ni atama wo butskete shine*' means '[go] hit your head on the corner of tofu and die'. It comes from a *rakugo* play called 'Ana-doro', taken from a collection of stories (*Kotoshi wa nashi*, something like *This Year's Tales*) published in the Kaei era (1848–54).[2] The story begins when a woman kicks her husband out of the house on Ōmisoka (New Year's Eve) for not being able to come up with the money needed for their bills, uttering the idiom above as she does so.[3] To make up for it the man attempts to steal something from a merchant's house but ends up falling into an *ana-gura* (a type of basement used for storing valuables).[4] Online Japanese dictionary Weblio defines the idiom as a 'way to ridicule those who don't take jokes well' and also a way to 'jokingly say *shine*'.[5] *Shine* (pronounced 'shi-neh') literally means 'die' in the imperative sense, an interjection often glossed in English as 'go to hell'.[6] It is possible that the original phrase had more to do with soft-headedness, that is, stupidity, tofu being notoriously soft, than its more recent mantle of disparaging humourlessness. The phrase gets around; mystery writer Jun Karachi published a novel in 2021, roughly called *The Case of Death by Head Hitting the Corner of Tofu*, a locked-room mystery in which a man is found dead with chunks of tofu around his head.[7]

The importance and prevalence of tofu in Japan are so great that the food finds its way into modern media, including video games. The Japanese company Capcom included a game mode in their 2019 release of the *Resident Evil 2* remake in which players can opt to play as a block of tofu – 'Code name: Tofu'. The loading screen, which shows 'Tofu' being picked up with giant chopsticks looming from the right of the screen, gives the following description, a knowing nod to the versatility of tofu itself: 'A shadowy intelligence agent who's known for his ability to adapt to a wide variety of situations. He's only as good as the water he's made from. His low costs and good results have seen him serve active duty around the world in recent years.' Armed only with combat knives and a few healing herbs, players must dodge zombies and navigate to an escape route in 'survivor mode', a task made more difficult given the softness of tofu. Completing the stage reveals more gelatinous characters including 'Uiro-Mochi' (representing the steamed rice flour cakes of the same name) and 'Annin Tofu'. It is possible that the otherwise eccentric inclusion of tofu in a survival horror game about zombies taking over a city is actually a pun, fu in tofu meaning 'rotten' and zombies being quite heavily associated with decomposition. Dodging zombies as a human-sized block of tofu may seem like an entertaining non sequitur, but for centuries tofu has been associated with death, the afterlife and the supernatural. It is a surprisingly gory foodstuff in this regard. Let us not forget that one of its origin stories involved it being born from the brains of a violently murdered mutant child god.

DEATH, FLESH AND TOFU: A SACRIFICIAL SUBSTITUTE

For the zombies of *Resident Evil* to be chasing a giant block of tofu instead of meat is fitting, and makes for an interactive pun, doubtless unintentional, in the case of the Cantonese phrase *aak gwai sik dau fu*, which literally means 'trick a ghost into eating tofu' and is used in the sense of 'you're kidding' or 'no way'.[8] Alternatively it also means to 'cheat somebody into the belief' of something.[9] This idiom originates with the Hungry Ghost Festival, which involves the placating of wandering, unfulfilled and otherwise 'hungry' spirits through prayers, burning incense and leaving gifts of food, including rice, roast meat and tofu. The family would later take the former dishes home, leaving the ghost 'tricked' into eating tofu. It could also be that lower-income families, unable to afford meat, would leave tofu, a cheap alternative, for hungry ghosts instead. Still another apocryphal story has it that, long ago, a scholar was visited by a ghost who wanted to eat him. 'You don't want to eat me!' the scholar said. 'I haven't bathed for days, my flesh is smelly and sour. I wouldn't taste good. This tofu here would be much better.' He gave the hungry ghost some tofu and it was a hit. Telling the villagers about the incident the next day, they said to the scholar, 'Wow, you really tricked that ghost into eating tofu instead of meat!'[10] It may not have been much of a trick. Tofu has been associated with the dead and funeral customs for hundreds of years in China. In the eighteenth century, the Qing scholar Wang Ji wrote: 'Tofu is made from the soul of beans, so it is called ghost food.'[11] This appellation, 'ghost food', alludes to tofu's historical and continuing association with funeral activities. A 2019 paper analysing the symbolism of funeral banquets (chi doufu fan, literally 'eating tofu rice') that comprise practices in some parts of China, makes it clear that 'tofu is an indispensable dish.'[12] In Hong Kong and Cantonese-speaking areas the mortuary significance of tofu is exemplified in the phrase dung gwaa dau fu. This refers to winter melon and tofu, 'two foods [that] were customarily served to people who helped out in arranging the funeral' and also 'fed to ghosts during the ghost festival'. Dung gwaa dau fu is charged with negative connotations and is used to mean 'misfortune' or 'serious emergency', among other ways to express bad things happening.[13] The severest meaning of the term is death itself ('especially death').[14]

Its legacy as a 'ghost food' is underlined in The Death of Mr. Wang (2021), a book that delves into the subject of death in urban China. While planning the funeral of the eponymous Mr Wang, his family members are told that it is traditional to serve *baicai doufu* (stir-fried cabbage and tofu) at funeral banquets.[15] Later, at the graveyard after sealing Mr Wang's burial chamber, 'Mr. Chen [who organized the funeral] then took out the five plates of sacrificial food (rice, meat, tofu, fish, and bok choy) and arranged them on top of the grave. At the center he placed an incense burner with a candle on either side.'[16] At another burial ceremony, a different family leaves bananas, dumplings and a tofu dish as sacrificial offerings on a grave. The daughters of the deceased are told to take the bananas home, the son the dumplings, and eat them; supercharged with ancestral energy, the foods would now be beneficial for reproductive health.[17]

The tofu, 'ghost food', was left for the departed as a symbol of sacrifice. This symbolic use of food extends to mortuary customs in Korea, where traditional funeral rites, though largely superseded since the 1980s with the advent of modern funeral halls, are called *sungbok-je*.[18] During these rites ritual clothing is worn, and offerings for the dead are placed on a table, including incense, fermented fish, *yumil-gwa* (a type of biscuit) and tofu.[19] Given that certain offerings embody certain qualities due to their colours, for example the red of *yukgaejang* (spicy beef soup) as a fire for 'defeating the evil spirit',[20] the whiteness of tofu adds to its emblematic standing, signifying purity alongside the significance of tofu as 'the soul of beans'. This has found its way into a more modern tradition that is often depicted in Korean pop culture: the gifting of tofu to, or eating of tofu by, people just released from prison. It is detailed in countless Korean films and TV series, from applauded titles such as *Lady Vengeance* (2005) to historical dramas like *Flower in Prison* (2016). The theories as to why were discussed during a tofu-themed episode of the Korean TV show *Wednesday Food Talk* in 2015. Hong Shin-ae, a culinary researcher, said, 'It's difficult to get the same exact taste every time, so much so that tofu craftsmen say, "No tofu has been made twice in my life",' due to the various factors involved such as exact temperature and speed or force of stirring. In response, food columnist Hwang Kyo-ik extrapolated the penitential connection. 'That's what it means to eat tofu when you come out of prison,' he said. 'The same tofu can never happen twice, so it symbolizes that bad things won't happen again.'[21] Another theory was put forward by novelist Park Wan-suh, who detailed the connection between tofu and prison in a 2002 essay, 'Dubu'. She explained that a life behind bars is a life of 'eating rice and beans' (another idiom: 'doing time'). With this in mind, tofu is 'released' from beans, can never return to beans, and symbolically tofu acts like a 'charm' to never find oneself in prison again.[22] Here again tofu is ghost food, the ritualistic consumption of which symbolizes rebirth and new beginnings, purifying the newly freed individual before the next stage in their life just as it accompanies ancestral spirits into the afterlife.

There is great reverence attached to tofu in this setting. Its status as an offering for the deceased could be an extension of its curative use on elderly parents, an act of filial piety, as shown in an origin story told in Chapter One. Namely this would be the legendary invention of tofu in the third century BC by Yue Yi, who ingeniously or accidentally created tofu as a nourishing medicine for his elderly parents in an act of care and devotion. It may have simply been practical. In his late Yuan dynasty (1279–1368) work *Gui Chao Gao* (Turtle Nest Compositions), the scholar Xie Yingfang (1296–1392) wrote that tofu was 'good for the elderly' who could no longer eat meat.[23] When exactly the Yue Yi legend arose is unknown, but it has strong parallels to the historical practice of *gegu*. This refers to offering parts of one's own flesh, usually a sliver of thigh, for medicinal consumption by an ailing parent. This was 'a socially accepted expression of love and respect in

China which began in the ninth century'.[24] And it was an idea potentially imported to Tang dynasty China via various tales of gory selflessness that came with the Silk Road transmission of Buddhism.[25] For tofu to vicariously become part of such rituals, as expounded in the case of the legend of Yue Yi, who gave his parents tofu possibly in lieu of his own flesh, lends it a status higher than that of simple culinary meat substitute, elevating it to the form of an avatar for human sacrifice itself. According to Sinologist Keith Knapp, 'the idea of eating the body of one's own flesh and blood was not particularly alien to mediaeval Chinese.'[26] However, several thirteenth-century edicts banned the use of eyeballs, liver and thigh for *gegu*.[27] Moreover, there was a scholarly shying away from its 'crassness',[28] suggesting that an alternative may not only have been welcomed but actively endorsed in the form of tofu-substituting myths like that of Yue Yi.

Human flesh has long been used in a ritualistic way, and not always volunteered out of filial piety. Throughout much of the Shang dynasty (*c.* 1600–1046 BC), 'human sacrifice of captured peoples was frequent and numerous,' and continued, though to a lesser extent, into the Warring States era.[29] Human parts would, on occasion, be 'served' to ancestral spirits. Constance A. Cook, a specialist in excavated texts of ancient China, writes: 'The sharing of this meal by the living transformed this semi-symbolic cannibalistic feast into a communion of the living and the dead.'[30] Shocking as this sounds to modern-day ears, the 'practice of cannibalism is not exceptional in Chinese history,'[31] with 'Chinese literary and historical sources [providing] wide-ranging examples of both survival anthropophagy and ritualistic endo-cannibalism'.[32] It was noted by external observers; for instance, the tenth-century Arabic commentary in the *Account of India and China* touches on cannibalism in China. It describes how, in war-time, the vanquished would be 'barbarously devoured', something allegedly allowed by the 'laws of their religion', which also '[permitted] human flesh to be exposed to public sale in the markets'.[33] Xie Yingfang also mentions that, in 1356, he fled his home town in the wake of the army of Zhu Yuanzhang (1328–1398), founder and first emperor of the Ming dynasty (1368–1644), who 'set everything on fire and ate the flesh of those who died'.[34] One wartime story in the Warring States period of Chinese history showcases an allegorical link between flesh and tofu. At the time seven major states battled it out for supremacy, two of the strongest being Qin and Zhao. The state of Qin employed the fearsome general Bai Qi to finally quash the Zhao, culminating with the Battle of Changping, which Bai Qi decisively won in 260 BC. Rather than letting captured Zhao soldiers go, allowing them to potentially raise a rebellion, or keeping them as prisoners (which wouldn't be cheap), it is said that Bai Qi had 400,000 of them killed, leaving 240 alive, presumably to spread the story and inspire fear.[35] The local people, enraged by this ruthless mass murder, vented their hatred towards Bai Qi via the medium of food, creating *bai qi rou*, literally 'Bai Qi meat'.[36] This dish, in which tofu is grilled like meat and served in a sauce to resemble Bai Qi's head smashed into mud, can be seen as an allegory of punitive cannibalism, a physical representation of the vengeful idiom *shi rou qin pi* (eat their flesh and sleep on their skin).[37] Here tofu plays the part of stand-in for the body of Bai Qi, though whether the dish really originates at that time is highly doubtful (and would make tofu older than the purported Liu An legend). Due to its fleshy semi-resemblance to meat in general, the likelihood is that tofu later stood in for all and any flesh, the human variety being historically just one type of these. Even before tofu, soybeans were a significant part of sacrifice, 'likely a staple as early as the Shang period'.[38] Comprising one of the Five Grains (though not the most common), they likely played a part in grain sacrifices, which, as Cook explains, served 'as a primary symbol of state creation in ancient times'.[39] Thus associated with nationhood itself, tofu takes it one step further. As the 'soul of beans', extracted after an alchemical, medicinal process, the reverence attached to tofu is unambiguous. It is both grain and meat, sustenance and sacrifice.

As well as being a proxy for meat or flesh, even of the human variety, it is also frequently used to describe or allude to women's bodies in a sexual context. For example, the Cantonese slang term *dau fu po*, literally meaning 'tofu woman', figuratively refers to lesbians.[40] The connotation is twofold: the phrase reduces the woman in question to a non-autonomous object – tofu – rather than a human being; and it is used metonymically to refer to female genitals. That is, *dau fu po*, roughly translated, means 'a woman who likes women's bodies'. To be clear about its skewed meaning, the equivalent phrase for men, *dau fu lou* (tofu guy), does not mean a man who likes women's bodies, but is used to refer to a male tofu-seller.[41] Somehow when women come in contact with tofu in a lexical context, the connotations are sex and objectification. Further illustrating the association of tofu with female bodies is the phrase *mo doufu*. Though it innocently refers to grinding tofu, the slang meaning of *mo doufu* is sexual in nature, as it is 'frequently . . . used to signify mutual clitoral stimulation by lesbians'.[42] As sociologist James Farrer notes, the longevity of the Spanish-language *panochita* (from *panocha*, a type of pudding) as a slang term for female genitals 'points to the resonance of food–sex metaphors'.[43] In a more general sense, to say you are eating tofu, or are going to eat tofu, have eaten tofu, will eat tofu, or any other tense of consuming bean curd sounds harmless enough, but in Chinese languages eating tofu (Mandarin: *chi doufu*) should not always be taken literally, roughly meaning to take advantage of, flirt with or sexually harass a woman.[44] There are two possible reasons for the meaning. The first is thought to come from the funeral custom of *chi doufu geng* (literally 'eating tofu soup'), or *chi doufu fan* as mentioned earlier, a tradition in Zhejiang, Hunan and Hubei provinces, among other places. In this context, 'eating tofu' referred to a freeloader, somebody who goes to a funeral not to lend a hand, but for the occasion – to literally eat the tofu on offer, thus taking advantage of the situation.[45] Another folk etymology cites a Qing-era novella, *Jing Meng Ti* (A Waking Cry), which features a tofu maker, Li Dalang, and his wife, Chuntao. Such was Chuntao's beauty that word spread around the neighbours, who said Li Dalang's tofu was delicious; everyone came to his house on the pretence of buying it, but really to flirt with Chuntao.[46] Either way the phrase caught on, and the meaning of both sexual harassment and taking advantage of others suggests that both origins have intermingled.

The phrase is far from a historical side note, remaining very much charged with meaning today. In 2019 an advert by Ikea for tofu-flavoured ice cream in their Hong Kong stores caused uproar for its inclusion of the phrase 'You guys can eat my tofu whenever you like.' On social media, the picture was accompanied by a note encouraging consumers 'to be gentle'.[47] Hong Kong activist group Gender and Sexual Justice in Action criticized the advert and demanded that Ikea remove it, saying that 'the ice-cream ad once again treats woman's body as an object . . . to be taken advantage of.' Ikea refused, stating that the brand had tried hard to communicate in a 'playful yet positive manner', despite their use of a phrase that is used to refer to sexual harassment. Here the symbolism of tofu as analogous to flesh can be extended to the female body, an objectified, pre-sacrificed form with no more agency than a plate of bean curd. Depending on the context or idiom in which it is used, the connotations of the word 'tofu' can be powerful, charged with contempt, humour, death and ridicule, let alone the symbolic role played by the literal physical presence and use of tofu as a foodstuff and offering.

GODS, SPIRITS AND SUPERSTITION IN JAPANESE TOFU

Whether tofu made its way over to Japan with a delegation of Chinese Buddhist monks over a thousand years ago, or its first outing in Japan was in 1183 as an offering at a Shinto shrine, the hallowed status of tofu in the country stuck.[48] One tradition emblematic of this status is hari-kuyō. Literally meaning 'needle memorial service', this ceremony is held among seamstresses in Japan as a 'funeral' for broken needles and pins. Part of the koto-yoka tradition of cleaning up tools and equipment observed by artisans (shokunin), it was originally a day of rest but was later attributed to warding off a diminutive one-eyed yōkai ('strange apparition') called hitotsume-kozō, who is incidentally sometimes depicted carrying tofu.[49] During the hari-kuyō, which is believed to have originated at Awashima-jinja shrine in Kada, Wakayama Prefecture, in the Edo period and spread from there, the broken or bent needles and pins are stuck into tofu (or konnyaku, konjac jelly) as a mark of respect for the tools' hard work.[50] Granted their final resting place within ghost food itself, these inanimate but spirit-imbued objects get the same sort of respect as a human, both receiving the honour of the tofu offering and becoming a sacrifice themselves. Tofu as a communion between higher powers and earthly spirits in Japan has better currency in the case of Inari, the kami (deity) of rice cultivation, merchants and general prosperity. Inari is depicted variously as female, male or neither; a genderless, graceful bodhisattva or a smiling, bearded figure. They are often conflated with Dakiniten, a made-in-Japan deity (sometimes represented riding on a white fox) based on ḍākinī, flesh-eating female spirits in Hindu and Buddhist tradition.[51] Though

Students at the Kōran College of Fashion Design in Fukuoka City, Japan, stick bent and broken needles into tofu during the *hari-kuyō* (literally 'needle memorial service') as a mark of respect for their hard work.

Inari was cited as a disciple of Buddha, their close association with Buddhism in an 'official' sense ended on 28 March 1868, when the newly instated Meiji government passed the *Shinbutsu Hazen-rei*, an edict that brought about a campaign of *shinbutsu bunri*, 'separating the [native Shinto] gods from the Buddha'.[52]

While Dakiniten has a majestic white fox as their steed, Inari instead has a fleet of foxes (kitsune in Japanese) serving as their messengers. Those looking to seek the favour of Inari traditionally leave inari-zushi, vinegared rice wrapped in a thin slice of salty-sweet abura-age (fried tofu), as offerings at Inari shrines as it is a favourite food of the fox. In return, the fluffy messenger is expected to report back to Inari with only good things about the worshipper, acting as a conduit between the earthly and the divine.[53] Shape-wise, inari-zushi are said to resemble bales of rice, the crop for which Inari is venerated, or else the pointed edges of the snack are made to look like fox ears. Given that inari-zushi is filled with rice, this may stem from another tradition to get on the good side of kitsune. This is mentioned by the Swiss connoisseur of Japanese crafts and folklore Ugo Alfonso Casal (1888–1964), later head of the Section for Foreign Interests of the Swiss consulate, Kobe, in a 1959 essay about 'witch animals' such as foxes, badgers and snakes:

> You have to tie three balls of rice (nigiri-meshi . . .) to a strawrope [sic] a hundred handbreadths long. For one hundred consecutive nights, at midnight, this charm must be taken to an Inari shrine, and each time one handbreadth of the rope must be deposited as an offering to the deity. In the end a fox will come and eat the rice-balls . . . and 'provided you have a pure heart' this fox will become your humble servant for the rest of your days.[54]

These foxes are partial to some particular foods. Kitsune-udon, thick, wheat noodles (udon) swimming in dashi broth and topped with a spongy slab of abura-age, is another favourite. One variety, shinoda udon, features thinly sliced strips of abura-age instead. The name derives from Shinoda, the once-forested setting for the legend of Kuzunoha, a byakko (white fox) who acts as a shinshi (divine messenger) of Inari. In the story, Kuzunoha is saved from hunters by Abe no Yasuna, who is subsequently injured and later visited by a mysterious woman who nurses him back to health. The two have a child together, the Merlin-esque figure Abe no Seimei. Later it is discovered the woman is none other than the human form of Kuzunoha the fox.[55] Shinoda-maki, which involves rolling thin abura-age around vegetables, meat and other ingredients before simmering or serving in oden (a type of Japanese stew), is also derived from this legend. This can be compared to kinchaku (literally meaning 'purse'), a pouch of abura-age stuffed with ingredients, sealed with a toothpick or tied with kanpyō (strips of dried gourd). Today's Izumi City keeps a connection to the legend alive with a yuru-chara (mascot) named Kon-chan. A cartoon fox wearing festival clothing, and named after the onomatopoeic word for the sound foxes make in Japanese (kon-kon), Kon-chan is determined to 'liven up school lunches' in line with shokuiku (government-sanctioned food education).[56] Speaking of tofu-related mascots, there's also Tofucchi, a cute little figure with a lacquered bowl of tofu for a head, a mascot of Iwate Prefecture.

In folktales featuring foxes, the animals are supposed to be 'fond of fried rats' to such an extent that it often leads to their downfall. For example, an 'efficacious way to detect a bakemono [monster] fox is to depose a fried rat on the road along which the suspicious person comes in . . . he will immediately abandon his prank and pounce upon the tidbit'.[57] In the noh play Tsuri-gitsune, a shapeshifting fox is lured into a trap with a fried rat.[58] It could be that the predilection of foxes for abura-age comes from the rabid, all-too-keen response they have for fried rats, 'such a luscious dish' for them that, maybe, they prematurely jump on anything that could even half-resemble a frittered rodent.[59]

The appearance of Inari, the dazzling deity, accompanied by their *byakko* (white fox) messenger, *c.* 1840, woodblock print by Utagawa Kuniyoshi.

Indeed, 'the fox is greedy and loves tidbits'.[60] It may be that *abura-age* is a vegetarian, that is, Buddhist-friendly, substitute for the fried rat which the *kitsune* so likes. But perhaps *kitsune* are not all that picky: 'The badger [*mujina*, another supernatural, shape-shifting prankster] will steal fish . . . as the fox will steal anything fried.'[61] Foxes are not the only messenger of Japan's *kami* connected with tofu. Basil Hall Chamberlain (1850–1935), a prominent Japanologist, makes mention in his A Handbook for Travellers in Japan: 'There is a current belief to the effect that Koya-san [Mount Koya] is so precipitous that such luxuries as bean-curd (*tōfu*) cannot be carried up to it, but that the priests place coppers on the temple balustrade, with which the crows fly off to Kumano and bring back bean-curd in return.'[62]

The association of tofu with supernatural animals is not always so curiously buoyant, particularly in the case of *kitsune*, who have an unshakeable association with madness and possession (*kitsune-tsuki*). This specific form of possession by unseen forces has long been documented in Japan, with cases recorded as recently as 2011. Even while possessing a human, *abura-age* apparently continues to be an obsession. According to an anonymous letter dated to 14 August 1916, 'The man whom fox possessed wants to eat "*Aburage*" (fried bean-curd) or becomes like a mad man.'[63] Lafcadio Hearn describes a type of 'fox-superstition in Izumo', in the westerly Chugoku region of Japan, which is directed not only towards foxes themselves, but anything associated with them. He describes a shrine devoted to Inari at Zuikozan-Kiyomizudera, a Buddhist temple in Yasugi, Shimane Prefecture:

Beside it is a sort of huge trough filled with little foxes of all shapes, designs, and material. If you want anything, you pray, and put a fox in your pocket, and take it home. As soon as the prayer is granted you must take the fox back again and put it

Hundreds of fox statues at a shrine dedicated to Inari.

just where it was before. I should like to have taken one
home; but my servants hate foxes and Inari and *tofu* and
azuki-meshi and *abura-gi* [*abura-age*] and everything related
to foxes. So I left it alone.[64]

It is clear to see that the image projected by *kitsune* is one 'both
admired and feared'. As early as the eleventh century, the fox had
become a 'troubling animal in the mind of the Japanese people',
feared for their ability to shapeshift and possess people.[65] Indeed
'accusations of being foxes' were 'often leveled against wealthy
families [and] served in small, close-knit Japanese hamlets as a
way of expressing envy and jealousy in a form that was mythically
and socially acceptable.'[66] It is therefore very possible that Inari

shrines, foxes and their culinary accoutrements would have been actively avoided by Hearn's servants owing to this fox phobia.

The Edo-period Confucian scholar Nakai Chikuzan (1730–1804) characterized 'reckless talk of badgers and foxes' as 'deviant beliefs [jakyō] . . . and nothing but techniques to confound the ignorant masses'.[67] This wariness against kitsune-tsuki was particularly detrimental to the merchant class of which Nakai was a part. Even into the modern period, wealthy homes of the merchant classes in rural villages were known to be shunned due to accusations of being kitsune-mochi (fox possessors), those with the ability to get a fox to do their bidding, which includes possessing people.[68] This stigma reached well into the twentieth century; in 1952 (also in Shimane Prefecture), a young couple committed suicide due to the generations-old belief that the woman came from a fox-possessing family.[69] It was contagious; simply by marrying into such a family you could become 'one of them'. Even the term itself, kitsune-mochi, is taboo.[70]

Shimane, Japan's second-least populous prefecture, epitomizes Japan's agricultural population, whose imaginations worked in complex ways to 'understand the incursion of capitalism and

A SCENE OF SORCERY.

An illustration of 'sorcery' by Aimé Humbert (1819–1900) in *Japan and the Japanese Illustrated* (1874). One fox blows a *horagai* (conch shell horn), the other shakes an *ōnusa* (sacred wand).

the accumulation of wealth', symbols of which were the fox, Inari and anything associated with Inari worship. As late as the 1990s, certain families in Shimane (in the village of Kamo, for example) have been labelled as fox-possessors. Interestingly, these are 'new money' families who came into their wealth in the seventeenth and eighteenth centuries, 'the period that saw the shift from bartering to currency exchange in rural Shimane'.[71] Kitsune-mochi began with families who migrated to rural communities; they held influential economic positions and became landowners. They ended up being scorned and rejected by the community and 'in extremely brutal cases, their houses were attacked and burnt down by peasants with torches in hand.'[72] With these acts of violence in mind, it's no wonder that 'everything to do with foxes', tofu included, no matter how integral to Japanese cuisine, would be so shunned.

The kitsune is not the only yōkai with bean curd connections. There is also tōfu-kozō – tofu boy, named for the plate of tofu he carries. This (sometimes) one-eyed, big-headed, long-tongued, claw-footed child wears a big kasa (umbrella) hat and a toy-patterned kimono. He first appears in illustrated woodblock print works called kusazōshi and the more satirical kibyōshi, both written in vernacular Japanese and popular with ordinary people, between 1775 and 1806. Smallpox at the time was raging, as it did throughout the Edo period, and hōsōe (smallpox pictures) depicting various types of hōsōgami (smallpox gods) were popularly used to ward off the disease. It is theorized that tōfu-kozō may be a parody of such deities, being a cheeky-looking child rather than the ogre or adult figures commonly used otherwise.[73] As smallpox can cause blindness, the one-eyed variety of tōfu-kozō makes sense. Two other yōkai seem like variations: ō-atama-kozō (big-head boy) and hitotsume-kozō (one-eyed boy), both of which sometimes carry tofu. There are many different depictions of

Meet *tōfu-kozō*, the non-threatening *yōkai* (apparation). He has clawed feet, almost like talons, in this illustration by Kitao Masayoshi (1764–1824) in *Bakemonochakutōchō* (1788).

tōfu-kozō. He appears often in manga artist Shigeru Mizuki's iconic *GeGeGe no Kitaro* franchise, while mystery writer Natsuhiko Kyogoku has written a whole series of books, the *Tofu Kozo Series*, which was adapted into a film in 2011 – *Tofu Kozu* (published in English as *Little Ghostly Adventures of Tofu Boy*) directed by Gisaburō Sugii and Shimmei Kawahara. It's plain to see that the cultural weight of tofu in Japan, from myth to manga, equals its physical prevalence in the country.

THE USE OF TOFU IN IDIOMS RELATING TO WEAKNESS

Much has been said thus far regarding the symbolic strength of tofu, its use as a stand-in for the human body as well as a representation of life-to-death transition observed at funerals across China and Japan. Then there is the physicality of tofu, a structural integrity that is less than strong. This, and its virtues of affordability, lead to idioms and phrases that showcase the weakness of tofu, and which have historically been used to denigrate those who subsist on it. Its softness is used in a Cantonese phrase for making a mess of things, *daan faai jyu sau + fa dau fu – gaau wo saai* ('trying to eat tofu with one chopstick makes a messy mix').[74] Tofu is implicated in an idiom for a fence-sitter: *dau fu dou – leung bin min* ('a bean curd knife is sharp on both sides').[75] Speaking of knives, in Mandarin you can have 'a tongue like a knife, but a bean-curd (soft) heart' (*daozi zui, doufu xin*).[76] It is also possible for things to be 'higgedly-piggeldy' if you *putao pan doufu, yi dou lu yi gui de* (literally, 'muddle grapes and tofu, here a piece, there a bunch').[77] In addition to this language relating to mess, in China tofu has often been used to allude to shortcuts, malpractice and bad workmanship. The epithet 'bean-curd official' (*doufu guan*) was used, at least while H. A. Giles was compiling his Chinese–English dictionary in the latter years of the Qing dynasty, for 'flabby or unenergetic officials'. It was also 'a term of contempt applied to certain of the poorer classes of official servants who are compelled to feed largely on this cheap food [tofu]'.[78] There appears to be a connection between tofu and the lower classes and in some cases, maybe by extension, with inferiority – a far cry from the noble poverty that provides the origin story of the deified general Guan Yu, once a humble tofu seller.

In Giles's dictionary the term *doufu lou* ('tofu building') refers to a cheap restaurant.[79] People nowadays may associate a 'tofu building' with shoddy workmanship, due to the existence of a more recent idiom, 'tofu-dreg construction', which circulated widely in the aftermath of the Great Sichuan Earthquake in 2008.

> Beichuan was once a picturesque town. It became well
> known because of the high number of casualties caused
> by the earthquake. Over half the population of Beichuan
> was killed in the earthquake. The city center was flooded
> by media from all over the world because many students
> from Beichuan high school died in the earthquake.

So writes journalist Lee Yee-chong in an account of the quake. The school in question, one of many destroyed, 'is an icon of tofu-dreg construction'.[80] A direct translation of the Chinese term *doufuzha gongcheng*, this turn of phrase was coined by Zhu Rongji, Chinese premier between 1998 and 2003, to describe a flimsy set of flood defences along the Yangtze River during a tour of dikes in 1998.[81] But 'tofu construction' may have begun earlier than this, with the Banqiao Dam that collapsed during a typhoon in 1975, killing tens, perhaps hundreds, of thousands, of people; cracks began to show not long after the dam's completion in 1952. Since 2007, there have been at least nineteen major bridge collapses in China, resulting in over 140 deaths. And, according to a statement by one Water Resources Ministry official in 2006, 'in a given year around 68 (mostly small) dikes . . . collapse in China.'[82]

Lee's account of the Sichuan earthquake states 'even reconstruction efforts are not problem-free.' Alongside missing donations and embezzlement, 'tofu-dreg problems are reappearing,' with rumours of 'tofu bricks' and 'tofu rods'. Lee states they were able to find evidence of shoddy 'tofu bricks' in the countryside.[83] With the advent of the Belt and Road Initiative, and construction along the New Silk Road, the use of the term 'tofu-dreg construction' has spread across the globe. In 2017 the Chinese-built Sigiri Bridge in western Kenya collapsed, injuring nineteen workers; two years later, 28 construction workers were killed when an unfinished, Chinese-funded condominium block crumbled in Sihanoukville, Cambodia – all signs of a 'ticking time-bomb' regarding tofu-dreg construction, according to a 2021 article in the *American Affairs Journal*. The same article states: 'Tofu-dreg construction persists because many Chinese construction companies cut corners, rush jobs, ignore safety standards, and use poorly trained workers to save costs and meet deadlines. Inside China, companies get away with this by bribing officials and stifling popular protest.'[84] These issues, though occurring within China and Chinese construction companies, are not exclusive to either. The ease with which the term 'tofu-dreg construction' is picked up outside China to speak of Chinese construction controversies, rather than using neutral words like 'malpractice', is reflective of the ease with which anti-Chinese sentiment is elicited from Western audiences. Its use does not feel too far away from the negative press that tofu itself gets, which may or may not be laced with a certain amount of racism and, in particular, Sinophobia. Such sentiment in Western countries seems easily whipped up, especially in light of anti-Chinese sentiment following COVID-19. Using this Chinese foodstuff to describe only

Chinese failings in construction serves to other the people, the government and even the cuisine of the country, as if making shortcuts in this way were a China-specific phenomenon, which clearly it is not. The stigma already attached to tofu makes it easier for commentators to attach negative sentiment to the phrases in which it is used, trickling down into a vague uneasiness or mistrust about tofu's country of origin. The use of 'tofu-dreg construction' in the West hints at this, but in the past decade or so, tofu has found itself weaponized in the seemingly eternal slanging match between liberal and conservative political camps.

TOFU-EATING: EFFEMINATE, DISRUPTIVE, LIBERAL

In a similar way to terms like 'snowflake', tofu has become something of a synecdoche for veganism and vegetarianism,[85] and by extension used in epithets for male effeminacy and left-leaning or liberal politics. In 2022 the British Home Secretary Suella Braverman made comments in the House of Commons that brought bean curd into the spotlight. Reacting to Just Stop Oil protestors who had forced a major London river crossing to close, Braverman blamed 'Guardian-reading, tofu-eating wokerati' for the disruption. In response, David Knibbs, co-founder of British tofu company Tofoo, stated, 'She's got what we call tofuphobia . . . It's a phrase we use a lot: the fear of the white block.'[86] Extending from mere mistrust and dislike of tofu on a culinary level, this 'tofuphobia' permeates the political landscape today on both sides of the Atlantic, both creating a loaded term out of tofu and putting it in the firing line of xenophobia masquerading as rhetorical banter. A Vice article documenting the use of tofu to denigrate certain groups of people states, '[American] conservative pundits, cartoonists, and columnists have fallen back on tofu as a specific way to insult liberals for at least the past decade-plus.'[87] Among all of this is the obvious, or perhaps not-so-obvious to some: that tofu is an Asian import to the West. For it to be used as a pejorative either displays ignorance of its Asian origins, thus negating the experience of minorities (tofu being 'culturally white'), or actively seeks for tofu, as a foreign food, to be reviled. Describing people as 'tofu-eating' to insult them could be held up as an ethnic slur, but there is a paradox at work: tofu's dual existence as both a commonplace Asian food *and* a foodstuff of Western vegetarians. However, by assuming the acceptability of this phrase, by brushing aside tofu's Asian-ness, we delete not only the origin of tofu and the communities who eat it, but the process of the white assimilation of a product once, and to some extent still, held in pariah limbo by Western diners.

The historical denigration of an Asian diet is not a new thing. It goes back over a century, to a time when it was used as part of the rhetoric surrounding white supremacy and as a justification or an explanation for colonialism. Referencing the supposed scientific inferiority of a plant-based (in this case, Asian) diet, American neurologist James Leonard Corning wrote in 1884, 'The effeminate rice eaters of India and China have again and again yielded to the superior moral courage of an infinitely smaller number of meat-eating Englishmen.'[88] Corning was not alone in his views. Calling rice a 'wretched article of diet', Australian doctor and author S. M. Caffyn wrote in 1883: 'We might expect to find rice-eaters everywhere a wretched, impotent, and effeminate race, and such is the case.'[89] Far from being 'discredited or fringe ideas', this type of thinking prevailed in the mainstream during the late nineteenth century.[90] By the First World War, 'the Asian body came to represent nutritional deficiency in American gastropolitical discourse,' and an apparent threat to white, working-class America.[91] This can be exemplified in the report *Meat vs Rice: American Manhood against Asiatic Coolieism, Which Will*

Survive? written in 1902, two decades after America's 1882 Chinese Exclusion Act, by Samuel Gompers, founder and president of the American Federation of Labor. By consuming little, according to the report, the Chinese immigrant worker 'underbids all white labor . . . until the white laborers come down to the scanty food and half civilized habits' of Chinese immigrants themselves.[92] The title of the report, combined with its contents, is highly indicative of hostility towards the Asian, rice-eating 'coolie' and the imagined plight of a supposedly superior white American meat-eating 'man'.

This speaks to carnophallogocentrism, a term coined by French philosopher Jacques Derrida, drawing on and evolving his previous neologism, phallogocentrism, 'a male-centred point of view expressed in and through language'.[93] The addition of *carno* adds 'flesh-eating' into the bargain. With this, 'Derrida [attempts] to name the primary social, linguistic, and material practices that go into becoming a subject within the West and how explicit carnivorism lies at the heart of classical notions of subjectivity, especially male subjectivity.'[94] This subjectivity skews imagery and ideology in favour of masculine meat-eaters in everything from political debates to advertising. Writer and activist Carol J. Adams, author of *The Sexual Politics of Meat* (1990), among other works, reflecting on the topic in discussion with animal philosopher Matthew Calarco, described an advert that illustrates carnophallogocentrism at work:

A 2006 Hummer advertisement features a man buying tofu in a supermarket. Next to him a man is buying gobs of raw meat. The tofu-buying man notices this and becomes alert to and anxious about his virility, apparently compromised by his tofu-buying. He hurries from the grocery store and heads straight to a Hummer dealership.[95]

The implication with this particular advert is that the vegetarian man must buy a Hummer to compensate for the emasculating protein (tofu) he was about to buy. A similar advert, released in 2011, by New Zealand beer company Red Lion, citing in a press release that 'the modern man is in a state of turmoil' and 'traditional male values are being eroded,' promulgated 'Man Points' whereby 'pursuits such as building a barbecue get man points, but cooking tofu on said barbecue . . . gets negative man points.'[96] Adams's suspicion here is that unlike a library card (her example) masculinity needs constant renewal as it can be depleted with apparent ease. The lack of masculinity ascribed in Western culture to tofu and its consumption is telling of two things: a mistrust of Asian cuisines, long seen as 'effeminate', that encroach on traditionally 'Western' culinary spaces (that is, barbecues), and a prevailing view that is carnophallogocentric in nature. To illustrate the point further, consider the critic A. A. Gill's point of view that steak is 'manly': 'Women can eat it, they can appreciate it, but [doing so is] a cross-gender impersonation.'[97] Therefore in this masculine, carnivorous world, tofu is the anti-steak, anything but manly.

According to some, eating tofu is not just a symbolic relinquishing of 'male values' but a very real threat to manhood, whereby consuming it can literally reduce one's masculinity. This anxiety finds its origin in claims that tofu actively boosts oestrogen and lowers testosterone. As one *Men's Journal* article bluntly put it, soy (tofu included) is 'perceived as being a man boob-giving, estrogen-bestowing testosterone-killer'.[98] Or take the language of this 2004 *New York Post* article entitled, 'DOCS: SOY BOYS SHOOT BLANKS', which states that soy 'may contribute to male infertility . . . because soy contains the female hormone estrogen – and eating too much of it has been linked to poor-quality sperm'.[99] This term 'soy boy' has more recently become a term used by the alt-right on social media, originating on 4chan in April 2016, to refer to what they deem to be effeminized males.[100] The 'discredited science about phytoestrogens in soy foods', combined with soy's association with 'traditional and current Asian popular culture', has made it a target for the alt-right.[101] On the other hand, as opposed to the feminine nature of soy milk, dairy milk has frequently been associated with masculinity and superiority, and more recently as 'a symbol of alt-right hyper-masculinity', well illustrated at what has since been dubbed the 'milk party', a gathering of angry milk-toting white nationalists in February 2017.[102]

Despite this, as the next chapter will discuss, tofu is growing in popularity. Xenophobia, partisan politics played out on social media and misinformation apparently have not affected the tofu market. While COVID-19 and subsequent 'anti-China rhetoric' saw Chinese-owned restaurants in the United States experiencing an 18.4 per cent decrease in customers (equivalent to a $7.42 billion loss), the same year witnessed record figures for tofu. Nielsen data revealed sales of tofu were up 40 per cent in the first half of 2020 compared to the same period of 2019.[103] Pulmuone, a South Korean company that owns America's top-selling tofu brand, Nasoya, experienced such high demand that their three U.S.-based plants working six days a week couldn't keep up.[104] The UK brand Tofoo has seen a massive surge in popularity, 'in just six years [growing] annual sales from £426,000 to £18.6m in 2021'.[105] With a history of two millennia, give or take a few centuries, on its side, tofu has become a firmly entrenched foodstuff across the world. Its expansion beyond the kitchen and into conversations, political debate and ad campaigns speaks volumes to its ubiquity and versatility. A rarer item of food may not have made it into Suella Braverman's speech, or into the hearts and minds of alt-right social media users. Neatly mirroring its culinary utility is its cultural mobility.

Tofu means different things to different people. It is a funeral offering, a symbol of new beginnings, the folkloric favourite food of shapeshifting foxes, and a metaphor for human flesh, the female form, un-manliness, poverty, stupidity and shortcuts in construction. There is no denying the culture that stems from bean curd, both in the enduring traditions and languages of Asian nations and communities, and in how it is viewed and used today in the West where tofu is a newer food, a threat and a saviour. Its continued survival looks promising. And with technological innovations to further bend and stretch tofu to the will of humanity (and its tastebuds), the ancient invention has an interesting future.

SIX
TOFU INC.,
THE BUSINESS OF BEAN CURD

Tofu has had a rocky road towards gaining acceptance in the West. But what was the road less travelled is today a highway of bean curd goodness. The house that tofu built, once a niche outbuilding, is in these allegorical terms a shiny skyscraper today. From cottage industry to lucrative enterprise, tofu has become a big hitter in the food world, with multinational companies purveying it in various forms. In general meat-free alternatives are doing well: 27 per cent of households in the UK alone purchase alternatives to meat.[1] However, the global meat-alternatives market has slumped in 2023, despite being hailed as possibly 'the biggest single trend in the history of food' by Walter Rob, former Whole Foods co-CEO, in February 2021.[2] Since then, the *Financial Times* reports, it's been 'a painful two-and-a-half-year journey for investors in the sector'. Teething issues in the form of development, trying to match the flavour, texture and cost of actual meat, are cited by some analysts of the trend. Tofu, on the other hand, requires far less lab time for product development. It is a tried-and-tested formula. In short, what the twentieth century started, from Li Shizeng and Kin Yamei to The Farm and

The Book of Tofu, the twenty-first will continue. As this chapter will reveal, with its market and consumption set to increase, tofu is being recast. Not only are long-standing tofu brands modernizing, conjuring protein bars and burgers out of bean curd, but eateries primed for twenty-first-century dining experiences are also appearing. And as demand increases, so will production, resulting in more soybean crops, more tofu being made, more environmental impact and ways to improve its sustainability from bean to boxed product; novel solutions for tofu waste products look set to power homes and cars, while elsewhere soy-less bean curd is making its debut. The future looks bright.

Despite the negative press, people are evidently more accepting of tofu today and the food is seeing a surge in popularity, raising its profile from dud to darling. Several factors, including

The original tofu burger: *ganmodoki* is a deep-fried wonder studded with your favourite vegetables.

the zoonotic nature of COVID-19 and an increase in the number of people cooking from scratch at home, saw the sales of tofu surge as the pandemic took hold in 2020. In the USA the country's largest tofu provider, Pulmuone, experienced shortages that had to be bolstered by sending extra tofu from South Korea; once present in just 5 per cent of U.S. homes, six months into the pandemic that rose to 16 per cent.[3] Sales of tofu in the UK increased by 87 per cent in the twelve weeks leading up to June 2020.[4] The UK tofu market is expected to see a compound annual growth rate of 14.68 per cent between 2021 and 2026.[5] Worldwide, it will see growth of 11.56 per cent between 2016 and 2028.[6] A report by *Bloomberg Intelligence* predicted in 2021 that the value of the plant-based foods market as a whole would increase from $29.4 billion in 2020 to $162 billion by 2030.[7] Even in Italy, a country not at all associated with tofu consumption, Nielsen reported a 12.4 per cent rise in value (13.4 per cent in volume) of the Italian tofu market from 2021 to 2022.[8] Kenyan tofu brand Mtofu, which started life in 2019, could be leading the way for modern, home-grown tofu in East Africa. Mtofu director Quinter Katuyi explained in a 2022 interview with the Kenyan newspaper *Business Daily* that it was hard to find tofu 'because no one was actually making it'.[9] With investment interest from Tanzania, while eyeing expansion across East Africa, Mtofu has the makings of a pioneering brand: they sell to young adult Kenyans and market their products, which include meat alternatives, via Facebook and Instagram. Mtofu also uses soybeans grown in Kenya, cutting the need for imports. In doing so they join various brands across the world who use only domestically grown soybeans as demand for GMO-free and deforestation-free soy increases.[10] Tofu companies across the globe, big and small, are taking up the bean curd baton and running with it. In 2021 the U.S. subsidiary of Japanese brand House Foods began construction of a new 32,500-square-metre

A selection of tofu products available in UK supermarkets as of 2022.

(350,000 sq. ft) tofu plant in Louisville, Kentucky. Costing $146 million to build, it won't be complete until 2025 – a sure sign of the company's betting on bean curd futures.[11] Hundreds of tofu brands do business across the globe, the biggest players being Japan's House Foods, Kikkoman and Morinaga, Singapore's PSC Corporation (owner of Fortune Foods) and Hong Kong's Vitasoy. There are plenty of honourable mentions. In the UK there is Tofoo, whose sales grew by 89 per cent in 2020.[12] The company had to import new machinery from Japan the same year to keep up with demand,[13] ultimately increasing production capacity by 70 per cent.[14] Other companies also include Tofu King, which in 2020 established the UK's largest factory dedicated to tofu, as well as veteran brands Clearspring and Cauldron.[15] SoyBoy and Meiji Tofu are well known in the United States, Fortune Beancurd and

Blue Lotus Foods in Australia, not to mention other Japanese brands like Asahico, Sagamiya and Yamami.

Although the tofu market has been experiencing massive growth in the West particularly, Japan's tofu industry as a whole has been declining over the years. According to the Ministry of Health, Labour and Welfare, the number of tofu factories has dwindled significantly from the 1960 peak of 51,596. In 2018, just 6,143 of these facilities remained. The existence of the humble *machi no tōfu-ya-san* (neighbourhood tofu shop) is also threatened. According to Japan's Zenkoku Tōfu Rengō-kai (National Tofu Federation), this is due to both the age of their owners, many of whom are in their seventies now, and the lack of eligible or willing successors to businesses. The organization credits stay-at-home requests ordered by the Japanese government to combat COVID-19 with the survival of some *tōfu-ya* in bedroom communities around metropolitan areas.[16] But the fading of traditional tofu producers is not a Japan-only phenomenon. For example,

Tama dare tōfu, served with salty-tangy soy sauce, is a variety of *yose* or *oboro tōfu* – soybean curds served fresh without pressing. It is sold at Hagino Tofu, a two-hundred-year-old tofu shop ticking by in a popular *onsen* (hot spring) resort.

San Jose Tofu, a stalwart of San Jose's historic Japantown for 71 years and which acted as 'a community center of sorts', shut up shop in 2017; 'For many longtime Japanese residents, it was a bitter reminder that historic Japantown's original businesses – often born on the backs of working-class immigrant families – are slowly disappearing.'[17] In the wake of such closures and the general decline of traditional shops, it could be that tofu in general is losing this connection to its more lowly roots. While it remains cheap to produce, modern brands with a strong identity, and those which are willing or can afford to innovate, seem to be faring better than those rooted in the past.

INNOVATION IN JAPAN'S TOFU SCENE

'Deliciousness alone does not sell. What do you need to stand out?'[18] This was the musing of Shingo Ito, president of Kyoto-headquartered Otokomae Tofu-ten (literally 'Handsome Tofu Shop'), in a 2021 interview. Otokomae is anything but old hat. Founded in 2005 when Ito took over a flailing tofu business, the brand comes complete with its own non-cutesy mascot – a punk rocker named Jonny (Ito's nickname), who is often depicted standing stoically on the prow of a boat – and an equally punk approach to selling tofu. 'Many punk bands have no other way to promote their music than to make very attractive and impactful CD sleeves. I had to do the same with my tofu,' Ito explained in the interview. Short of sampling the product itself, the only thing customers in a retail setting, either online or offline, have to guide them to a decision are visual cues.[19] Thus Japanese customers, part of a market already familiar with tofu, need only to inwardly subscribe to the visual appeal of Otokomae in deciding whether to purchase or not. With these individualistic brand aesthetics decided upon, Ito set about targeting an upscale department store in the affluent riverside development of Futako Tamagawa, Tokyo.[20] Otokomae's website has an approachable, friendly design, but it also has a separate site to sell all-important merchandise; the site boasts a DIY aesthetic, echoing a Web 1.0-era site for band merch. It stocks T-shirts (for example, 'TOFU' emblazoned on the front, 'NICE COLD BEER' on the back), beer mugs, keyrings, even a branded *beigoma* (traditional metal spinning top), among other items.[21] With a masculine lilt far from the 'soy boy' pejorative, the brand rings of irony and a genuine love of retro apparel. It seems the visual appeal of Otokomae has caught on, making its way over to the United States. The recommendation by New York Times food critic Florence Fabricant to eat Otokomae's tofu 'as you would Greek yogurt, for dessert, topped with good preserves, even yuzu marmalade, or coated with a spoonful of caramel dessert' feels fittingly akin to the unconventional brand

Shingo Minatochō ('Shingo Port Town'), a generous 500 g (1 lb) slab of *kinu* (silken) tofu by Otokomae.

Tokunō Ken-chan tōfu: these 'richly flavoured' mini-portion multipacks are Otokomae's best-selling product.

itself.[22] Unlike much cheap tofu available in Japan, which is often made using soybeans from the USA and Canada, the soybeans used in the creation of Otokomae's products are sourced from Japan. This could be seen as a mirroring of trans-local music scenes, fostering a sense of togetherness as if importing soybeans were 'selling out' in the same way a punk band 'sells out' by signing with a major record label, though it may have been a practical decision, not one driven by ideals. This further contributes to its grassroots, DIY image. On this level Otokomae is to tofu what Scottish brand BrewDog is to craft beer or London's Black Sheep Coffee is to coffee: an alternative, independent brand targeting a new generation of consumers tired of the same old stuff.

Beyond Otokomae's punk tofu lie many other innovations in Japan that look firmly to the future of tofu in the country. General price increases, a weaker yen and increased imports by

China have put a strain on the already flailing and shrinking tofu market. Prices of soybeans produced overseas increased by 30 per cent in 2022 compared with 2021, and 75 per cent compared with 2015.[23] Despite the enduring status of tofu in Japan, the country's tofu market, which peaked at ¥338 billion in 2016, has since been decreasing. While this negatively affects traditional bastions of the soybean curd – neighbourhood tofu shops, for example – it allows innovative makers to take advantage of a more health-conscious market. With protein forming a large part of modern dieting trends, culminating in something of a 'protein mania', tofu companies like Japan's Asahico are taking note.[24] Their 'Toffu' bar, packing 10 grams of protein, is their bet to 'revitalize the tofu market by evolving it into a form that fits the modern food scene'. While you would need to eat around 200 grams (7 oz) of regular silken tofu to get 10 grams of protein, Asahico's ultra-compressed tofu bars weigh in at just 68 grams (just over 2 oz); flavours include umami *konbu* (kelp) and salted basil.[25] By the start of 2022, convenience store giant 7-Eleven had begun stocking its own-brand 10-grams-of-protein tofu bars, showcasing the profitability and power of the healthy-protein-snack world in Japan and the starring role tofu can play therein.

Aside from these concentrated doses of protein, there are also emerging players in the meat-alternative market, hoping to match or surpass the successes of Beyond Meat and Impossible Foods. One of them is Sagamiya, whose humble origins date to 1951, when Hisa Ebara, who lost her husband in the Second World War, started up Sagamiya Tofu Shop to support her livelihood.[26] Over seventy years later, now a much bigger company, Sagamiya is known for its Beyond Tofu range, which includes the *piza-shreddo* (pizza shred) offering, designed to look, feel and taste like grated cheese thanks to 'fermentation technology'.[27] It won an award at the *Japan Food Journal*'s 39th Hit Food Awards in 2020.[28] It doesn't stop at vegan cheese. Sagamiya Foods extended its Beyond Tofu line to include a tofu approximation of uni (sea urchin), and inaugurated an 'Innocent Meat' range with Niku-nikushii *Ganmo* ('meaty meat *ganmodoki*'). The latter recalls a staple of *tōfu-ya* in Japan, *ganmodoki*, a tofu fritter studded with vegetables, though Sagamiya's version is a wholly modern, meaty, burger-like mass. *Ganmodoki* already has some prestige as a meat substitute of sorts, *gan* meaning 'goose' and *modoki* meaning 'imitation' – mock-goose, you could say. This joined other meatless, animal-named dishes of *shōjin-ryōri* such as *kiji-yaki dōfu* (grilled pheasant tofu).[29] This is tofu cut into 6.5-centimetre-square (1 sq in.) pieces, sprinkled with salt, coated in sake and soy sauce, then grilled.[30] Another is *shigi-yaki*, which began as grilled sandpiper but ended up as aubergine *miso dengaku*.[31] Also capitalizing on Japan's growing flexitarian

Beyond tofu: tofu as an alternative, rather than as an everyday item, is catching on in Japan. Thanks to a fermentation process, it can even act like grated mozzarella on pizza.

Even imitation *uni* (sea urchin) is now available in Japanese supermarkets thanks to Beyond Tofu.

market is long-standing purveyor of tofu Somenoya. Though their pre-pandemic sales of meat alternatives were 'not very good', the company has since seen success with its Someat range experiencing a 384 per cent growth from 2019 to 2020; Somenoya tofu sales also increased by 122 per cent between 2020 and 2021.[32] The tofu brand, which was founded in 1862, is also a sponsor of the global initiative Meat Free Monday. It is this levelling up of traditional tofu brands in Japan into a proponent of the meat-alternative market that showcases the potential of tofu. The Western development of brands such as Tofurky, and the vegetarian-coded nature of tofu in general, have contributed to this, feeding back into an ingredient unchanged for many centuries and altering its DNA. It would not have happened in the same way without tofu's eventful and arduous journey to the West.

Sagamiya, once a humble tofu shop, is really taking Japan's meat alternatives up a notch from tofu. This giant meatball/hamburger is made to a similar specification as the more traditional *ganmodoki* (fried tofu fritters).

The same is not necessarily the case for tofu brands across the world, where on a general level they exist separately to meat alternatives rather than being branches of the same tree. The evolution of tofu companies in Japan reflects modernization and a desire to keep up with global trends, but the very existence of homegrown tofu companies in the West is in itself an innovation, a radical shift in a world of bread and casseroles. For example, in the UK companies such Tofoo (tagline: 'TOFU with TASTE'), founded in 2015 and advertising itself as 'not the soggy, tasteless stuff you might be thinking of',[33] provide 'extra firm' tofu in an array of shapes and sizes, including flavoured blocks, pre-seasoned chunks and crispy, breadcrumbed bites. Tofoo's claim of their product being based on 'a traditional Japanese recipe' heightens itself with an imagined prestige of 'tradition' and, as is sometimes the case with Japanese products, projects a superficial sheen of modernity. Older UK tofu stalwart Cauldron, which was founded in 1979, appeals to the UK's love of ready meals and ready-to-cook meals.[34] Its various products include 'Hoisin Tofu Pieces' (an 'easy swap for those weekend takeaway classic dishes')[35] and 'Quick And Tasty Tofu Block with Italian Herbs and Tomato', which is flavoured with basil, marjoram, rosemary, thyme, bay, dried onion, garlic and paprika and advertised as 'the perfect flavourful addition to throw into your pasta, salads and favourite Italian dishes'.[36] The tofu offerings from both Tofoo and Cauldron are entirely moulded for a Western market, and like many varieties of tofu in the West, are extra-firm. This allows for ease of cooking (especially frying) for those unaccustomed to working in the kitchen with tofu.

This extra-firm variety also results in a texture that is more akin to meat than softer types: a more familiar texture for Western palates. For example, silken tofu has a texture like crème caramel or blancmange, and beyond a dessert setting this kind of texture may flummox a Western eater if not disgust them outright. American food writer Ligaya Mishan noted in 2023 that English '[lacks] a robust vocabulary for food textures', which possibly signifies anglophone nations' lack of texturally diverse cuisine, and reflects a yearning for 'food that simply oblige[s]' rather than challenges the palate.[37] Consider that while English has approximately 77 words or phrases to describe the texture of food, there are 445 words and phrases in Japanese to do the job.[38] In this instance, familiarity of texture is likely to further drive the tofu market in the UK, at least, into a place of plant-based meat alternatives. The lack of access in the UK particularly to tofu products such as *abura-age*, *yuba*, or the extra-meaty *dougan*, let alone fresh silken tofu, puts the development of bean curd into a one-track, one-size-fits-all offering in which variation can be experienced only in terms of flavour. As forecasts earlier in this chapter make clear, the profitability of tofu is only likely to increase, but whether this will attract innovation in the form of a richer tofu-scape, or will result in new producers making more of the same, remains to be seen. In the grand scheme of things, a richer selection of pre-existing East Asian tofu products wouldn't exactly be ground-breaking but it would transplant some deeper-rooted tofu traditions into a somewhat monotonous market. In reality, with the 'mechanized manufacturing of tofu . . . still at its infancy' and much production 'confined to cottage level', the limits of what can be done with tofu still have yet to be fully defined.[39]

THE AESTHETICIZATION OF TOFU
FOR MODERN DINING EXPERIENCES

Social media has proven to be a huge factor in the world of food today. Online communities play a big role in influencing our behaviours; 'influencers' are named so for a reason. Eating behaviour is strongly determined by seeing what and how much others around us are eating, and with constant access to such cues on social media apps like Instagram, what and where we choose to eat is on one level predetermined by the countless foods we see daily snapped, shared and consumed.[40] Compounding our readiness to associate with people like ourselves, or at least with whom we identify (a phenomenon called homophily), it is ever easier for food trends to spread among the complex, interwoven webs of followers and followings that overlap between online communities.[41] This network of people translates to a powerful marketing tool, attracting potential customers to any number of carefully curated culinary experiences that they will, in turn, share online. Therefore whether they are tofu connoisseurs or not, consumers nowadays can easily be attracted to an establishment that serves tofu dishes simply by its alignment with their interests or aesthetic preferences.

Such is the case of a slew of unrelated but intrinsically linked eateries themed on the popular *Initial D* franchise. Starting as a manga by Shuichi Shigeno, serialized between 1995 and 2013, it's centred around the illegal street-racing exploits of high-school student Takumi Fujiwara. His father is Bunta Fujiwara, former drifting legend turned owner of Fujiwara Tofu Shop. Takumi makes tofu deliveries along a mountain road using his father's car, a black-and-white Toyota AE86 emblazoned with the name of the family business. *Initial D* spawned multiple anime series, games and films, not to mention a global fanbase, in its wake. Many locations mentioned in Shigeno's manga are actual places, the tofu shop included; the real-life Fujino Tofu Store in Shibukawa, Gunma Prefecture, had the honour of being converted into the Fujiwara Tofu Shop for the 2005 live-action film adaptation, a Hong Kong venture directed by Andrew Lau and Alan Mak. Though the shop has since been demolished, the fandom of *Initial D* is such that reincarnations of the tofu shop live on around the world, servicing a cross-section of petrolheads, Japanophiles and foodies alike. For example, Fujiwara Tofu Shop Malaysia serves Japanese dishes alongside Malaysian favourite *tau foo fah* (tofu pudding) and speciality homemade black tofu at its location in Subang Jaya, which opened in April 2022. The shop interior also features a roped-off Toyota AE86 and multiple arcade machines carrying the video game *Initial D Arcade Stage 3*.[42] Another, Indonesia Fujiwara Tofu Shop, is a more out-of-the-way venue in Batam, Riau Islands. At the beginning of 2023, a separate *Initial D*-themed Fujiwara Tofu Concept Shop opened in Singapore, serving Japanese food and its signature dish, 'Fujiwara tofu'. The phenomenon is not limited to Southeast Asia. Fujiwara Tofu Cafe opened on 20 January 2022 in El Monte, California, to a fanfare of crowds and souped-up

Japanese cars. The cafe, which stemmed from a series of *Initial D*-themed pop-ups beginning in 2017 at the Los Angeles 626 Night Market and the Asian American Expo in Pomona, features a menu of soy-based boba tea, soy milk and tofu pudding with toppings like sweet red bean and brown sugar. In an interview with *Eater* magazine, owner Vincent Chan revealed that he grew up around tofu: 'When I was a kid, my family used to make tofu and soy milk every other week. I know which ones are good and which ones are bad. Once we started this idea, we tried to make everything on our menu tofu and soy-related.'[43] This and the Southeast Asian themed cafes provide an innovative if gimmicky vehicle for tofu, introducing it to a niche, non-gastronome consumer base. Without the strong visual branding tethering the restaurants to a much-loved Japanese franchise, it is doubtful that these tofu-based eateries would have received the attention that they have garnered. Using the shell of *Initial D*, Vincent Chan is able to successfully showcase the heritage of tofu and soy milk he grew up with; otherwise it is likely that an aesthetically discernible, easily digestible physical space would have been necessary to attract anywhere near the same attention. In a similar way to Otokomae, it says much about the highly visual nature of the gastronomic landscape today, in which establishments stand to gain traction if their identity can be slotted into an aesthetic, relatable corner of Instagram or TikTok. This development of tofu today contrasts greatly with the dusty, utilitarian guise of tofu in late twentieth-century vegetarian cookbooks.

While the Fujiwara Tofu Shop concept trades on the romanticization of a retro Japanese tofu shop within the setting of a manga, other restaurants instead aim to elevate tofu as an ingredient with luxury settings and sumptuous visuals to match. Case in point: Mora, a Hong Kong restaurant created in 2021 by Hong Kong chef Vicky Lau and based entirely on soy. 'I can't think of another ingredient that has such a wide range of textures, from super-soft silken tofu to super-firm mock meat,' said Lau in an interview with CNN Travel.[44] Lau came up with the idea for the new venture – 'modernizing a tradition like tofu and educating people to incorporate it in their diet' – while assembling a tofu-focused tasting menu ('Ode to Tofu') at the two-Michelin-starred TATE Dining Room, also in Hong Kong. Mora's side hustle, a luxury soy milk brand named Ān, similarly brings the ancient legend of Liu An into the modern day with Instagram-friendly bottles and indulgent flavours like Chinese almond and pistachio.[45] In the same kind of vein, 'discreet eatery' Mihara Tofuten in Bangkok has been hailed by Time Out Thailand as 'Thailand's, and probably the world's, first tofu omakase diner'.[46] The bean-curd-based venture by chefs Gaggan Anand and Goh Fukuyama constitutes a 'challenge' to Thai tastes, as an interview with the pair by Michelin Guide Bangkok discovered.[47] Anand reveals that Mihara Tofuten is all about bringing the Japanese experience to Bangkok, which includes shipping water in from Saga Prefecture and snow salt from Okinawa, eliciting a sheen of authenticity – an importantly Japanese 'taste of nowhere else' that is a commodity in the 'gourmet age of food'.[48] It's big business: food exports from Japan were worth ¥1,238.5 billion (around £6.8 billion) in 2021, a 25 per cent rise from 2020.[49] Like the claim of Tofoo and its basis in specifically Japanese tradition, this tofu venture is garnished with tradeable Japanese credentials, ultimately a result of Japan's 'state-led culinary politics' that promote the 'Japan brand'.[50] It also associates Japanese cuisine with healthiness and being light.[51] Within Japan, where tofu is a given, stylish Instagrammable interiors can be found at various venues, including Tofu Sorano, a Japanese outfit with two branches in Tokyo and one in Osaka. Their interiors are Zen-inspired, a triumph of minimalism and modern dining with tofu at its centre.[52]

It's not just restaurants; tofu-making facilities themselves are also dragging tofu into the twenty-first century. Caizhai Tofu Workshop, the brainchild of Chinese architectural firm DnA_ Design and Architecture, in China's Zhejiang province does just this, transforming the tofu experience from workaday to speciality. Finished in 2020, the beautiful building tucked away in the village of Caizhai, Songyang County, was created to keep the village's tofu economy going, consolidating local traditional tofu makers unable to fit into the modern era of supermarket-ready food certificate standards. It is a sprawling, minimalist space, a marriage of stone and vernacular wooden building techniques, that is both a working factory and an education centre for children to learn more about the tofu-making process.[53] In essence, tofu is modernizing. Traditional tofu shops may be slowly disappearing in some places, notably Japan, but a fresh dedication to tofu as an ingredient, whether served casually in the novelty *Initial D*-themed eateries or elevated to luxurious levels in strongly aestheticized spaces, could contribute to a more widespread reinvention of tofu. Alongside this novel, superficial change in fortune for tofu in some corners of the world, plus the general growth in the tofu market, as well as behind-the-scenes tinkering for new types of meat alternatives, the question of supply, demand and sustainability naturally comes into the equation.

WASTE NOT WANT NOT: THE SUSTAINABILITY OF TOFU

To consume tofu is a guilt-free, karma-friendly undertaking, at least on the surface of it. Not unfounded: the consumption of meat and dairy alone has been forecast to be responsible for over half of all global warming over the next century.[54] With calls to eat less meat, particularly beef, to decrease greenhouse gas emissions and curb the use of nitrogen fertilizer and water, alternatives such as tofu seem the natural substitute.[55] Indeed soybeans have been touted as the 'crop of the century'.[56] Briefly, in 2018, soybeans surpassed corn as the most planted crop in the United States.[57] There are issues surrounding the production of tofu, however, from enormous tracts of land set aside for soybeans, notably in Brazil, and the use of GMO crops to the massive volumes of water used in its production and the question of what to do with waste products of the tofu-making process. Looking ahead to the future of tofu therefore necessarily includes not only the modest niche of its aesthetics-coded gastronomic breakthrough and the place of its manufacturers, and their innovations, in the meat-alternatives market, but its ecological and economic sustainability. The impact of scaling up the industry could be massive. In 2020 Swedish researchers modelled a scenario in which 50 per cent less meat is consumed in Sweden, finding that it would reduce the environmental impact of the Swedish diet by 22 per cent and land needed to supply it by 23 per cent, but noted a lack of legume-processing facilities as one of several barriers to this hypothetical reality.[58]

Being the chief raw ingredient in tofu production, soybeans naturally get the most attention when taking into account the process, but a far greater amount of water goes into each and every batch. As reported by the Vienna-based organization Renewable Energy and Energy Efficiency Partnership (REEEP), the amount of water required for tofu production is massive: for 80 kilograms (176 lb) of tofu, 60 kilograms (132 lb) of soybeans and 2,700 litres (91,300 fl. oz) of water are required.[59] This puts a strain on both local water supplies and poses an issue in the form of tofu wastewater (that is, the whey). For each kilogram of tofu produced, you're left with 7 to 10 kilograms (15–22 lb) of tofu wastewater, the disposal of which is not as simple as pouring it down the drain and starting again. In 2022, *Business Insider* reported that tofu wastewater runoff in Indonesia pollutes rivers, causing an unpleasant smell and killing fish.[60] This 'nutrient-rich' water is brimming with ideal conditions for the cultivation of micro-organisms, not all of them good, presenting enough environmental concern to prompt manufacturers to recycle and treat it despite the increased cost of doing so.[61] But because of its composition there is great potential in this by-product. One solution taking hold in Indonesia is the reuse of tofu wastewater in the production of biogas, which can be used as a source of renewable energy. In 2012, Indonesia's Agency for the Assessment and Application of Technology (BPPT), with funding from REEEP, developed a plant for the production of biogas from tofu wastewater at Banyumas, Central Java. It was the first step in a scheme that, nationwide, could see 56,000 tonnes of fossil fuels substituted each year with biogas from tofu industry wastewater in Indonesia.[62] By 2016 in Kalisari village, Banyumas, tofu wastewater was being treated with bacteria in tanks to provide dozens of homes with power.[63] One study in 2019 described pipes leading directly from a tofu factory, via the biogas plant, and onward to supply homes with biogas for cooking, cutting monthly household expenditure on fuel by at least two-thirds.[64] Diverting tofu wastewater from rivers into biomass converters for biogas helps keep rivers clean, provides renewable energy and supplies homes with a reliable way to cook. This is a particularly good opportunity in Indonesia, where the number of tofu-making facilities has increased from an estimated 84,000 small to medium-sized enterprises (SMEs), many family-run, in 2012 to around 100,000 a decade later.[65] Thanks to its make-up, tofu wastewater can even be used as the raw material in the production of bioethanol, which is a major fuel substitute for petrol-powered road vehicles.[66]

As well as being employed as a renewable energy source, tofu wastewater also has the potential to be used in other ways.

Even though it is not commonly used to create products destined for human consumption, it seems that research into making the most of tofu wastewater is proving to be an important endeavour if the tofu market is to increase as predicted.[67] For example, tofu wastewater is a good substrate for the cultivation of several moulds, namely *Aspergillus awamori*, used for making *awamori* and *shōchū*, and *Rhizopus oryzae* for *tempeh* production and brewer's yeast.[68] According to a 2021 study, tofu wastewater can also be used as the nitrogen source needed to create nattokinase, an enzyme found in *nattō* (fermented soybeans) that has potential in treating cardiovascular diseases and combatting obesity.[69] In general, tofu whey has potential to be utilized as a 'cheap, nutritional and functional food additive', and sustainably too, thanks to it being a recycled waste product.[70] Over in Singapore it's more of a water-into-wine situation. Sachi is a new alcoholic beverage launched in November 2021, made using soy whey, the wastewater involved in the tofu-making process. Though dubbed 'soy wine', Sachi (5.8 per cent ABV) reportedly has more of an *umeshu* (plum wine) lilt to it. The venture began life in 2016 when its founder, Chua Jian Yong, was studying the potential uses of soy whey at the National University of Singapore.[71] One recent paper from 2023 underlined the importance of the circular economy of tofu production, using a Swiss company, Tigusto, as a case study. Soybean hulls and straw can be burned to generate electricity, the whey can, as mentioned above, be used for biogas (among other things), and the *okara* or dregs can be used either as animal feed or as an ingredient for soy-based foods. The study found that 'the benefits of processing [tofu] by-products to generate energy were significant in terms of moving toward more sustainable methods of tofu production', positioning its future as a low-impact alternative to other sources of protein, particularly beef.[72] The use of *okara* has already been mentioned in Chapter Two, where it was described as a key ingredient in making the Indonesian fermented product *oncom*. *Okara* can be purchased as is from supermarkets in Japan, where it is used to make *unohana*, a side dish in which *okara* and various vegetables are simmered in soy sauce and mirin. In 2023 researchers at the University of Belgrade found *okara* to be a favourable ingredient in gluten-free bread, resulting in a product with nutritional proteins, fewer saturated fatty acids, antioxidants, low energy content and, importantly, good texture and taste.[73] Research from Singapore has also posited *okara* as a possible alternative serum in lieu of the morally questionable, not to mention expensive, use of fetal bovine serum (FBS, derived from unborn calves) to grow animal cells used in the creation of so-called 'clean meat', that is, lab-grown cultured meat, which Singapore was the first government in the world to allow the sale of.[74] With FBS costing the equivalent of between £300 and £700 per litre, and *okara*-based alternatives costing as little as $2 per litre, the pursuit of its usefulness in the cellular-agriculture world is not only ethical and sustainable in nature, it is also economic.[75]

The economical sustainability, that is, profitability, of tofu production has been noted since Song dynasty China (remember: learn the arts of Huainan and you can reap money), and that was without considering the potential of its various waste products. For example, another way to mitigate the environmental pollution caused by the waste products of tofu production is to manufacture 'whole-bean tofu' instead, thereby also saving on the cost of either recycling or reusing tofu waste products.[76] This can be achieved by using a high-speed pulverizer, resulting in a smoother-textured tofu, a more complex flavour and higher nutritional value compared to 'commercial tofu'.[77] But on a less technologically advanced level, the ability to simply and cheaply create tofu and other soy products, and a push for food security, are the driving force behind purpose-built soy-processing machinery developed by Canadian charity Malnutrition Matters. This is currently being used by NGOs, schools and cooperatives in North Korea, Myanmar and Thailand, and across Africa, where it has been implemented in several countries, including Ghana, Malawi, Zambia and Guinea.[78] One piece of kit, dubbed SoyCow, gives means to those in 'high-need' situations to make nutritious food or simply provide 'new income streams for rural micro-entrepreneurs', while the VitaGoat system is a pedal-powered alternative that does not require electricity, further increasing the scope for grass-roots tofu production in areas where food security is not guaranteed.[79] In 2013 the VitaGoat was trialled as a microenterprise at Chewaqa Union, 'the most successful' soybean-growing cooperative in Ethiopia.[80] Here, where more than 32 million people abstain from animal products for almost two hundred days each year, the reach of tofu has the potential to grow immensely.[81] Since soybeans were introduced in the 1950s, they have been widely grown in Ethiopia, with production increasing to an estimated 120,000 tons in 2018–19 'due to an increase in area planted', more than tripling production from 35,000 tons in 2011–12.[82] For 2022–3, this is estimated to rise to 150,000 tons.[83] Given the utilization of soy products, 'especially . . . tofu' in some regions (Jimma, for example), at the domestic level, there seems to be an acceptance of tofu that should see it make further inroads into Ethiopian cuisine.[84] The use of domestic soybeans in Ethiopia decreases the dependence on imports, increasing food security and making tofu production more viable.[85] It also lessens the environmental impact caused by 'food miles'.

Transporting food contributes 6 per cent of the global total of carbon emissions, with fruit and vegetables being the biggest culprits, so for the tofu industry to remain sustainable much needs to be done to keep soybean production on a local level.[86] This is not necessarily possible. In the case of Indonesia, there are several challenges to securing enough domestic production to satisfy demand, including low fertility of available land, 'lack of market quality traits' and lower prices of locally grown soybeans.[87] Indonesia is 'the world's second-largest consumer of soybeans for direct human consumption', and there is a high dependence on imported soybeans, 70 per cent of which are destined for foods.[88] For example, in 2020, with total need approaching 3.29 million tons, and domestic output about 0.63 million tons, approximately 81 per cent of soybeans used in Indonesia had to be imported.[89] But the rising cost of soybean imports to Indonesia has seen tofu producers on the verge of unrest. In 2021 tofu and *tempeh* producers stopped producing and selling their products in response to an increase in the price of soybeans from Rp. 7,200 to Rp. 9,200 per kilogram.[90] And in February 2022, the Center for the Indonesian Tempe and Tofu Producers Cooperative (Puskopti) held a three-day production strike, setting off 'alarm bells' for Indonesia.[91] This was reflective of a global price hike that year in the cost of soybeans by 30 per cent, largely owing to a drought in South America affecting the harvests of Argentina, Brazil and Paraguay, which together account for more than 50 per cent of the world's supply of soybeans.[92] Indonesia's own production of soybeans fell that year to 425,000 tonnes from 475,000 the previous year, further compounding the issue.[93] Imports of food to the global South, of which Indonesia is a part, are set to increase in the coming years – not necessarily a problem in itself but indicative of ever-increasing reliance on staple crops such as soybeans, and the 'potential problematic exposure . . . to tele-connected food supply shocks'.[94] The South American soybean shortage and strikes of Indonesian tofu and *tempeh* producers in 2022 show how easily this can happen. That a bad harvest in South America can affect the most local of tofu producers in

Indonesia says much about the globalized nature of soybeans and of the world at large.

The global demand for soybeans, grown mostly as livestock feed, has seen vast swathes of land occupied by the crop. Because of this tofu and other soy-based products have, in recent years, been associated with deforestation. Being the world's largest supplier of soybeans, Brazil is a focus point, particularly the Cerrado, a vast savannah ecoregion now inundated with soybean farms and other agriculture. The UK alone imports around 3.3 million tonnes of soy, which requires an area of 1.68 million hectares (4.1 million ac) to grow (almost eleven times the area of Greater London).[95] But in the UK, where 77 per cent of the soy eaten is done vicariously through eggs, dairy products and meat, tofu is not to blame: instead it is chickens and livestock being fed soy.[96] Farmers around the world recognize the nutritional triumphs of soy; in 2021 it was the largest protein source for livestock globally.[97] An estimated 75 per cent of all soy produced worldwide is destined for animal consumption. Despite this, Andrew Stephen, CEO of the Sustainable Restaurant Association, told HuffPost in 2020 that 'tofu made with soya from the deforested land in the Brazilian rainforest will have a carbon footprint twice that of chicken'.[98] Sound logic, maybe, but this is provided only that this hypothetical chicken wasn't fed using soybeans grown on deforested lands. Notwithstanding, a push for locally grown soy would shift the burden from areas high in biodiversity, the Amazon and the Cerrado, and redistribute soybeans more evenly around the world. Ironically, climate change may lead to a more extensive range for soybean cultivation. According to a paper by scientists from Rothamsted Research, soybeans could be widespread crops across England and Wales by 2050, thanks to an increase in both temperature and CO_2 levels.[99] However, by increasing the yield capabilities of soybean crops, the farmed area itself need not necessarily increase. A study in 2019 found that the soil-born bacteria Rhizobia 'talks' to soybean plants via ribonucleic acid (RNA), together forming atmospheric nitrogen-fixing nodules along soybean roots, theoretically leading to an increase in soybean yield and negating a need for fertilizer.[100] Commenting on the study, Argentinian biologist Flavio Blanco noted that 'it is much easier to manipulate bacteria than to make transgenic [genetically modified] plants.'[101] Ease of manufacture aside, finding an alternative way to improve soybeans without using genetically modified methods to do so may ultimately be in the best interests of consumers.

THE 'SCIENTIFIC CONSENSUS' ON GENETICALLY MODIFIED SOYBEANS

Search and you will find that genetically modified organisms (GMOs) have been largely acquitted of their risk to human health, often citing a 'scientific consensus'. But an article co-signed by more than three hundred scientists and legal experts in 2015 claims such a consensus is fabricated.[102] 'Decisions on the future of our food and agriculture should not be based on misleading and misrepresentative claims by an internal circle of likeminded stakeholders that a "scientific consensus" exists on GMO safety,' the article states. One variety of GM soybean developed by American agrochemical giant Monsanto (now owned by Bayer) is dubbed 'Roundup Ready' due to its tolerance of glyphosate (the principal ingredient in Roundup, a herbicide). However a 2015 study noted that industry testing on this particular soybean did not include 'application of representative dosage of herbicides as well as subsequent analysis of herbicide residues', suggesting that there were holes in the research behind the 'consensus'.[103] Most telling, a 1996 study authored by Monsanto researchers into a product 'currently under development', that is, the glyphosate-tolerant soybean, claimed there was no difference in the seeds of both plants.[104] Simply worded and easy to digest, the results of the study weren't untrue; they just missed out the part where their soybeans would be doused with glyphosate and non-GM soybeans would remain un-doused. Various glyphosate formulations can be detrimental to the nervous system, and have been linked to the development of breast cancer.[105] Another recent study sounded a note of concern due to the lack of availability of glyphosate-tolerant soybeans for independent, as opposed to industry, testing.[106] It also noted that late-season spraying of soybeans increased the amount of glyphosate residue on plants and products, which is not taken into account during testing.

Similarly to the 1996 study, a group of researchers in 2017 found another Monsanto-developed GM soybean, this time tolerant to the herbicide dicamba, to be 'compositionally equivalent' to non-GM soybeans.[107] Again, however, the issue is with the use of herbicides themselves, which as different weeds develop resistance to them results in a 'herbicide treadmill' of using more and stronger herbicides to do the job, like the old woman who swallowed a fly.[108] To illustrate, in American states where glyphosate-resistant weeds have been found, more dicamba-tolerant soybean seeds are used. In 2018 dicamba was classified as a 'restricted-use pesticide', limiting its use to certified applicators who must complete training specific to dicamba.[109] Other mandates in the United States require dicamba to be applied in low winds, not used if other non-dicamba-tolerant crops are downwind of its application, and applied during daylight hours, with equipment to be thoroughly cleaned and detailed records kept following each application.[110] These precautions make dicamba seem dangerous, though 'few studies have been conducted on its environmental safety and health effects'.[111] A 2023 study of its effects on zebrafish (which are often used in laboratory research) hints at health risks, reporting haemorrhage, spinal and eye malformations, developmental delay and oxidative stress (an imbalance between free radicals and antioxidants that can cause damage to organs) due to dicamba exposure.[112] In 2022 a team from Beijing University of Chinese Medicine conducted a review of hundreds of studies, sourced from databases between 1983 and 2020, on the adverse effects of consuming genetically modified products, including soybeans. Accepting the limitations of animal studies, they concluded that further clinical trials 'are still warranted', and that GM food should be labelled as such 'so that consumers can make their own choice'.[113] Looking into two varieties of GM soybeans and their risk assessment by the European Food Standard Authority (EFSA), a 2023 article highlighted that analysis undertaken by the EFSA has long been 'criticized for its limitations with respect to a restricted and "biased" selection of compounds that can be analyzed, as the detection of unknown toxins or anti-nutrients is not possible using this method'. The study concluded that EFSA guidance is 'not fit for purpose and needs to be improved'.[114] If testing methods themselves are not stringent enough, there is bound to be uncertainty surrounding the use of GM foods. In short, the scientific consensus seems fabled in light of this flurry of continued research into GM crops and foods. The debate, far from over, is very much ongoing.

BEYOND SOYBEANS: MAKING THE TOFU OF TOMORROW

The future of tofu may not even contain soybeans. Of all legumes, tainted as they are with a legacy of deforestation, herbicides and the mostly unfounded effects of phytoestrogens, soybeans have possibly the worst reputation. The intrigue they posed to Western agriculturalists and nutritionists in the late nineteenth and early twentieth centuries led to relatively quick and wide-spread adoption in the United States and Europe. The American Soybean Association was founded in 1919, and by 1952 soybeans had become a staple for animal feed, nowadays rivalling corn, the former American crop of choice. But if soy was the bean of the twentieth century, the bean of the twenty-first century, at least as far as tofu is concerned, needs to be something that fits with the pragmatic climate-change-busting ethos of the present day. While in theory we could lean into growing soybeans in areas that previously would not have made for stable or efficient growth, and noting the wisdom of this sort of adaptation, more can be done with regard to the search for a soy substitute. With food production requiring a 50 per cent increase if it is to meet the demands of the forecast 9 billion world population in 2050, and with soybean limited due to 'rising prices, ethical issues, environmental impact, and competition for feed/food for land use', alternative protein sources for use as animal feed instead of soy have been explored in recent studies, from pigs to poultry.[115] The focus on moving food production away from meat and dairy towards plant-based diets also brings the search for a nutritious stand-in for soy into the equation. With food intolerances also an important factor in shaping twenty-first-century diets (soy and gluten, often used to create meat analogues, being the most common), the search for a substitute in the meat-free market is as personally practical as it is universally ecological.[116]

One of these could be fava beans. It has been noted as a potential alternative for soybeans in tofu since at least 1987, when a Canadian team created fava bean tofu with a similar firmness and texture to soybean tofu;[117] the following year the same team found that, compared to soybean tofu, fava bean tofu contained fewer lipids (1.5 per cent compared to 34.4 per cent), had lower antinutritional factors (those that interfere with the body's absorption of nutrients), and boasted comparable digestibility and amino acid availability.[118] Now, with soybeans seen as a crop with dubious environmental credentials, the reality of fava bean tofu is even closer. 'Many consumers are crying out for alternatives to soy,' said Danish scientist Iben Lykke Petersen in a 2020 interview.[119] Petersen was the co-author of a study looking into the viability of using fava bean protein powder as an alternative to soy used in plant-based foods; its propensity for gelation, that is, the formation of a gel, makes it ideal for use in the production of tofu and meat alternatives, outperforming lentils, amaranth grains, quinoa and buckwheat.[120] One of the main benefits of fava beans is their ability to grow in colder climates, Petersen explained, meaning that ingredients for tofu and other plant-based foods can be grown locally in countries like Denmark rather than imported at great economic and environmental cost.[121] Fast-forward two years to 2022 and the first commercial fava bean tofu is available for purchase. It's a trans-local Canadian enterprise, developed at Red River College in Winnipeg, made using fava beans grown by Prairie Fava in Glenboro, Manitoba, and sold by Vancouver's Big Mountain Foods.[122] The female-owned company announced in 2022 that it would be opening a new facility capable of producing more than 900,000 kilograms (2 million lb) of tofu per year – and 'inclusive of upcycling, with a goal to be zero-waste', explained Big Mountain Foods CEO Jasmine Byrne.[123] The company recently received $1.4 million of government funding 'to increase production capacity of its locally-sourced, whole-food alternative proteins', part of which will include the development of chick-pea tofu.[124] As described in Chapter Three, chickpea tofu exists already as to hpu, also known as Shan, or Burmese, tofu. As well as paying heed to allergens, nutrition is also clearly playing a large part in the reinvention of tofu beyond the coagulation of soybeans. In 2021 researchers from Chiang Mai Rajabhat University experimented with tofu created using a blend of soybeans and chickpeas 'to increase the amount of dietary fibre and reduce fat levels', but found that a soybean–chickpea blend of 70:30 resulted in an end product too hard and crumbly.[125]

Plenty of food blogs and recipe sites showcase the reasons for and efficacy of using various legumes to create tofu. Fava beans are currently making big waves, but other non-soy tofu exists in the world. An Italian company called Armonia e Bontà (no longer in business) once offered a soy-free, gluten-free tofu variety made of hemp that they called 'Hemp-Fu';[126] this was dubbed 'Tempt' by Portland, Oregon, company Living Harvest, who expound hemp seeds' nutritional value (omega 3, omega 6, dietary fibres, amino acids, antioxidants and protein).[127] A British start-up called Peafu aims to create tofu using yellow peas, usually grown for animal feed in the UK.[128] But as food writer Kate Williams notes, 'you can't just pull another dried bean out of your pantry and follow soy tofu directions,' mainly because of the unique composition of soybeans that allows them to be curdled.[129] Another alternative may have been found in the form of lupin beans, claimed to be 'sustainable and healthy', ticking both the nutrition and ecologically sound boxes.[130] The lupin may be better known to gardeners as a brightly coloured early spring plant, but the beans they produce have long been eaten, having been mentioned by Greek physician Hippocrates, who 'considered lupin . . . nutritious food', in the fifth century BC.[131] Today lupin beans are a popular snack in Italy (lupini), Egypt (termes) and Portugal (tremoços), among other European and Mediterranean nations. 'Move over soy, because lupini are ready to take center stage in the plant-based revolution,' wrote journalist Haldan Kirsch for Tasting Table in 2023.[132] Kirsch is not wrong. A review the same year found 'high acceptability rates' for lupin-derived foods, revealing a 'possible wide utilization in different food product types, such as meat alternatives, dairy alternatives, snacks and desserts'.[133] Another in 2021 stated that though they have been 'overlooked for decades, interest in lupins is undergoing a revival due to the health benefits of their fibres, proteins and phytochemicals content'.[134] Dubbed a superfood, with apparently as-yet untapped nutritional benefits, lupin beans deserve further research.

As of 2018, more than 85 per cent of the world's lupins have been grown in Australia, where it has been predominantly used for livestock feed.[135] Though it requires a bit more processing (lupin beans are toxic if not prepared correctly), lupin tofu seems promising. A 2010 study looked into the sensory acceptability of a soy–lupin tofu blend, finding that a lupin content of up to 40 per cent had 'no significant changes in quality' and actually 'improved the appearance of deep-fried tofu samples'.[136] Companies are beginning to take note of lupin as a protein source, with Malaysian firm CK Ingredient selling a powdered form of what they dub the 'rebel bean' to add additional protein to meals.[137] In the agricultural homeland of the lupin, Australian venture Eighth Day Foods has invented Lupreme, 'a plant-based alternative . . . customised for Asian cuisine', made from the lupin beans.[138] Echoing the promise heralded by American tofu pioneers of the late twentieth century is LuFu (tagline: 'Bringing you the food of tomorrow'). The Swedish venture claims that lupin-based products have the same protein as soy foods but are 'significantly richer in fiber content and have lower levels of phytoestrogen'. Founded in late 2021 by four master's students at Lund University, LuFu is 'aimed at Swedish customers who want to live healthily while protecting our planet'.[139]

After these centuries of soybeans, perhaps it is time for a change. Diversifying the legumes that go into making tofu beyond soy seems bound to have several advantages. First, there are the environmental considerations. By relying less on soybeans there is less dependence on imports, resulting in fewer food miles, decreased use of GM crops and therefore of herbicides and, in theory, fewer acres set aside for soy monoculture. This could also result in the revival or shoring up of local, domestic industries devoted to various legumes. Second, there are health implications. Making tofu out of legumes other than soy addresses the issue of plant-based alternatives for those who have soy intolerance or a soy allergy, while also adding the potential for consuming beneficial nutrients from a variety of grains, beans and seeds (fava, chickpea, lupin and hemp being highlighted above). Researchers from the American Gut Project discovered in 2018 that eating a more varied selection of plants led to an increase in gut microbe diversity, likely to be be beneficial to one's health.[140] To illustrate, in 2023 a team from the University of Copenhagen discovered high levels of biological diversity in gut bacteria among centenarians, suggesting that those with a healthy gut microbiome are 'better protected against aging related diseases', and are therefore better equipped to live to one hundred.[141] Diversity in tofu could help to contribute to these sorts of health benefits, especially as a plant-based, or at least plant-heavy, diet becomes more desirable. There is great potential in tofu, whether made with soybeans, other legumes, or a mix of both. As Li Shizhen wrote in his *Compendium of Materia Medica*, 'black beans, soybeans, white beans, autumn soybeans, peas, mung beans and the like' can be used, suggesting there is no room for purism in the world of tofu.

We come full circle. So old that nobody knows where it came from and beginning, maybe, with Taoist alchemists and agricultural experimenters who crushed and boiled beans in water, adding gypsum or whatever coagulant was close to hand, we have arrived at another time of idealistic experimentalism in the food world. Tofu can be lab-manipulated into modern meat substitutes, sating a desire for meat alternatives that echoes Buddhist cuisines of China and Japan, complete with their ingenious mock-animal products of yesteryear. It has developed generally in step with the industrial and social progression of the world; becoming a popular street food in Japan's peaceful Edo period with its emerging middle class; attracting the attention of fin de siècle chemists and biologists eager for discovery and industry; embraced by Western, countercultural vegetarians in a post-war period still fascinated with East Asian culture. Along the way, tofu has remained a powerful totem, symbolic of piety, ingenuity and poverty; of death, misfortune, mental and physical instability; and of alternative lifestyles and femininity. Bland though it has been touted as, the depictions and reactions it elicits and has inspired, in poetry, video games, comics, media and political rhetoric, are indicative of something much more polarizing and divisive than drab or dull. It has been an epic journey. And now, in an age of globalized food networks, technological advances, endless research into the applications of tofu in diets, and an increased awareness of healthy eating as much as our collective impact on the environment, tofu and its descendents, this family of soy-based meat alternatives, look set to play a leading role in the diets of the future.

GLOSSARY

abura-age Japanese word for fried tofu

abura-age tsukeyaki fried tofu marinated in soy sauce and grilled. Japanese dish

annin dofu a type of tofu made with apricot kernels; rather than being curdled with a coagulant, the mixture is solidified with starch. Japanese term; *xingren doufu* in Chinese. Also called 'almond tofu'

awayuki-dōfu 'snowflake tofu' in English. A very soft Japanese dessert historically sold by vendors along the Sumida River in Tokyo's Ryogoku district. It is also a speciality of a confectionary store in Okazaki, Aichi Prefecture, called Bizen-ya (established 1782)

Bai Qi *c.* 332–257 BC. Chinese general of Qin state during Warring States period. Supposedly unbeaten during his career

bai qi rou tofu dish created out of vengeance felt towards Bai Qi, who oversaw the massacre of 450,000 Zhou prisoners of war. Literally 'Bai Qi meat', it is made to resemble the general after which it is named

bai ye 'hundred pages'. See *qian zhang*

baojiang doufu a variety of tofu in China. Cubes of tofu are marinated in a mixture containing bicarbonate of soda, which softens it further, before the tofu is deep-fried, retaining a melt-in-the-middle aspect

banzuke   rankings for upcoming sumo tournaments originally painted on wood but later printed on paper (and still produced today)

benikōji   Japanese term. See red yeast rice

Changsha stinky tofu   a type of stinky tofu from Hunan province. It has a black, crispy crust and is renowned as an integral part of Hunan cuisine, which is noted for its hot-and-sour character

chaokuai   grass jelly, a dessert in East and Southeast Asia; often used in boba tea

chifa   fusion food of Peru that mixes Chinese (specifically Cantonese) cuisine with Peruvian traditions, sometimes with Japanese influences

chou doufu   stinky tofu, a type of fermented tofu that typically has a shorter marination period. Typically served fresh (in soup) or deep-fried

chou ganzi   a type of stinky tofu local to Changsha, Hunan province. Literally means 'stinky jerky'. See Changsha stinky tofu

coagulant   a substance used to create curds from milk and soy milk. For tofu, salts such as gypsum and nigari have typically been used. Acids including lemon juice and vinegar are also used in the curdling process

cu   Mandarin Chinese term for vinegar, one of the coagulants listed for use in tofu production in the sixteenth-century *Compendium of Materia Medica*

Dao Yi Zhi Lue   known as *A Brief Account of Island Barbarians* in English. Travelogue featuring descriptions of various Asian nations. Published in 1349, written by Wang Dayuan

doenjang   Korean fermented soybean paste

dotori-muk   acorn jelly

dou bian   dried tofu skin

doufu   the Mandarin Chinese word for tofu. Written using the characters for 'bean' and 'rotten'

doufu pi   tofu skin, a by-product of tofu production by which the skin of simmering soy milk is removed and (often but not always) dried. See *yuba*

doufupian   'tofu slices', made by pressing and rolling *dougan* into sheets

dougan   a form of dried tofu in which tofu is pressed for extra, almost meaty, firmness and texture. Flavoured with star anise, among other herbs and spices

douhua   literally 'tofu flower', the Mandarin Chinese word for tofu pudding, a soft variety of freshly made tofu that is served either savoury or sweet

edamame   steamed or boiled young green soybeans, a common food item in Japan. Served salted or with other condiments

edamame tofu   made using young green soybeans (edamame) mixed with soy milk and solidified with gelatin

Eight-Nation Alliance   a coalition that launched an invasion of Qing dynasty China in 1900, responding to the anti-Western Boxer Rebellion. Made up of Austria–Hungary, France, Germany, Italy, Japan, Russia, the UK and the USA.

fu pi   another word in Mandarin for dried tofu skin

furu   fermented tofu. See *sufu, rufu*

fuzhu   literally 'preserved bamboo'. Sheets or bunched sticks of dried tofu skin. See *dou bian, fu pi*

ganlao   dried yoghurts. Ancient Chinese dairy product

goma-dōfu   sesame tofu (Japanese). Made by mixing ground sesame (sesame paste) with water and arrowroot starch

hachihaidōfu   simmered eight-cup tofu

hei doufu   Mandarin term for black tofu. Typical of northeast China, where it is made using black soybeans. Has a higher protein content and more elasticity than tofu made using regular soybeans

higan-e   Buddhist festival in Japan

hijiki shiroai   tofu with hijiki seaweed

hiyayakko   cold tofu topped with a variety of condiments, including (but not always or limited to) spring onions, ginger paste, *katsuobushi* and soy sauce

Ho-ling   name of a Javanese kingdom that began trading with China in the seventh century. See Kalingga

hongfuru   literally 'red fermented tofu', this variety, which is named after its colour, hails from Fujian province, China. The red colour comes from the red yeast rice used in its production

hoshi abura-age   dried fried tofu. See *Matsuyama-age*

Huogongdian   a historic restaurant in Changsha, Hunan province. The name, meaning Fire Palace, relates to the building's previous life as a temple dedicated to a god of fire (not specified). Famed for its stinky tofu

imogara abura-age   simmered taro stems and fried tofu

iri-ni   Japanese cooking technique. Refers to ingredients cooked in sesame oil before simmering them in a mixture of soy sauce, *dashi*, mirin, sake and sugar

jidou liangfen   Mandarin word for chickpea jelly, native to Sichuan and Yunnan

jimami-dōfu   peanut tofu (Japanese). Made by solidifying peanut extract with potato starch

Kalingga   see Ho-ling

Kan'ei Great Famine   a famine that occurred in Japan from 1640 to 1643, during which time 50,000 to 100,000 people are estimated to have died

kata-dōfu   Japanese name for hard tofu. Also called *kazura tōfu* (*kazura* being a type of rope that can be tied around this variety without it crumbling) and *kashi no ki tōfu* (oak tree tofu)

katsuobushi   flakes of skipjack tuna (*katsuo* in Japanese). The fish is filleted, simmered, smoked over a month or so, sprayed with *Aspergillus glaucus* to aid in fermentation and then sun-dried

kedelai   Indonesian word for soybean

kinome dengaku   grilled tofu on skewers slathered with kinome miso, made with the addition of citrusy sansho (Japanese pepper)

kinugoshi tōfu   Japanese word for silken tofu. A soft variety that is not pressed and therefore retains more water

kobu abura-age   fried tofu and kelp

kombu   Japanese word for edible kelp. Also kobu. See yudōfu

kona-dōfu   Japanese powdered dried tofu, usually created as a by-product of kōya-dōfu

kona-dōfu jiru   powdered tofu soup

kona-dōfu no iri-ni   dish in which kona-dōfu is simmered with other ingredients, giving it a kind of scrambled-egg texture

kokkeibon   a sort of comic novel popular in Edo-period Japan

konnyaku   a type of jelly made from the tuberous roots of of the konjac plant

kōji   a mould used in the creation of various fermented products in Japan, for example sake

kōya-dōfu   Japanese freeze-dried tofu, originally made using the ichiya-gōri technique of drying. See shimi-dōfu

kurumi-tōfu   walnut tofu. Made by grinding walnuts, simmering with water and adding arrowroot starch

liangfen   literally 'cold powder', refers to a type of Chinese jelly, made from a variety of ingredients. Similar to a Korean dish, muk

Lingqing Jinqing Rufu   a variety of fermented tofu, its name (literally Lingqing Entering-the-Capital rufu) refers to its acceptance in imperial cuisine in the early nineteenth century

li qi   mysterious ancient word for tofu in China. Purportedly the name for bean curd in Shu Han (today's Sichuan and Yunnan), written two different ways using Chinese characters. Also lai qi

lulao   ancient Chinese strained yoghurt

maboroshi no ippin Japanese word meaning 'phantom dish'. Refers to a rare food that is found only in a few places in the country

mao doufu hairy tofu, a type of fermented tofu from Anhui province, named for the hair-like mould that grows over its surface

mapo doufu a Sichuan dish consisting of cubes of tofu and minced pork in a numbing-spicy sauce. Literally means 'pockmarked woman tofu', allegedly owing to the nickname of the woman whose shop the dish originated in. Popular dish in Japan

Matsuyama-age see *hoshi abura-age*

memil-muk a type of Korean jelly made of buckwheat

mitate banzuke rankings of various subjects based on sumo *banzuke*; ranked topics include things such as natural disasters, comedians, foods, etc.

momendōfu Japanese word meaning 'cotton tofu', that is, firm tofu. Covered with a cloth and weighted to remove water

muk a kind of hard-ish jelly native to Korea. Various ingredients can be used such as acorns and mung beans

nanru literally 'southern milk'. Another word in Mandarin for red fermented tofu. See *hongfuru*

nigari a type of salt left over from the production of sodium chloride from seawater (brine). Used as a coagulant to create curds in soy milk. Contains several chemicals originally present in brine, including magnesium chloride. See *yanlu*

nikudofu a Japanese dish of simmered beef and tofu

nokdu-muk mung bean jelly

oboro tōfu super soft variety of Japanese tofu that has not been strained or pressed. Also called *sukui* (scooped), *zaru* (colander) and *yose* (gathering) *tōfu*. See *awayuki-dōfu*

okara the Japanese (common) word for tofu dregs or soy pulp. It is a by-product of soy milk and tofu production, what remains after grinding and filtering the soybeans

okazu   side dish

oncom   a fermented soybean product hailing from Java, Indonesia. Made by pressing tofu dregs (*okara*) and other food by-products (peanut, cassava and coconut) into a block

oncom hitam   orange/red oncom

oncom merah   black oncom

pehtze   'fresh soybean curd overgrown with fungal mycelium', also *pizi*

qian zhang   'thousand sheets'. See *bai ye*

Qingyilu   written by the scholar Tao Gu (903–970), this text contains the earliest known appearance of the word *doufu*, that is, tofu

qiu you furu   a variety of fermented tofu. Literally 'autumn oil' furu due to the time of year when the particular soybeans and sesame seeds used in its production were harvested. Emperor Wanli of the Ming dynasty is believed to have called it 'a treasured pickled food, king of furu'. It was admired by Empress Dowager Cixi, who sampled it for herself in 1902 and ordered it made a part of the imperial menu

red yeast rice   see *benikōji*

rokujō-dōfu   way of preserving tofu in Japan by which the tofu is salted and then left out to dry in the sun. Also called *shōjin-bushi* due to its similarity to *katsuobushi* (dried bonito flakes), as a replacement for which it is used in *shōjin-ryōri* (Japanese Buddhist cuisine)

rutuan   'milk balls'. Ancient Chinese dairy product

Ryukyu Islands   a chain of islands stretching southwest of the Japanese mainland, today part of Kagoshima and Okinawa prefectures. It once made up part of the Ryukyu Kingdom, which flourished as a tributary of Ming dynasty China. Later invaded by the Satsuma Domain, becoming its vassal in 1609, and finally incorporated as part of Japan in 1879

shaoxing furu   a type of fermented tofu from Shaoxing, Zhejiang province, China. Made using Shaoxing wine

shigao   gypsum, one of the coagulants listed for use in tofu production in the sixteenth-century *Compendium of Materia Medica*

shimadōfu   'island tofu' made in Okinawa, noted for the slight difference in production when compared to the method of the Japanese mainland

shimi-dōfu   see kōya-dōfu

shin-no-udon tōfu   tofu cut into thick strips (like udon noodles) using a tool called a *tokoro-ten tsuki* and served in a broth of soy, sake and *dashi*, garnished with grated *daikon*, diced root of a spring onion, *mikan* (satsuma) peel, Asakusa *nori* seaweed and chilli powder

shu   an ancient Chinese word for 'bean', later superseded by *dou*

so   a type of ancient cheese. Called *su* in Chinese

Srivajaya   a maritime empire centred on Sumatra with territory on the Malay peninsula and Java. Flourished between the seventh and eleventh centuries

stinky tofu   English translation of *chou doufu*, a type of fermented tofu product

su   a Chinese character referring to vegetarian cuisine, the colour white and plainness

suan jiang   commonly called 'Chinese lantern', a member of the physalis family. Listed as a coagulant for making tofu in Li Shizhen's *Compendium of Materia Medica*

su ji   Chinese 'vegetarian chicken' created by layering simmered mushrooms and other vegetables alternately with tofu skins, before rolling tightly and frying

su shao'e   vegetarian roasted duck

suyou   ancient Chinese clotted cream

taho   the name of *douhua* (tofu pudding) in the Philippines. Served cold with syrup and other sweet accoutrements

tahu   tofu in Indonesian. First appeared in an inscription ('Watakura A') dated to AD 902, making it the first recorded Chinese-origin loanword in the region.

tahu takwa   deep-fried tofu with a crispy outside and soft centre, like *baojiang doufu*

tamago-dōfu   egg tofu, made by mixing egg with *dashi* and soy sauce before steaming

tao hu dam   Thailand's 'black tofu'. A speciality of Photharam, Ratchaburi, brought there by Chinese immigrants. Given its colour and distinctive *palo* (herbal stew) flavours by prolonged immersion in a mixture of cinnamon, five-spice powder, sea salt, star anise and sugar

tempeh   a fermented soybean product from Indonesia made by wrapping boiled soybeans that have been mixed with a fermentation starter in leaves

tihu   ancient Chinese ghee

Tofu Hyakuchin   translates as A Hundred Tricks with Tofu in English. Landmark recipe book featuring one hundred ways to cook and serve tofu, published in 1782. Followed by two sequels: *Tōfu Hyakuchin Zokuhen* (Sequel to a Hundred Tricks with Tofu) and *Tōfu Hyakuchin Yōroku* (A Hundred More Tricks with Tofu)

tōfu no misozuke   Japanese pickled tofu. Listed in *Tofu Hyakuchin* as *tōbei*, today a famous food product of Kumamoto Prefecture. Tofu is cut into cubes and fermented in miso over several months. A particular variety, said to have the texture of sea urchin (uni), is called *yama-uni tōfu* (mountain sea urchin tofu). According to legend it was the warriors of the Heike clan who preserved tofu in this way using *kata-dōfu*

tōfuyō   Okinawan fermented tofu, made using *benikōji* (red yeast rice), *kōji* and *awamori*, local rice-based alcohol. It has a striking red colour and is thought to be derived from *hongfuru*

to hpu   Burmese tofu, also known as Shan tofu, not strictly tofu as such given that the raw materials involved, chickpeas, congeal into a solid form by themselves without the need for a coagulant

tokwa't baboy   a common dish in the Philippines. Comprises deep-fried tofu, pork belly, pig's ear, chilli and spring onions with pork broth, soy sauce and vinegar

unohana   simmered vegetables and okara. Staple Japanese side dish

wara   West African curd milk product often approximated with soy milk. Other names include *warankashi* (Fulani), *awara* and *woagachi* (Nigeria), *wagashi* (Benin, Togo, Ghana), *touzia* (Algeria), *amo* (Fon language), *gasaru* (Bariba), *wangash* (Mina). See *beske*

Watakura   a *rakrayan* (chiefdom) of central Java where an inscription made under the rule of Balitung, king of the Javanese Mataram kingdom, was discovered to contain the word *tahu* (tofu), in reference to a dish at a feast

xiaochi   small snacks

yakidōfu suishitaji   grilled tofu simmered in soy sauce soup

yanlu   Chinese term for bittern. See *nigari*. Listed in *Compendium of Materia Medica* as a coagulant for tofu production

yubuchobap   Korean word for *inari-zushi*

yudōfu   simmered tofu. Japanese dish whereby silken tofu is simmered in water with *kombu*

yu doufu   Chinese word for fish tofu, made from fish paste and resembling tofu

zha gutou   literally 'fried bones', a type of cheese-based mock meat made out of *rutuan*

zhai   vegetarian food/dishes

zyu hung   Cantonese term for pig blood curd, also called blood tofu (*xue doufu* in Mandarin)

RECIPES

At some point, Asian cooking in general lost the edge of disgust that has dogged it since its discovery by unimpressed Westerners. Japanese cuisine in particular seems to have come a long way. As well as the disparaging remarks made against it by Ernest Satow and Isabella Bird, among other big names, there was a very real separation of Westerners from the cuisine of the country in which they were living. Westerners in late nineteenth-century Japan lived 'inside a self-created socio-cultural bubble, separate from everyday Japanese life . . . rejecting Japanese food' among other things, employing Chinese cooks to supply them instead with approximations of home comforts and Western food.[1] As a side note, this is not dissimilar to the situation in the modern-day 'Chinese camps' of Zambia (see Chapter Four), to take one example, in which Chinese workers of state-owned enterprises are sequestered in comfortable Chinese bubbles, complete with pork and tofu.

Even so, Asian recipes – some of which call for tofu – made their way over to the West, and much earlier than the famous 1945 tome *How to Cook and Eat in Chinese*. First, there was *Chinese Cookery in the Home Kitchen*, written by Jessie Louise Nolton and published in 1911 and, three years later, the *Chinese–Japanese Cook Book* by Sara Bosse and Onoto Watanna (better known as Winnifred Eaton). At the time, Chinese food or any approximation of it was considered 'at best exotic and at worst dangerous',[2] and quite widely, too, if the damning opinion of it put forward in *King's Handbook of New York City* (see Chapter Four) was the prevailing one.

Things have changed. According to a 2015 article in the *Washington Post*, 'global sales at Asian fast food restaurants have grown by nearly 500 percent since 1999', clear evidence that Asian cuisine has 'gone from being a niche food obsession to one of the most popular around the world'.[3] As the final chapter of this book highlighted, it seems tofu has come along for the ride. Though still misunderstood by many, social media is boosting interest in tofu, with '#tofurecipe' on TikTok garnering 220.8 million views ('#tofu' has 2.1 billion) – fewer than '#chickenrecipe' (1.8 billion) but more than '#porkrecipe' (82.8 million) – as of July 2023.[4] This easy access to a diversity of tofu recipes shows how far it has come from the days of 'Layered Casserole' (as seen in Louise Hagler's 1982 *Tofu Cookery*),[5] for example, when tofu had to be hidden and mashed beyond recognition to be appreciated. The following recipes are a taster of thousands out there, some traditional, others vegetarian in origin, and a few leaving out soybeans altogether.

HIYAYAKKO

1 pack (350 g/1 lb) kinu (silken) tofu, drained and lightly pressed
1 tbsp *ssamjang* (for the topping)
1 (thin) spring onion, finely sliced
soy sauce to taste

This is barely a recipe, but it's a classic across Japan: tofu in all its raw glory, topped with various ingredients like a bean curd smorgasbord. It's a common menu item in *izakaya* (Japanese pubs), which may be down to its shareability. The toppings are usually *katsuobushi* (bonito flakes) and sliced *negi* (spring onion) with soy sauce to taste. It's not usually cut either, but my first experience of *hiyayakko* was in this more flavour-absorbing form. The addition of extra soy goodness from the rich, fiery *ssamjang* is certainly not canon, but it is a go-to topping for me.

Make a horizontal slice through the middle of the tofu so there's now a top and bottom layer. Cut vertically, separating your block into squares. How large you make your cubes is up to you, but too small and you'll have long, thin cuboids; too big and it'll be unmanageable. Once this is done drip soy carefully across the surface. The aim is to get it to run down between the cubes. Then grab your *ssamjang*. You can either place it on top artfully or spread it over the surface of the cut tofu. Sprinkle with cut spring onion (you probably won't need it all) to finish. Best eaten in summer.

HIRYŪZU/GANMODOKI
From *Tofu Hyakuchin* (1782)

2 packs (700 g/2 lb) momen (firm) tofu
1 medium egg
60 g (2 oz) kuzuko or potato starch
1 medium carrot (50 g/⅓ cup)
50 g (⅓ cup) burdock root
20 g (¾ oz) konbu
4–5 ginkgo nuts, halved
sugar
salt
vegetable oil (for frying)

Called hiryūzu in the *Tofu Hyakuchin*, ganmodoki has long been an easy-to-grab snack from tofu shops across Japan. Essentially these are tofu fritters, shallow-fried for deliciousness. The 240-year-old recipe goes:

> Drain the tofu and grate it well. Add kudzu powder as a binder. For the filling you can use any favoured ingredients such as burdock root, ginkgo nuts, wood ear mushroom and the like. Stir-fry these in a little oil then wrap them in a suitably sized tofu package and fry in oil. Serve with *irizake* and grated wasabi or white vinegar and grated wasabi.

Some of the ingredients may be hard to find. If you can't find burdock root, use *daikon* (also known as *mooli*). For ginkgo nuts, substitute edamame beans or double up on ordinary garden peas. Start by draining and pressing your tofu. The least moisture possible makes a better mixture, so wrap the tofu in a cloth or several pieces of kitchen paper, put it in a suitable tray and weigh it down with a heavy object. Refrigerate and leave for three or four hours. Julienne the carrots and burdock root; make sure they're not too long. Boil them for one minute, don't let them get too soft. Drain and dry.

Once the tofu is ready, remove and unwrap. Push it through a colander into a mixing bowl. Add potato starch into the mixing bowl and knead by hand. Throw in a pinch of sugar and salt. Depending on the wetness of the mixture, you may not need all the egg. Add it gradually. Fold in the vegetables and mix until evenly distributed. Form into little patties (should make 8–10) and fry in a tablespoon or so of cooking oil. Remove after six or seven minutes or when the colour is an appetizing golden brown all over. The original recipe suggests serving with *irizake* (sake boiled down with dried plums and bonito flakes) and grated wasabi, but soy sauce for dipping will do just fine.

COLD SOY MILK NOODLES
Recipe from columnist and food writer Susan Jung, inspired by a similar dish at Mora, Hong Kong

100 g (1 cup) medium wheat or rice noodles
250 ml (1 cup) unsweetened soy milk, chilled
1 tsp clear soy sauce
60 g (2 oz) *dougan* (seasoned pressed tofu)
60 g (2 oz) Asian cucumber
15 g (½ fl. oz) *doubanjiang* (hot fermented bean paste)
toasted sesame seeds
ice cubes

'I first tasted a version of these cold soy milk noodles at Mora, the soybean-focused restaurant by chefs Vicky Lau and Percy Ho,' said Jung. 'The Mora version uses shredded chicken, but I've substituted seasoned pressed tofu [*dougan*] to give the dish a double dose of soybeans.' *Dougan* has a firm, meaty texture, but can be hard to find. Substitute regular firm tofu and season with a tiny bit of soy sauce and sesame oil, just enough to moisten the bean curd. 'The quality of the soy milk is important – try to avoid mass produced types,' Jung adds. And whatever you do, go for unadulterated soy milk, no added sugar or anything.

Doubanjiang is Sichuan fermented broadbean chilli paste. Clear soy sauce, also called white soy sauce (*shirojōyu* in Japanese), looks like slightly tinted water. Jung uses it so it doesn't discolour the soy milk as regular soy sauce would. 'If you can't find it, season the soy milk with about ⅛ tsp fine sea salt, or to taste,' she wrote.

Heat a pan of water until boiling. Add noodles, cook until tender. Drain, rinse with cold water, drain again. Replace noodles in pan and cover with cold water, adding ice cubes so the noodles are very cold. Pour soy milk into serving bowl, stir in the soy sauce (or season). Add a few ice cubes to the soy milk to get it very cold. Cut tofu into thin strips. Julienne the cucumber. Put noodles into the bowl, place tofu on top, add the cucumber. Top with *doubanjiang* and sprinkle some sesame seeds. Add a few drops of chilli oil into the soy milk for further appearance and zing.

TOFU CHEESECAKE

Base
1 pack (300 g/2½ cups) Hobnob biscuits or similar
100 g (½ cup) salted butter

Filling
1 pack (350 g/½ lb) silken tofu
tahini
2 lemons (for zest and juice)

Cheesecake, except (mostly) vegan. Essentially, the main difference with cheesecake here is swapping ricotta or mascarpone for tofu. I saw a recipe for this while looking back through the archives of *Vegetarian Magazine* (June 1997). There are plenty of others out there. This one is a chimaera of several. What's interesting about vegan cheesecake is how you decide to retain the rigidity of the filling. Use cacao butter and it'll be chocolatey; opt for tahini and you'll get a rich, sesame depth; almond butter has a nuttier feel. This may alter how you choose to flavour the cheesecake, but for this one I've gone for refreshing lemon. The same goes for the base. While this recipe uses butter, coconut oil or syrup would work in theory.

For the base, blitz biscuits using a food processor or, if you don't have one, use a rolling pin to crush them in a mixing bowl. Add the butter and mix into a thick paste. Use some of the butter to line a tin. Spoon the base mixture into it. For the filling, ensure the tofu is well drained first. Zest and juice lemons. Add these ingredients to food processor, setting aside extra zest to garnish. Refrigerate for three to four hours or overnight before serving.

KURUMI-TŌFU (WALNUT TOFU)
From Yamagata City, Japan

50 g (½ cup) walnuts
50 g (½ cup) kuzu powder (arrowroot starch)
400 ml (13½ fl. oz) water
90 g (½ cup) sugar
⅛ tsp salt

Sauce
½ tbsp potato starch
½ tbsp sugar
½ tbsp soy sauce
2½ tbsp water
½ tsp sake
1 small piece ginger, grated

Tofu by name, but perhaps not tofu by nature. This is a speciality of Yamagata Prefecture, Japan, and often used in shōjin ryōri. If you can't get kuzu powder, substitute ground arrowroot or tapioca starch. Grind the walnuts into a powder, either in a food processor or using a pestle and mortar. Add the kuzu powder, water, salt and sugar (in that order). Mix well and strain. Pour resulting mixture into a pan and stir on a low heat. Keep stirring so it doesn't burn. Stir for 20 minutes or until it becomes a thick paste. Pour this into a mould and leave for about two hours. For the sauce, put the ingredients into a saucepan and heat until thickened, stirring the whole time. Place the set walnut tofu in a serving bowl or plate, pour the source over. Top with grated ginger.

CRÈME OF ALMAUNDES
From *The Forme of Cury* (c. 1380)

150 g (1¼ cups) blanched almonds
1½ tbsp distilled (white) vinegar
450 ml (¾ pint) water
sugar
salt

Medieval European 'almond tofu'. The original recipe isn't overly detailed, so some steps from the tofu-making process can be observed.
Cover almonds in water and soak them overnight. Drain them and whiz
them up into a paste in the food blender. Stir them into your water and
bring to the boil. Eventually the mixture will become homogenized.
Strain through a cloth or sieve. Pour the almond milk into the saucepan.
On a medium heat, while continually stirring, add the vinegar. Curds
will form. Add sugar and salt in the final moments. Stand for five minutes and place on a muslin cloth or similar. Twist it tight, allowing
excess water to drain. Allow to cool. Slice and serve.

TO HPU (BURMESE TOFU)

150 g (1 cup) *besan* (gram flour)
450 ml (¾ pint) water
turmeric, a pinch
salt to taste

In the realm of tofu-adjacent products, nothing could be simpler to
make than *to hpu*. All you need is *besan* (also called gram flour), which
is readily available even in mainstream supermarkets, and water, plus
a little turmeric for colouring. It sets by itself and is generally low-
maintenance. In a mixing bowl, whisk gram flour and water together
with turmeric until it attains a smooth consistency. I recommend adding
salt as it can be a little bitter.

Spoon mixture into a saucepan and cook on a medium heat,
stirring all the while. Ensure the mixture is very thick, as in hard to
stir (this should take around ten minutes), before you spoon it into a

container to set, using a spatula to reach all the mixture. Cool for a further ten minutes and refrigerate for around one hour. Remove and slice into whatever size chunks suit you. Though it can be eaten as is, to *hpu* is much better shallow fried in oil and served as a side dish or stir-fried with other ingredients.

REFERENCES

INTRODUCTION

1 Fina Wahibatun Nisa, 'Resep Gulai Tambusu, Usus Isi Tahu Telur Khas Minang yang Lezat Banget', IDN Times, www.idntimes.com, 28 February 2022.
2 Tan Yunfei, 'How to Make Salty and Delicious Crab Roe Tofu', *The World of Chinese*, www.theworldofchinese.com, 6 July 2021.
3 Carla Nappi, 'Li Shizhen – Brief Life of a Pioneering Naturalist: 1518–1593', *Harvard Magazine*, CXII/3 (2010), pp. 30–31.
4 Li Shizhen, *Bencao Gangmu* [本草綱, 1596], ebook, *Chinese Text Project*, www.ctext.org, accessed 8 July 2022.
5 Tan Yunfei, 'Flavor Wars', *The World of Chinese*, www.theworldofchinese.com, 6 December 2017.
6 Simon Rabinovitch, 'Chinese Petition Obama on Invasion, Poisoning and Tofu', *Financial Times*, www.ft.com, 8 May 2013.
7 R. S. Raghuvanshi and Kavita Bisht, 'Uses of Soybean: Products and Preparation', in *The Soybean: Botany, Production and Uses*, ed. Guriqbal Singh (Wallingford, 2010), p. 421.
8 Woon-Puay Koh et al., 'Gender-Specific Associations between Soy and Risk of Hip Fracture in the Singapore Chinese Health Study', *American Journal of Epidemiology*, CLXX/7 (2009), pp. 901–9.
9 Ho N. Nguyen et al., 'Dietary Tofu Intake and Long-Term Risk of Death from Stroke in a General Population', *Clinical Nutrition*, XXXVII/1 (2018), pp. 182–8.

10 Kyoko Taku et al., 'Soy Isoflavones Lower Serum Total and LDL Cholesterol in Humans: A Meta-Analysis of 11 Randomized Controlled Trials', *American Journal of Clinical Nutrition*, LXXXV/4 (2007), pp. 1148–56.

11 Le Ma et al., 'Isoflavone Intake and the Risk of Coronary Heart Disease in U.S. Men and Women', *Circulation*, CXLI/14 (2020), pp. 1127–37.

12 Megan Ware, 'Everything You Need to Know about Tofu', *Medical News Today*, www.medicalnewstoday.com, 27 September 2017.

13 'The Master Cooks of King Richard II', *The Forme of Cury* [*c.* 1390], ebook, trans. and ed. Samuel Pegge (1780), available at www. gutenberg.org, accessed 3 June 2022.

14 David E. Zaurov et al., 'Genetic Resources of Almond Species in the Former USSR', *HortScience*, L/1 (2015), p. 19.

ONE LIU AN AND LI QI: ANCIENT ORIGINS OF TOFU

1 See 'Where Does Tofu Come From?', *Tofoo*, www.tofoo. co.uk, accessed 20 June 2023; Pallavi Kanugo, 'Tofu: The Meat Alternative That Originated 2,000 Years Ago in China', HT *School*, *Hindustan Times*, htschool.hindustantimes.com, 2 December 2022; 'How to Cook Tofu: The Ultimate Guide', www.veganuary.com, accessed 20 June 2023.

2 Robin D. S. Yates, 'Huang-Lao', in *The Encyclopedia of Taoism*, ed. Fabrizio Pregadio (Abingdon and New York, 2008), pp. 508–10.

3 Corina Smith, *The Wholeness of Early Chinese Texts: Mu Shi* 牧誓, *Huainanzi* 淮南子, *and Wu Cheng* 武成 (Oxford, 2021), p. 25.

4 Evan Morgan, *Tao, the Great Luminant: Essays from the Huai-nan-tzu* (Shanghai, 1933), p. xliii.

5 David Dawson, 'Cradle of Tofu', *The World of Chinese*, www.theworldofchinese.com, 10 January 2016.

6 Li Shizhen, *Bencao Gangmu* 本草綱目[1596], ebook, *Chinese Text Project*, www.ctext.org, accessed 8 July 2022.

7 Carla Nappi, 'Li Shizhen – Brief Life of a Pioneering Naturalist: 1518–1593', *Harvard Magazine*, CXII/3 (2010), pp. 30–31.

8 Li, *Bencao Gangmu*.

9 'Tofu 豆腐', *Five Seasons* TCM, www.fiveseasonstcm.com, 21 February 2021.

10 Jiuquan Zhang, 'Textual Research on Tofu Poetry in the Song
    Dynasty', *Journal of Anhui University of Science and Technology (Social
    Science)*, xxii/5 (2020), pp. 73–7.
11 Tao Gu, *Qing Yilu* [10th century], ebook, *Chinese Text Project*,
    www.ctext.org, accessed 8 July 2022.
12 Zhang, 'Textual Research on Tofu Poetry in the Song Dynasty'.
13 David Bradley, *Southern Lisu Dictionary* (Berkeley, ca, 2005), p. 329.
14 Thomas M. Pinson, ed., *Naqxi–Habaq–Yiyu Ceeqdiai (A Naxi–
    Chinese–English Dictionary)* (Kunming, 2012), pp. 293, 238.
15 'Ancient Chinese Folk Epic Published', *China Internet Information
    Center*, www.china.org.cn, 3 April 2002.
16 'Shennong', *Britannica*, www.britannica.com, accessed
    16 June 2022.
17 Morgan, *Tao, the Great Luminant*, pp. 220–21.
18 Gillian Daniel, 'The Legend of the Divine Farmer', *Public Domain
    Review*, www.publicdomainreview.org, 3 November 2015.
19 Sissi Wachtel-Galor et al., '*Ganoderma lucidum* (Lingzhi or Reishi):
    A Medicinal Mushroom', in *Herbal Medicine: Biomolecular and
    Clinical Aspects*, ed. Iris F. F. Benzie and Sissi Wachtel-Galor,
    2nd edn (Boca Raton, fl, 2011), p. 174.
20 Lihui Yang, Deming An and Jessica Anderson Turner, *Handbook
    of Chinese Mythology* (Santa Barbara, ca, Denver, co, and Oxford,
    2005), pp. 190–99.
21 Liao Kaishun and Shi Jianeng, 'The Aesthetic Gene of the
    Ancient Myths and Legends of the Dong Nationality', *Guizhou
    Ethnic Studies*, xvii/3 (1995), pp. 111–19.
22 Wang Xianzhao, 'Minority Creation Myths: An Approach to
    Classification', in *China's Creation and Origin Myths: Cross-Cultural
    Explorations in Oral and Written Traditions*, ed. Mineke Schipper,
    Shuxian Ye and Hubin Yin (Leiden and Boston, ma, 2011),
    pp. 197–218.
23 Yang, An and Turner, *Handbook of Chinese Mythology*, p. 177.
24 James Legge, trans., 'The Shih King; or, Book of Poetry', in *Sacred
    Books of the East*, vol. iii, ed. F. Max Müller (Oxford, 1879), p. 398.
25 Gyoung-Ah Lee et al., 'Archaeological Soybean (*Glycine max*)
    in East Asia: Does Size Matter?', *plos One*, vi/11 (2011), p. 9.
26 Emily Mark, 'Xia Dynasty', *World History Encyclopedia*,
    www.worldhistory.org, 10 January 2016.

27 Wolfram Eberhard, A History of China (Berkeley and Los Angeles, CA, 1969), p. 7.

28 Siwei Yue, 'Functionalism Theory Applied in C–E Translation of Chinese Food Culture Text', Theory and Practice in Language Studies, III/1 (2013), pp. 61–8 (p. 62).

29 E.T.C. Warner, Myths and Legends of China (London, 1922), p. 174; Chen Kaiwen, 'Hangye shen', Encyclopedia of Taiwan, https://nrch.culture.tw, 9 November 1998.

30 Zeng Xueying, Chinese Culture Series: Tofu (Taipei, 2019), p. 11.

31 Trấn Văn Mỹ, 'Hội Vật Mai Động', in Lê hội Việt Nam, ed. Lê Trung Vũ and Lê Hồng Lý (Ho Chi Minh City, 2005), p. 11.

32 Ibid., p. 12.

33 'Annual Wrestling Festival in Mai Dong Village', Vietnam Investment Review, www.vir.org.vn, 16 March 2018; 'Mai Dong Wrestling Village in Spring', The Voice of Vietnam, www.vovworld.vn, 13 February 2016.

34 'Đậu phụ Kẻ Mơ', Tuổi Trẻ Online, www.tuoitre.vn, 30 October 2009.

35 'Kẻ Mơ – một vùng văn hóa cô Thăng Long', Sở Văn hóa và Thể thao Thành phố Hà Nội, http://sovhtt.hanoi.gov.vn, 4 February 2021.

36 Miriam T. Stark, 'Early Mainland Southeast Asian Landscapes in the First Millennium AD', Annual Review of Anthropology, XXXV (2006), pp. 407–32 (p. 414).

37 Michel Ferlus, 'A Layer of Dongsonian Vocabulary in Vietnamese', Journal of the Southeast Asian Linguistics Society, I (Honolulu, HI, 2009), pp. 95–108 (p. 105).

38 Ernest Caldwell, 'Promoting Action in Warring States Political Philosophy: A First Look at the Chu Manuscript Cao Mie's Battle Arrays', Early China, XXXVII (2014), pp. 259–89 (p. 259); Su Li, The Constitution of Ancient China, trans. Edmund Ryden (Princeton, NJ, and Oxford, 2018), p. 104.

39 Yu Jinshou, 'Jade of the Bean House', in Shanhai jing Tales Series: The Legend of the Three Hundred and Sixty Lines of the Patriarch, ebook, ed. Chen Delai (Hangzhou, 2013).

40 Herbert A. Giles, A Chinese–English Dictionary (Shanghai and London, 1892), p. 658.

41 'Zhongxiang's Characteristics Are World-Renowned – The Fragrance of Shipai Tofu Floats at Home and Abroad', Shipai Tofu, www.spdoufu.com, 23 February 2023.

42 'Belief in Industry Gods – Tofu Industry', *Sanching Temple*, www.sanching.org.tw, accessed 21 June 2022.

43 'Social Responsibility', *Tramy Group*, www.sh-tramy.com, accessed 24 July 2023.

44 Zhang, 'Textual Research on Tofu Poetry in the Song Dynasty'.

45 Yimin Yang et al., 'Proteomics Evidence for Kefir Dairy in Early Bronze Age China', *Journal of Archaeological Science*, XLV (2014), pp. 178–86.

46 Karine Taché et al., 'What Do "Barbarians" Eat? Integrating Ceramic Use-Wear and Residue Analysis in the Study of Food and Society at the Margins of Bronze Age China', PLOS One, XVI/4 (2021), p. 18.

47 Francesca Bray, 'Where Did the Animals Go? Presence and Absence of Livestock in Chinese Agricultural Treatises', in *Animals through Chinese History: Earliest Times to 1911*, ed. Roel Sterckx, Martina Siebert and Dagmar Schäfer (Cambridge, 2020), p. 120.

48 Bryan K. Miller, 'Power Politics in the Xiongnu Empire', PhD thesis, University of Pennsylvania, 2009, p. 102.

49 Katarzyna Cwiertka and Yujen Chen, 'The Shadow of Shinoda Osamu: Food Research in East Asia', in *Writing Food History: A Global Perspective*, ed. Kyri W. Claflin and Peter Scholliers (London, 2012), p. 182.

50 Zhang, 'Textual Research on Tofu Poetry in the Song Dynasty'.

51 Alexander Savelyev, 'Farming-Related Terms in Proto-Turkic and Proto-Altaic', in *Language Dispersal beyond Farming*, ed. Martine Robbeets and Alexander Savelyev (Amsterdam and Philadelphia, PA, 2017), p. 140.

52 Ibid., p. 131.

53 Carla Nappi, *Translating Early Modern China: Illegible Cities* (Oxford, 2021), p. 218.

54 'The Issue Surrounding the Arrival of Tofu in Japan', *Shibata Shoten*, www.shibatashoten.co.jp, 25 January 2011.

55 Fuchsia Dunlop, 'Chinese Cheese: A Taste of "Milk Cake" in Yunnan', BBC, www.bbc.co.uk/news, 19 May 2012.

56 C. Culas and J. Michaud, 'A Contribution to the Study of Hmong (Miao) Migrations and History', *Bijdragen tot de Taal-, Land- en Volkenkunde*, CLIII/153 (Leiden, 1997), pp. 211–43.

57 Bryan Allen and Silvia Allen, 'Mozzarella of the East
(Cheese-Making and Bai Culture)', *Ethnorêma*, I (2005)
pp. 19–27; Don Otter, 'Etymology', in *The Oxford Companion
to Cheese*, ed. Catherine W. Donnelly (Oxford, 2016), p. 256.

58 Anooja Nair, Dechen Choden and Monika Pradhan, 'Chemical
Composition and Microbial Quality of *Datshi and Zoety*, Unripen
Cottage Cheese of Bhutan', *Food Science and Nutrition*, X/5 (2022),
pp. 1385–90.

59 Yang Fuquan, 'The "Ancient Tea and Horse Caravan Road,"
and "Silk Road" of Southwest China', *Silk Road*, II/I (2004),
pp. 29–32.

60 Chee-Beng Tan, 'Tofu and Related Products in Chinese
Foodways', in *The World of Soy*, ed. Christine M. Du Bois, Sidney
Wilfred Mintz and Chee-Beng Tan (Champaign, IL, 2008), p. 102.

61 Duk-Kyung Choi, 'Reexamination of the Origin of Soybean
and the Distribution of Soybean Sauce, Soybean Malt, and
Tofu from the Documentary and Excavated Data from Ancient
China', *Korea Society for Historical Folklife Studies*, XXX (2009),
pp. 363–427.

62 Robert Guang Tian et al., 'Food Culture in China: From Social
Political Perspectives', *Trames*, XXII/4 (2018), pp. 345–64 (p. 351).

63 Ibid.

64 Bray, 'Where Did the Animals Go?', p. 118.

65 Tian, 'Food Culture in China', p. 8.

66 Bray, 'Where Did the Animals Go?', p. 125.

67 Vincent Goossaert, 'Animals in Nineteenth-Century
Eschatological Discourse', in *Animals through Chinese History*,
ed. Sterckx, Siebert and Schäfer, p. 190.

68 Dagmar Schäfer, Martina Siebert and Roel Sterckx, 'Knowing
Animals in China's History: An Introduction', in *Animals through
Chinese History*, ed. Sterckx, Siebert and Schäfer, p. 2.

69 Bray, 'Where Did the Animals Go?', p. 119.

70 For the dairy of the Tibetan Plateau, see Li Tang et al.,
'Paleoproteomic Evidence Reveals Dairying Supported
Prehistoric Occupation of the Highland Tibetan Plateau', *Science
Advances*, IX/15 (2023).

TWO WHAT'S THAT SMELL? PRESERVING TOFU AND ITS BY-PRODUCTS

1 Jiuquan Zhang, 'Textual Research on Tofu Poetry in the Song Dynasty', *Journal of Anhui University of Science and Technology (Social Science)*, XXII/5 (2020), pp. 73–7.
2 Miranda Brown, 'Mr. Song's Cheeses: Southern China, 1368–1644', *Gastronomica*, XIX/2 (2019), pp. 29–42 (p. 38).
3 Herbert A. Giles, *A Chinese–English Dictionary* (Shanghai and London, 1892), p. 259.
4 Bei-Zhong Han, Frans M. Rombouts and M. J. Robert Nout, 'A Chinese Fermented Soybean Food', *International Journal of Food Microbiology*, LXV/1–2 (2001), pp. 1–10 (pp. 2–3).
5 Li Anlan, 'China's "Vegetarian Cheese" Has Health Benefits', *Shine*, www.shine.cn, 15 August 2018.
6 Cathy Erway, 'These Umami-Packed Tofu Cubes Are Vegetables' Best Friends', *Food and Wine*, www.foodandwine.com, 3 February 2021.
7 Michael R. Godley, 'China's World's Fair of 1910: Lessons from a Forgotten Event', *Modern Asian Studies*, XII/2 (1978), pp. 503–22 (p. 503).
8 Cherl-Ho Lee and Moonsil Kim, 'History of Fermented Foods in Northeast Asia', in *Ethnic Fermented Foods and Alcoholic Beverages of Asia*, ed. Jyoti Prakash Tamang (2016), p. 7.
9 Ibid.
10 Han, Rombouts and Nout, 'A Chinese Fermented Soybean Food', p. 2.
11 Yukio Magariyama, 'Tofuyo and Furu', *Journal of the Brewing Society of Japan*, CIX/11 (2014), pp. 785–90 (p. 786).
12 Masaaki Yasuda, 'Fermented Tofu, Tofuyo', in *Soybean: Biochemistry, Chemistry and Physiology*, ed. Tzi-Bun Ng (2011), ebook.
13 Chen Yunning, 'Fermented Bean Curd Brewed during the Dragon Boat Festival, Used as a Drinking Snack in the Mid-Autumn Festival', *Day to Day Guide*, http://yummy.greeninhand.com, 10 July 2018.
14 'Group Profile', *Beijing Capital Agribusiness and Foods Group*, www.bjcag.com, accessed 8 August 2022.
15 Brent Crane, 'Hairy, Stinky Tofu Is the Stuff of Smelly Dreams', *Vice*, www.vice.com, 29 August 2016.

16 See www.techanyi.com, accessed 8 August 2022.

17 See 秋油腐乳, *The People's Government of Lankao County*, www.lankao.gov.cn, accessed 8 August 2022.

18 Wang Zengqi, *A Taste of Life (Classic Works of Wang Zengqi)* (Tianjin, 2017), ebook.

19 Jiang Zhenyue, 'Netizens Commented on the Top Ten Local Cultural Specialties. Roast Duck and Stinky Tofu Were Selected', *China News*, www.chinanews.com, 12 April 2017.

20 Fan Minghui, 'Mao Zedong Dining in "Fire Palace"', *Huogongdian*, www.huogongdian.com, 19 October 2015.

21 Masaaki Yasuda, 'Sciences and Technical Developments of Tofuyo which Is the Unique Fermented Soybean Food', *Nippon Nōgeikagaku Kaishi*, LXXV/5 (2001), pp. 580–83 (p. 580).

22 Basil Hall, *Account of a Voyage of Discovery to the West Coast of Corea, and the Great Loo-Choo Island in the Japan Sea*, ebook (London, 1818), available at www.gutenberg.org, accessed 18 July 2022.

23 Yasuda, 'Fermented Soybean', p. 310.

24 'Tofuyo', *Taste Atlas*, www.tasteatlas.com, accessed 19 July 2022.

25 'What's the Story behind Stinky Tofu?', *The Loop HK*, www.theloophk.com, 1 October 2019.

26 Geoff Wade, 'Ryukyu in the Ming Reign Annals, 1380s–1580s', *ARI Working Paper Series*, XCIII (Singapore, 2007), pp. 1–120 (p. 3).

27 Ibid., p. 12.

28 Magariyama, 'Tofuyo and Furu', p. 786.

29 Shunzo Sakamaki, 'Ryukyu and Southeast Asia', *Journal of Asian Studies*, XXIII/3 (1964), pp. 383–9 (p. 384).

30 Dennis Normile, 'Update: Explorers Successfully Voyage to Japan in Primitive Boat in Bid to Unlock an Ancient Mystery', *Science*, www.science.org, 10 July 2019.

31 Michael Gold, 'Stinky Tofu: Taiwan's Tasty Snack Packs a Rotten Stench', *Reuters*, www.reuters.com, 5 August 2013.

32 Chris Horton, 'Where Stinky Tofu Is at Its Malodorous Best', *New York Times*, www.nytimes.com, 19 November 2017.

33 Randy Mulyanto, 'Taipei's Tasty "House of Stink"', *BBC Travel*, www.bbc.com/travel, 7 May 2019.

34 'City of Splendid Culture', *Taiwan Today*, www.taiwantoday.tw, 1 September 2016.

35 Lisa Kao, 'New Taipei City – Shenkeng Old Street', *TravelKing*, www.travelking.com.tw, accessed 18 July 2022.

36 Horton, 'Stinky Tofu'.

37 Mulyanto, 'House of Stink'.

38 'Taiwan's Stinky Tofu Is Not a Dish for the Faint-Hearted', *Saigoneer*, www.saigoneer.com, 27 June 2017.

39 Yuping Liu et al., 'Analysis of Organic Volatile Flavor Compounds in Fermented Stinky Tofu Using SPME with Different Fiber Coatings', *Molecules*, XVII/4 (2012), pp. 3708–22.

40 Silvia Marchetti, 'Cheese in China Has a Long History – Made with Buffalo, Yak, Goat's, Cow's and Sheep's Milk, and Everywhere from Taiwan to Tibet and 16th Century Shanghai', *South China Morning Post*, www.scmp.com, 6 August 2021.

41 Brown, 'Mr. Song's Cheeses', p. 38.

42 Dale Purves et al., eds, *Neuroscience*, 3rd edn (Sunderland, MA, 2001), p. 339.

43 Arnold Berstad, Jan Raa and Jørgen Valeur, 'Indole – The Scent of a Healthy "Inner Soil"', *Microbial Ecology in Health and Disease*, XXVI/1 (2015).

44 'Is Stinky Tofu the Cause of the Odor? Temporary Suspension of Operation', *Mainichi Shimbun*, 8 February 2016.

45 Tejal Rao, 'In a Tense Political Moment, Taiwanese Cuisine Tells Its Own Story', *New York Times*, www.nytimes.com, 16 August 2022.

46 Fernanda Guilherme do Prado et al., 'Fermented Soy Products and Their Potential Health Benefits: A Review', *Microorganisms*, X/8 (2022), p. 1606.

47 Jiayang Fan, 'The Gatekeepers Who Get to Decide What Food Is "Disgusting"', *New Yorker*, www.newyorker.com, 10 May 2021.

48 Andreas Ahrens, 'Most Disgusting Foods', *Disgusting Food Museum*, www.disgustingfoodmuseum.com, 10 August 2021.

49 Erika Chayes Wida, 'Twinkies, Jell-O and Root Beer Deemed "World's Most Disgusting" Foods – Here's Why', *Today*, www.today.com, 17 October 2018.

50 Fuchsia Dunlop, 'The Pleasures of Texture', *Fuchsia Dunlop*, www.fuchsiadunlop.com, 24 June 2013.

51 C. C. Ho, 'Identity and Characteristics of *Neurospora intermedia* Responsible for *oncom* Fermentation in Indonesia', *Food Microbiology*, III/3 (1986), pp. 115–32.

52 Ingrid S. Surono and Akiyoshi Hosono, 'Indigenous Fermented Foods in Indonesia', *Japanese Journal of Dairy and Food Science*, XLIV/3 (1995), pp. 91–8 (p. 91).

53 Dudi Djuhdia Sastraatmadja, Fusao Tomita and Takanori Kasai, 'Production of High-Quality Oncom, a Traditional Indonesian Fermented Food, by the Inoculation with Selected Mold Strains in the Form of Pure Culture and Solid Inoculum', *Journal of the Graduate School of Agriculture, Hokkaido University*, LXX/2 (2002), pp. 111–27 (p. 112).

54 Surono and Hosono, 'Indigenous Fermented Foods', p. 92.

55 Fadly Rahman quoted in Syifa Nuri Khairunnisa, 'The History of Oncom Typical of West Java, Processed Food Leftovers', *Kompas*, www.kompas.com, 9 August 2020.

56 Li Shizhen, *Bencao Gangmu* [1596], ebook, Chinese Text Project, www.ctext.org, accessed 8 July 2022.

57 Yuan Mei, *Recipes from the Garden of Contentment*, trans. Sean J. S. Chen (Great Barrington, MA, 2018), p. 269.

58 Ibid., p. 255.

59 Ibid., p. 257.

60 Wang, *A Taste of Life*.

61 Hiroyuki Horio and Tomoko Yokoyama, 'Food Culture of the Muromachi, the Azuchimomoyama Era', *Journal of the Natural Scientific Society of Nagoya Keizai University*, XLIX/1–2 (2016), pp. 35–50.

62 Tokuji Watanabe and Kyoko Saio, 'Considering Tofu', *Chemistry and Biology*, XI/10 (1973), p. 632.

63 Ministry of Education, Culture, Sport, Science and Technology, 'Notes on Food', *Standard Tables of Food Composition in Japan*, VII (2015), p. 39.

64 'Rokujo Tofu Soup, Refined Flavor Reminiscent of Yuba', *Yamagata News Online*, www.yamagata-np.jp, 17 January 2012.

65 'Kona-tōfu no iri-ni', Izumi City, www.city.osaka-izumi.lg.jp, 14 February 2022.

66 'Iri-ni', *Japanese Dictionary of Food Terms/Words of Traditional and Modern Japanese Food*, www.japan-word.com, accessed 22 August 2022.

67 Helen J. Baroni, *The Illustrated Encyclopedia of Zen Buddhism* (New York, 2002), p. 129.

68 'New Asahi Kona-dofu', *Asahimatsu Foods*, www.asahimatsu.co.jp, accessed 22 August 2022.
69 'Features of Matsuyama-age', *Hodono Shoten*, www.matsuyamaage. co.jp, accessed 4 August 2022.
70 'History of Matsuyama-age', *Hodono Shoten*, www.matsuyamaage. co.jp, accessed 12 August 2022.

THREE SPREADING THE CURD: HOW TOFU TRAVELLED THE WORLD

1 Jeffrey A. Bader, 'China's Role in East Asia: Now and the Future', *Brookings*, www.brookings.edu, 6 September 2005.
2 'Korean Confucianism', *Stanford Encyclopedia of Philosophy*, https:// plato.stanford.edu, accessed 13 December 2023.
3 Khin Khin Aye, 'The Nature of Sinitic Lexicon in Bazaar Malay and Baba Malay in Singapore', in *Sinophone Southeast Asia: Sinitic Voices across the Southern Seas*, vol. XX, ed. Caroline Chia and Tom Hoogervorst (Leiden and Boston, MA, 2021), pp. 129–52 (p. 130).
4 Antoinette M. Barrett Jones, *Early Tenth Century Java from the Inscriptions* (Dordrecht, 1984), p. 36.
5 Ibid.
6 Jan Wisseman, 'Markets and Trade in Pre-Majapahit Java', in *Economic Exchange and Social Interaction in Southeast Asia: Perspectives from Prehistory, History, and Ethnography*, ed. Karl L. Hutterer (Ann Arbor, MA, 1977), pp. 197–212 (p. 197).
7 Ibid.
8 Ibid., p. 204.
9 Nedi Putra Aw, 'Kediri's Bah Kacung Tofu: Tradition Matters', *Jakarta Post*, www.thejakartapost.com, 21 February 2017.
10 'Tahu Takwa', *Pemkot Kediri*, www.kedirikota.go.id, 8 April 2019.
11 Cornelius Helmy, 'Sumedang Tofu, Delicious Thanks to Tampomas Water', *Kompas*, http://travel.kompas.com, 7 January 2012.
12 Wang Dayuan, *A Brief Account of Island Barbarians* [1349], ebook, *Chinese Text Project*, www.ctext.org, accessed 30 July 2022.
13 See http://theuntoldhistoryofwomen.tumblr.com, accessed 1 August 2022.
14 'How to Grow Soya Beans', *Royal Horticultural Society*, www.rhs.org.uk, accessed 20 July 2023.

15 Joanna Rose McFarland, 'Language Contact and Lexical Changes in Khmer and Teochew in Cambodia and Beyond', in *Sinophone Southeast Asia*, vol. xx, ed. Chia and Hoogervorst, pp. 91–128 (pp. 101–2).

16 See 'Thailand: Chinese', *Minority Rights*, www.minorityrights.org, accessed 13 August 2022.

17 Aranya Siriphon Fanzura Banu and Pagon Gatchalee, 'New Chinese Migrants to Thailand Hit with Negative Stereotypes, Language Barrier Form "Parallel Communities"', *South China Morning Post*, www.scmp.com, 31 March 2022.

18 Ernest Young, *Kingdom of the Yellow Robe, Being Sketches of the Domestic and Religious Rites and Ceremonies of the Siamese* (London, 1898), pp. 9–10.

19 Ibid., p. 11.

20 'Grass Jelly (Chao kuai)', *Taste Atlas*, www.tasteatlas.org, accessed 13 August 2022.

21 'A Day in Ratchaburi: Savour the Flavours in the Land of the Thai–Chinese–Mon', *Michelin Guide*, https://guide.michelin.com, 2 October 2020.

22 Henri Mouhot, *Travels in the Central Parts of Indo-China (Siam), Cambodia, and Laos, during the Years 1858, 1849, and 1860*, vol. I (London, 1864), p. 44.

23 Ibid., p. 245.

24 David Chandler, *A History of Cambodia* (Boulder, CO, 2008), p. 12.

25 Ibid., pp. 80–81.

26 Ibid., p. 8.

27 Mouhot, *Travels*, p. 110.

28 Japan International Cooperation Agency, *Country Study for Japan's Official Development Assistance to the Kingdom of Cambodia – From Reconstruction to Sustainable Development* (Tokyo, 2002), p. 48.

29 See Stephanie Belfield, Christine Brown and Robert Martin, 'A Guide to Upland Cropping in Cambodia: Soybean', ACIAR *Monograph Series*, CXLVI (Canberra, 2011).

30 Tom Starkey, 'Multi-Billion $ Global Vegan Market Sprouting Roots in Cambodia', *Khmer Times*, www.khmertimeskh.com, 15 January 2021.

31 Mech Choulay, 'Cambodian Youth Go Vegetarian Out of Climate Awareness', *Newsroom Cambodia*, www.newsroomcambodia.com,

8 October 2019; 'u.s. Food Grade Soybeans Ship to Cambodia and Myanmar for First Full-Scale Trials', *Healthy Food Ingredients*, www.hfifamily.com, 5 March 2018; Sam Jones, 'Net Loss: Fish Stocks Dwindle in Cambodia's Tonlé Sap Lake', *The Guardian*, 1 December 2015.

32 R. Talbot Kelly, *Peeps at Many Lands: Burma* (London, 1908), p. 46.

33 Hla Kyi, 'Nutrition and Health of Tofu', *Taste Window Magazine*, www.tastewindowmagazine.com, 29 September 2015.

34 Thu Thu Aung and Poppy Mcpherson, 'Monk Militia: The Buddhist Clergy Backing Myanmar's Junta', *Reuters*, www.reuters.com, 8 December 2022.

35 International Crisis Group, 'Buddhism and State Power in Myanmar', *Asia Report*, no. 290 (Brussels, 2017).

36 Duncan McCargo, 'Buddhism, Democracy and Identity in Thailand', *Democratization*, XI/4 (2004), pp. 155–70.

37 Sophie Shiori Umeyama and Will Brehm, 'The Power of Identity in Hybrid Peacebuilding: Buddhist Monks in Post-Conflict Cambodia', in *Operationalisation of Hybrid Peacebuilding in Asia*, ed. Yuji Uesugi et al. (Cham, 2022), pp. 81–97.

38 James J. Steward, 'The Question of Vegetarianism and Diet in Pāli Buddhism', *Journal of Buddhist Ethics*, XVII (2010), pp. 100–140 (pp. 110–11).

39 Johanna Son, 'Plant-Based Food Finds Its Way into Post-Pandemic Menu', *Cambodianess*, www.cambodianess.com, 2 March 2021.

40 Jovan Maud, 'The Nine Emperor Gods at the Border: Transnational Culture, Alternate Modes of Practice, and the Expansion of the Vegetarian Festival in Hat Yai', in *Dynamic Diversity in Southern Thailand*, ed. Wattana Sugunnasil (Chiang Mai, 2005), pp. 153–78 (p. 166).

41 Andrew Spooner, 'Phuket Taoist Vegetarian Festival', *The Guardian*, www.theguardian.com, 20 November 2009; Maud, 'Nine Emperor Gods', p. 161.

42 Maud, 'Nine Emperor Gods', p. 173.

43 Ibid., p. 165.

44 Mark Padoongpatt, *Flavors of Empire: Food and the Making of Thai America* (Oakland, CA, 2017), p. 49.

45 Alphonse de Candolle, *Origin of Cultivated Plants* (New York, 1908), pp. 330–31.

46 Ibid., p. 330.

47 Ibid., pp. 331–2.

48 Hiroyuki Horio and Tomoko Yokoyama, 'Food Culture of the Muromachi, the Azuchimomoyama Era', *Journal of the Natural Scientific Society of Nagoya Keizai University*, XLIX/1–2 (2016), pp. 35–50.

49 'The History of Tofu', *Japan Tofu Association*, www.tofu-as.com, accessed 2 July 2022.

50 'Introduction to "Tofu"', *Minokichi*, www.minokichi.net, 11 April 2022.

51 Yoko Hatta, 'The Transition of Dengaku Cuisine from the Edo Period to the Present', *Journal of Food Culture Research*, XI (2015), pp. 25–34.

52 Nobuko Hashizume, 'Food Business: Ryōri Chaya', in *Fundamental Materials for Historical Research of Japanese Food Culture*, ed. Research Center for Japanese Food Culture and Kyoto Research Center for Japanese Food Culture (2019), pp. 54–61.

53 'Gion's Much Loved Dengaku Tofu at a 480-Year-Old Teahouse', *Kateigaho*, www.kateigaho.com, 11 May 2018.

54 Eric Rath, *Food and Fantasy in Early Modern Japan* (Berkeley, Los Angeles, CA, and London, 2010), p. 115.

55 Stuart Iles, 'Edict of 1635 and Its Inception', *Japanese History and Culture*, www.rekishinihon.com, 10 May 2013.

56 'The Flowering of the Ranking Chart (Banzuke) Culture', *Edo Tokyo Digital Museum*, www.library.metro.tokyo.lg.jp, accessed 8 August 2022.

57 Eric C. Rath, 'The Tastiest Dish in Edo: Print, Performance and Culinary Entertainment in Early-Modern Japan', *East Asian Publishing and Society*, III/2, ed. Peter F. Kornicki (2013), pp. 184–214 (p. 186).

58 Ibid., pp. 207–8.

59 'Tofu Hyakuchin: Tofu Cookbooks of Edo', *Toyama Prefecture Tofu Chamber of Commerce and Industry*, www.toyama-smenet.or.jp, accessed 8 August 2022.

60 See www.tofu-as.com, accessed 8 August 2022.

61 'Bizen-ya Main Store', *Okazaki Kanko*, www.okazaki-kanko.jp, accessed 11 August 2022.

62 Pauline Cherrier, 'Japanese Immigrants in Brazil and Brazilian Dekasseguis in Japan: Continuity of the Migration's Imaginary

vs. Reality', in *Japanese Society and Brazilian Migrants: New Paths in the Formation of a Network of Researchers*, ed. Chiyoko Mita et al. (Tokyo, 2008), pp. 37–43.

63 'Japanese Community Situations before and after the Outbreak of the War between Japan and the U.S.', *National Diet Library*, www.ndl.go.jp, accessed 22 July 2022.

64 Koji Sasaki, 'Between Emigration and Immigration: Japanese Emigrants to Brazil and Their Descendants in Japan', *Senri Ethnological Reports: Transnational Migration in East Asia Japan in a Comparative Focus*, LXXVII, ed. Shinji Yamashita et al. (Tokyo, 2008), pp. 53–66 (p. 54).

65 Célia Sakurai, 'From the Passengers of the Kasato Maru to Varig Airplanes: Who Were the Immigrants?', in *Resistance and Integration: 100 Years of Japanese Immigration in Brazil*, ed. Célia Sakurai (Rio de Janeiro, 2008), pp. 127–8.

66 See 'La colonia china en Nicaragua', *Noticias de Taiwan*, http://noticias.nat.gov.tw, 6 April 2011; 'Mandarin Chinese in Nicaragua', *Joshua Project*, www.joshuaproject.net, accessed 27 July 2022.

67 Lisa Lee, 'Instead of Silence: Chinese Nicaraguans and the Formation of Identity across Two Cultures', *Independent Study Project (ISP) Collection*, 2334 (2016), pp. 15–16.

68 Scarlett Lindeman, 'How Chinese Food Became a Mexico City Staple', *Eater*, www.eater.com, 23 May 2016.

69 Nico Vera, 'Tiradito Nikkei (Peruvian Sashimi)', *Pisco Trail*, www.piscotrail.com, 14 May 2015; Simona Stano, 'Glocalised Foodscapes: The Self, the Other and the Frontier', *Glocalism*, III (2020), p. 14.

70 Noe Tanigawa, 'Hawai'i Tofu Chronicles', *Hawaii Public Radio*, www.hawaiipublicradio.org, 10 May 2016.

71 Ibid.

72 Matteo Fumagalli, '"Identity through Difference": Liminal Diasporism and Generational Change among the Koryo Saram in Bishkek, Kyrgyzstan', *European Journal of Korean Studies*, ed. James Lewis and Robert Winstanley-Chesters, XX/2 (2021), pp. 1–47 (pp. 46–7).

73 Jayoung Francesca-Maria Shin, 'Being a "Soviet Korean" in Alma-Ata, Kazakhstan', PhD thesis, London School of Economics and

Political Science, British Library of Political and Economic Science, 2006, p. 22.

74 Ibid., p. 146.

75 'Sparzha – Asparagus', *Tasting Russia*, tastingrussia.blogspot.com, 8 November 2009.

76 'Sparzha – Kazakhstan-inspired "Korean" Salad * Салат со спаржей', at www.facebook.com/vegetaristan, 9 September 2016.

77 Sophia Rehm, 'Korean Sparzha: The Soy Dish That Took the USSR by Storm', *Folkways*, www.folkways.today, 21 November 2018.

78 Shim Seung-koo, 'Joposa Temple and Jingwansa Temple in the Joseon Dynasty – Focused on the Change of Joposa Temple and the Tofu of Jingwansa Temple', *Comparative Folklore*, LXX (2019), pp. 199–240.

79 'Joposa', *Sillokwiki*, http://dh.aks.ac.kr, accessed 28 August 2022.

80 Shin Seong-min, 'Explore the History and Culture of Jingwansa Temple through "Tofu"', *Hyundai Buddhist Newspaper*, www.hyunbulnews.com, 15 July 2019.

81 Shin, 'Being a "Soviet Korean"', p. 150.

82 Ibid., p. 153.

83 Ibid., p. 161.

84 Jie Wang and Josh Stenberg, 'Localizing Chinese Migrants in Africa: A Study of the Chinese in Libya before the Civil War', *China Information*, ed. Tak-Wing Ngo, XXVIII/1 (2014), pp. 69–91 (p. 78).

85 Ibid., p. 80.

86 Ibid., pp. 81–2.

87 Beibei Yang, 'Understanding Mobility: Motivation, Recruitment, and Migration of Chinese Foremen to Zambia', *Cambridge Journal of China Studies*, XI/1 (2016), pp. 129–40 (p. 137).

88 Zhengli Huang, 'Rwanda Market in Addis Ababa: Between Chinese Migrants and a Local Food Network', *China Perspectives*, IV (2019), pp. 17–25.

89 Ibid., pp. 20–22.

90 Seth Cook et al., 'Chinese Migrants in Africa: Facts and Fictions from the Agri-Food Sector in Ethiopia and Ghana', *World Development*, LXXXI (2016), pp. 61–70 (p. 65).

91 Seth Cook and Dawit Alemu, 'Jumping into the Sea: Chinese Migrants' Engagement in Non-Traditional Agricultural

Commodities in Ethiopia', *Future Agricultures: Working Paper* 121 (2015), pp. 1–26 (pp. 8–9).

92 Federica Guccini and Mingyuan Zhang, '"Being Chinese" in Mauritius and Madagascar: Comparing Chinese Diasporic Communities in the Western Indian Ocean', *Journal of Indian Ocean World Studies*, IV/2 (2021), pp. 91–117 (p. 94).

93 Ibid., p. 92; Yunnan Chen and David G. Landry, 'Where Africa Meets Asia: Chinese Agricultural and Manufacturing Investment in Madagascar', *SAIS China–Africa Research Initiative Working Paper Series*, V (2016), pp. 1–35 (p. 3).

94 Janice Leung Hayes, 'How Mauritius Became a Hotbed of Chinese Food', *South China Morning Post*, www.scmp.com, 29 December 2016.

95 J. B. Hussein et al., 'Chemical Composition and Sensory Qualities of West African Soft Cheese (Warankashi) produced from Blends of Cow Milk and Soymilk', *Nigerian Journal of Tropical Agriculture*, XVI (2016), pp. 79–89 (p. 80).

96 Dalia Mohamedkheir Khojely et al., 'History, Current Status, and Prospects of Soybean Production and Research in Sub-Saharan Africa', *Crop Journal*, VI/3 (2018), pp. 226–35.

97 Hirokazu Nakamura, 'Soya Bean Curd and Labyrinth of Its Distribution in Nigeria', in *A Great Scholar and Linguist: A Festschrift in Honour of Professor Ibrahim Ahmad Mukoshy*, ed. S. A. Yakasai et al. (Sokoto, 2016), pp. 578–91.

98 Haruki Ishikawa and Ryo Matsumoto, 'Diversified Approaches to Evaluate Wide Genetic Resources of Cowpea for Enhancing New Variety Development for West Africa and Its Social Implementation by Cowpea Research Program of IITA', *Japan Agricultural Research Quarterly*, LV (2021), pp. 443–62 (p. 450).

99 Bolaji O. Akanbi and Ekaete A. Usoh, 'Safety of Street-Vended Soy Wara in Nigeria', *Journal of Food Protection*, LXXIX/1 (2016), pp. 169–73; Nakamura, 'Soya Bean Curd', p. 1.

100 Nakamura, 'Soya Bean Curd', pp. 4, 7.

101 Ibid., p. 7.

102 Osamu Nakayama and Sidi Osho, *Tofu Recipes: Introducing Tofu (Soy Cheese) into Traditional African Foods* (Ibadan, 1996).

103 Khojely et al., 'History, Current Status, and Prospects of Soybean Production'.

104 Ibid.

105 Ibid.
106 'Chinese Taste for Tofu Fuels Kenya Soybean Boom', CGTN Africa,
      www.youtube.com, 22 September 2020.

FOUR TOFU'S JOURNEY TO THE WEST

1 Robert Kerr, ed., 'Travels of Two Mahomedans in India
    and China, in the Ninth Century', in A General History and
    Collection of Voyages and Travels, vol. 1 (Edinburgh and London,
    1824), p. 55.
2 Joumana Accad, 'Soapwort Meringue (Natef)', Taste of Beirut,
    www.tasteofbeirut.com, 23 April 2012.
3 Anissa Helou, 'Natef: A Miraculous Transformation', Anissas,
    www.anissas.com, 29 September 2022.
4 'Cold Food Festival and Annin Dofu', Kogetu, www.kogetu.co.jp,
    26 August 2016.
5 Jia Sixie, Qimin Yaoshu [544], ebook, ed. Miao Chiyu, The Annotated
    Qimin Yaoshu (Beijing, 1982).
6 Hyunhee Park, Mapping the Chinese and Islamic Worlds: Cross-Cultural
    Exchange in Pre-Modern Asia (New York, 2012), p. 25.
7 Ibid., pp. 68–9.
8 Vocabolario da lingoa de Japam, com adeclaracão em portugues, feito por
    alguns Padres e Irmãos da Companhia de Jesus (Nagasaki, 1603), p. 259.
9 John Saris, 'Eighth Voyage of the English East India Company,
    in 1611, by Captain John Saris', in A General History and Collection
    of Voyages and Travels, vol. IX, ed. Robert Kerr (Edinburgh and
    London, 1824).
10 Ibid.
11 Japan Dairy Association, The History of Milk in Japan: How Milk
    and Dairy Products Took Root in the Daily Lives of the Japanese (Tokyo,
    2020), p. 1.
12 Richard Cocks, Diary of Richard Cocks, vol. 1: Cape-Merchant in the
    English Factory in Japan 1615–1622 with Correspondence, ed. Edward
    Maunde Thompson (New York, 1883).
13 Thomas H. Reilly, The Taiping Heavenly Kingdom: Rebellion and the
    Blasphemy of Empire (Seattle, WA and London, 2004), pp. 43–51.
14 Domingo Fernández Navarrete, Tratados historicos, politicos, ethicos
    y religiosos de la monarchia de China (Madrid, 1676), pp. 347–8.

15 Isabella L. Bird, *Unbeaten Tracks in Japan: An Account of Travels in the Interior Including Visits to the Aborigines of Yezo and the Shrine of Nikko* (London, 1911), pp. 195–6.

16 Ernest Satow, *A Diplomat in Japan* [1921] (New York and Tokyo, 2003), p. 204.

17 Eliza Ruhamah Scidmore, *Jinrikisha Days in Japan* (New York, 1891), p. 161.

18 Julian Street, *Mysterious Japan* (Garden City, NY, and Toronto, 1921), p. 46.

19 Jukinchi Inouye, *Home Life in Tokyo* (Tokyo, 1910), p. i.

20 Ibid., p. 74.

21 Bird, *Unbeaten Tracks*, p. 74.

22 Ibid., p. 146.

23 Ibid., p. 148.

24 Ibid., p. 129.

25 Ibid., p. 19.

26 Frances Little, *The Lady of the Decoration* [1906], ebook, available at www.gutenberg.org, accessed 20 August 2022.

27 Elizabeth Bisland, *The Life and Letters of Lafcadio*, vol. I (Boston, MA, and New York, 1906), p. 91.

28 Ibid., pp. 91–2.

29 Marie Stopes, *A Journal from Japan* (London, 1908), p. 248.

30 Navarrete, *Tratados*, p. 348.

31 Ernest W. Clement, 'Japan as it Was and Is': *A Handbook of Old Japan* (Chicago, IL, 1906), p. 217.

32 Philip A. Towle, 'Japanese Treatment of Prisoners in 1904–1905 – Foreign Officers' Reports', *Military Affairs*, XXXIX/3 (1975), pp. 115–18; Eric Johnston, 'Civility Shown to Russo-Japanese War POWs Lives On as Matsuyama's Legacy', *Japan Times*, www.japantimes.co.jp, 22 August 2016.

33 Little, *Lady of the Decoration*.

34 J. W. Robertson Scott, *The Foundations of Japan: Notes Made during Journeys of 6,000 Miles in the Rural Districts as a Basis for a Sounder Knowledge of the Japanese People* (London, 1922), pp. 311–12.

35 Alexander Hosie, *Three Years in Western China: A Narrative of Three Journeys in Ssu-ch'uan, Kuei-chow, and Yün-nan* (London and Liverpool, 1897), p. 68.

36 George Ernest Morrison, *An Australian in China* (London, 1902), pp. 86–7.

37 John MacGowan, *Sidelights on Chinese Life* (London, 1907), p. 9.

38 Ibid., pp. 162–3.

39 Scott, *Foundations of Japan*, p. 251.

40 Roy Chapman Andrews and Yvette Borup Andrews, *Camps and Trails in China: A Narrative of Exploration, Adventure, and Sport in Little-Known China* (New York and London, 1918), p. 74.

41 Ibid., p. 106.

42 Ibid., p. 113.

43 Kate Rose, 'Just like Us: Elizabeth Kendall's Imperfect Quest for Equality', *Journal of Feminist Scholarship*, XIV (Spring 2018), pp. 40–54. See Elizabeth Kendall, *A Wayfarer in China: Impressions of a Trip Across West China and Mongolia* (Boston, MA, and New York, 1913), p. 110.

44 Kendall, *Wayfarer in China*, p. 144.

45 Ibid., pp. 109–10.

46 Ibid., p. 38.

47 Andrew Elliott, 'British Travel Writing and the Japanese Interior, 1854–89', in *The British Abroad since the Eighteenth Century*, vol. I: *Travellers and Tourists*, ed. Martin Farr and Xavier Guégan (Basingstoke, 2013), pp. 197–216.

48 Sarah Baxter, 'A Brief History of the Package Holiday', *The Guardian*, www.theguardian.com, 14 June 2013. See 'Inflation Calculator', *Bank of England*, www.bankofengland.co.uk, accessed 14 June 2023.

49 Pamela Roper Wagner, 'Tracking Down Tofu: Library Research in the U.S.', *Oxford English Dictionary*, https://public.oed.com, 14 August 2012.

50 Kaitlin Miller, 'United States of Food: Official State Foods', *Daily Meal*, www.thedailymeal.com, 13 November 2019.

51 See 'Eating Tofu: The Original Patriot Act?', PETA, www.peta.org, 27 October 2011.

52 'Of the Luk-Taw, or Chinese Vetches', *The London Magazine; or, Gentleman's Monthly Intelligencer*, XXXVI (1767), p. 237.

53 T. Hymowitz and J. R. Harlan, 'Introduction of Soybean to North America by Samuel Bowen in 1765', *Economic Botany*, XXXVII/4 (1983), pp. 371–9.

54 Alkira Reinfrank and Bernice Chan, 'How Tofu Made It to America, Was Disparaged for Decades but Went Mainstream When 1960s Counterculture Exploded', *South China Morning Post*, www.scmp.com, 15 November 2020.

55 *Quong Hop Soy Deli*, www.quonghop.com, 12 July 2000 [archived].

56 Katharine Mieszkowski, 'Tofu Maker Is Idled after Recall of Products', *New York Times*, www.nytimes.com, 5 August 2010.

57 'Soy Deli and Quong Hop Tofu Is Recalled', *United Press International*, www.upi.com, 20 September 2007.

58 Susan C. Kim, 'As American as Tofu', *Hyphen*, www.hyphenmagazine.com, 1 September 2010.

59 Shigeru Kojima, 'The Immigrants Who Introduced Japanese Foods to the Americas (Part 1: North America)', *Kikkoman Food Culture*, XXII (2012), p. 6.

60 Abby Narishkin et al., 'How America's Oldest Tofu Shop Makes 3,000 Pounds of Homemade Tofu Every Day', *Business Insider*, www.businessinsider.com, 7 December 2021.

61 Alphonse de Candolle, *Origin of Cultivated Plants* (New York, 1908), pp. 330–32.

62 Department of Home Economics, University of Illinois, *Let's Use Soybeans* (Urbana, IL, 1914).

63 Dr J. H. Kellogg, 'The Soy Bean', in *Northern Nut Growers Association: Report of the Proceedings at the Tenth Annual Meeting* (Battle Creek, MI, 1919).

64 Ibid.

65 Moses King, ed., *King's Handbook of New York City* (Boston, MA, 1892), p. 144.

66 Ibid., p. 214.

67 Tcheng-Ki-Tong [Chen Jitong], *Chin-Chin or The Chinaman at Home*, trans. R. H. Sherard (London, 1895), p. 97.

68 Morrison, *Australian in China*, p. 87.

69 Edward Spencer, *Cakes and Ale: A Dissertation on Banquets*, 4th edn (London, 1913), pp. 91–2.

70 Matthew Roth, 'The Chinese-Born Doctor Who Brought Tofu to America', *Smithsonian Magazine*, www.smithsonianmag.com, 13 August 2018.

71 Sun Yat-sen, *The International Development of China* (New York and London, 1922), p. 155.

72 Ibid., pp. 206–7.
73 John Gong, 'A New Republic Born Out of Tofu', *China Global Television Network*, http://news.cgtn.com, 1 April 2019.
74 Scott, *Foundations of Japan*, pp. 350–51.
75 Mildred M. Lager, *The Useful Soybean: A Plus Factor in Modern Living* (New York, 1945), p. 242.
76 B. Aubrey Schneider, 'The Useful Soybean: A Plus Factor in Modern Living. Mildred Lager', *Quarterly Review of Biology*, XXI/1 (1946), p. 99.
77 Bob Brown, *The Complete Book of Cheese* (New York, 1955).
78 Andrea Nguyen, *Asian Tofu: Discover the Best, Make Your Own, and Cook It at Home* (New York, 2012), p. 4.
79 Reinfrank and Chan, 'How Tofu Made It to America'.
80 David L. Wank and James Farrer, 'Chinese Immigrants and Japanese Cuisine in the United States: A Case of Culinary Glocalization', in *The Globalization of Asian Cuisines*, ed. James Farrer (New York, 2015), p. 82.
81 Ibid.
82 Pete Wells, 'When He Dined, the Stars Came Out', *New York Times*, www.nytimes.com, 8 May 2012.
83 Victoria Moran, 'Unsung Heroes: Where Would We Be without Them?', *Vegetarian Times*, CLX (1990), p. 22.
84 Nguyen, *Asian Tofu*, p. 4.
85 Patricia Wells, 'What Is This Thing Called Tofu?', *New York Times*, www.nytimes.com, 3 May 1978.
86 Sandor Ellix Katz, *The Art of Fermentation* (White River Junction, VT, 2012), p. 285.
87 Victoria Moran and Sharon Bloyd-Peshkin, 'Down on The Farm', *Vegetarian Times*, CLX (1990), p. 32.
88 Douglas Stevenson, *The Farm Then and Now: A Model for Sustainable Living* (Gabriola Island, 2014), p. 92.
89 Priya Fielding-Singh, *How the Other Half Eats: The Untold Story of Food and Inequality in America* [2021], ebook.
90 Lee Khang Yee, 'Making Better Tofu', *Woods Macrobiotics*, www.healthyfoodmalaysia.com, 28 September 2015.
91 Aindrisha Mitra, 'Not Just a Bland Cousin of Paneer: Why Tofu Is Finding Many Takers', *Reader's Digest India*, www.readersdigest.in, 27 August 2020.

92 Katherine Bishop, 'Who'll Sell Tofu Puffs after Co-Ops Are Gone?', *New York Times*, 6 June 1988.

93 Kathleen Doheny, 'The Joy of Soy', *Los Angeles Times*, 27 April 1998.

94 Joanne Ostrow, 'Tofu! Tofu! The Attack of the Orient's All-Purpose, Do-It-Yourself Miracle Food', *Washington Post*, 7 January 1983.

95 Wendy Lin, 'Breakthrough: Soy That Tastes Good!', *Washington Post*, 8 February 2000.

96 Jonathan Reynolds, 'Food; Do You Tofu?', *New York Times*, www.nytimes.com, 5 November 2000.

97 Oliver Thring, 'Consider Tofu', *The Guardian*, 3 August 2010.

98 Fuchsia Dunlop, 'Tofu Is a Cornucopia of Taste. No Really', *Financial Times*, www.ft.com, 25 June 2022.

99 Larissa Zimberoff, 'Tofu Goes Mainstream in America Thanks to Big Meat's Covid Crisis', *Bloomberg*, www.bloomberg.com, 11 June 2020.

100 Adam Brown, 'How Tofurky Carves up Profits', *Inc.*, www.inc. com, 23 November 2011.

101 Jane Kauer, 'The World of Soy' [review], *Expedition Magazine*, LII/2 (July 2010), available at www.penn.museum/sites/expedition, accessed 18 March 2024.

FIVE 'EATING TOFU' AND ITS PLACE IN CULTURE

1 Jia-Chen Fu, 'The World of Soy' [review], *East Asian Science, Technology, and Medicine*, XXXV/1 (2012), pp. 161–5.

2 'Ana-doro', CD Tacto, www.tacto.jp, accessed 11 August 2022.

3 'Ana-doro', *Rakugo Sanpo* 落語散歩, http://sakamitisanpo.g.dgdg.jp, accessed 11 August 2022.

4 'Walking on the Stage of Rakugo: Ana-doro', *Walking on the Stage of Rakugo*, http://ginjo.fc2web.com, accessed 11 August 2022.

5 'Go Hit Your Head on the Corner of Tofu and Die', *Weblio*, www.weblio.jp, accessed 11 August 2022.

6 'Shine', *Jisho.org*, www.jisho.org, accessed 11 August 2022.

7 'Tōfu no tsuno ni atama butsukete shinde shimae jiken', *Kinokuniya*, www.kinokuniya.co.jp, accessed 11 August 2022.

8 'Trick a Ghost into Eating Tofu', *Learn Cantonese!*, www.cantonese. sheik.co.uk, accessed 12 August 2022.

9 Chan Sin-wai, 'Cantonese Culture', in *The Routledge Encyclopedia of Traditional Chinese Culture*, ed. Chan Sin-wai (London and New York, 2020), pp. 132–68 (p. 138).

10 'Cantonese Encyclopedia: in "Trick a Ghost into Eating Tofu", Who Is Eating Tofu?', *Xinhua*, www.xinhuanet.com, 26 August 2017.

11 Wang Ji, *The Original Meeting of Things* [1796], ebook, *Chinese Text Project*, www.ctext.org, accessed 2 June 2023.

12 Jiang Qinjian, 'A Discussion of "Chi Doufu Fan" as a Funeral Activity', *Central Plains Culture Research*, II (2019), pp. 81–4.

13 Robert S. Bauer, *ABC Cantonese–English Comprehensive Dictionary* (Honolulu, HI, 2020), p. 245.

14 'Cantonese Proverbs in One Picture', *Blog of Cantonese Resources*, https://writecantonese8.wordpress.com, 25 February 2014.

15 Andrew B. Kipnis, *The Funeral of Mr. Wang: Life, Death, and Ghosts in Urbanizing China* (Oakland, CA, 2021), p. 7.

16 Ibid., p. 13.

17 Ibid., p. 58.

18 Hee Sup Kim, 'Funeral Foods and Its Role as Vehicle of Communication', *Social Systems Research* [special issue] (July 2017), pp. 47–54 (p. 47).

19 Ibid., p. 49.

20 Ibid., p. 47.

21 Hwang Kyo-ik, 'Revealing the Reason Why People Eat Tofu When They Go to Prison: "When One Gets Out of Prison . . ."', *Sports Seoul*, www.sportsseoul.com, 21 May 2015.

22 '"Tofu Powerhouse" South Korea Now Most Depressed among Korea, Japan and China', *Joong Ang Ilbo Japanese Version*, https://japanese.joins.com, 29 March 2013.

23 Xie Yingfang, *Tortoise Nest Compositions* [unknown], ebook, *Chinese Text Project*, www.ctext.org, accessed 27 June 2023.

24 Julie Washington, 'The Magical Power of Cannibalism', *Crossroads*, VI/1 (2012), pp. 46–57.

25 Keith N. Knapp, 'Chinese Filial Cannibalism: A Silk Road Import?', in *China and Beyond in the Mediaeval Period: Cultural Crossings and Inter-Regional Connections*, ed. Dorothy C. Wong and Gustav Heldt (Singapore, 2014), pp. 135–49.

26 Ibid., p. 143.

27 Washington, 'Magical Power of Cannibalism', p. 53.

28 Knapp, 'Chinese Filial Cannibalism', p. 146.

29 Constance A. Cook, 'Moonshine and Millet: Feasting and Purification Rituals in Ancient China', in *Of Tripod and Palate: Food, Politics, and Religion in Traditional China*, ed. Roel Sterckx (New York, 2005), pp. 9–33 (p. 16).

30 Ibid.

31 Xian Wang, 'Flesh and Stone: Competing Narratives of Female Martyrdom from Late Imperial to Contemporary China', PhD thesis, University of Oregon, Scholars' Bank, 2018, p. 43.

32 Stuart M. McManus and Michael T. Tworek, 'A (Dis)entangled History of Early Modern Cannibalism: Theory and Practice in Global History', *Transactions of the Royal Historical Society*, XXXII (2022), pp. 47–72.

33 Robert Kerr, ed., 'Travels of Two Mahomedans in India and China, in the Ninth Century', in *A General History and Collection of Voyages and Travels*, vol. I (Edinburgh and London, 1824), p. 71.

34 Patricia Buckley Ebrey, Cong Ellen Zhang and Ping Yao, eds, 'Peaceful Abodes: Account of Their Homes by Yelü Chucai (1190–1244) and Xie Yingfang (1296–1392)', in *Chinese Autobiographical Writing: An Anthology of Personal Accounts*, ebook (Seattle, WA, 2023).

35 Wicky W. K. Tse, 'Cutting the Enemy's Line of Supply: The Rise of the Tactic and Its Use in Early Chinese Warfare', *Journal of Chinese Military History*, VI/2 (2017), pp. 131–56 (p. 132).

36 Qian Guohong, 'Bai qi rou', *Minzhuxie Shangbao*, http://site.mzxsb. com, 24 December 2021.

37 Ibid.

38 Cook, 'Moonshine and Millet', p. 17.

39 Ibid., p. 18.

40 'Dau fu po', 豆腐婆, *Learn Cantonese!*, www.cantonese.sheik.co.uk, 28 May 2007.

41 'In Guangdong, Guangxi, Hong Kong and Macau, the One Selling Pork Is Called Pork Wing, and the One Selling Tofu Is Called Tofu Guy', *Toutiao*, www.toutiao.com, 29 September 2019.

42 Victor Mair, 'Vanity Plates, Writing Systems, and the Sexualization of Tofu', *Language Log*, https://languagelog.ldc. upenn.edu, 23 September 2011.

43 James Farrer, 'An Academic Diptych', *Gastronomica*, XXIII/1 (2023), pp. iv–ix.

44 Kiril Bolotnikov, 'Episode 7: Chinese Slang Game Show', *Asia Society*, www.asiasociety.org, accessed 1 August 2022.

45 Lin Chengyan, 'Sexual Harassment? Take Advantage? What Is the Origin of the Meaning of "Eating Tofu"?', *China Times*, www.chinatimes.com, 3 December 2017.

46 *A Waking Cry* [unknown], ebook, *Chinese Text Project*, www.ctext.org, accessed 1 August 2022.

47 Oiwan Lam, 'In Hong Kong, the Sexual Connotation of Ikea's New Tofu Ice Cream Ad Creates Controversy', *Global Voices*, www.globalvoices.com, 17 May 2019.

48 Matilda Baraibar Norberg and Lisa Deutsch, *The Soybean through World History: Lessons for Sustainable Agrofood Systems* (Oxford and New York, 2023), p. 63.

49 See 'Kotoyōka', *Kotobank*, www.kotobank.jp, accessed 15 August 2022.

50 See 'Hari-kuyō', *Kotobank*, www.kotobank.jp, accessed 15 August 2022. 'In Japan, There Is a Custom of Cleaning Up and Holding a Memorial Service for Tools that He or She Used over the Year. A Typical Event of Holding a Memorial Service for Tools is the "Hari Kuyo," a Requiem Service for Broken Needles', *Shokunin.com*, http://en.shokunin.com, 29 January 2021.

51 Michael Ashkenazi, *Handbook of Japanese Mythology* (Santa Barbara, CA, Denver, CO and Oxford, 2003), p. 133.

52 Ibid., p. 171; Klaus Antoni, 'The "Separation of Gods and Buddhas" at Omiwa Shrine in Meiji Japan', *Japanese Journal of Religious Studies*, ed. Paul L. Swanson, Thomas L. Kirchner and Robert J. Kisala, XXII/1–2 (1995), pp. 139–59 (p. 143).

53 Ibid., p. 170.

54 *84th Congress, 2nd session, House of Representatives, Report No. 1792* (1956), p. 5. U. A. Casal, 'The Goblin Fox and Badger and Other Witch Animals of Japan', *Folklore Studies*, XVIII (1959), pp. 1–93 (p. 23).

55 Kiyoshi Nozaki, *Kitsuné: Japan's Fox of Mystery, Romance and Humor* (Tokyo, 1961), pp. 110–11.

56 'In Charge of Healthy Lunches, Izumi City School Launches Food Education Character "Kon-chan"', *Izumi City Board of*

Education and Children Department School Management Office,
www.city.osaka-izumi.lg.jp, 2 March 2020.

57 Casal, 'Goblin Fox and Badger', p. 8.

58 Nozaki, Kitsuné, p. 94.

59 Casal, 'Goblin Fox and Badger', p. 87.

60 Ibid., p. 32.

61 Ibid., p. 51.

62 Basil Hall Chamberlain and W. B. Mason, A Handbook for Travellers
in Japan: Including the Whole Empire from Yezo to Formosa, 6th edn
(London, 1901), p. 387.

63 Casal, 'Goblin Fox and Badger', p. 37.

64 Elizabeth Bisland, The Life and Letters of Lafcadio Hearn, vol. II
(Boston, MA, and New York, 1906), p. 30.

65 Yuki Miyamoto, 'Possessed and Possessing: Fox-Possession
and Discrimination against the Wealthy in the Modern
Period in Japan', Culture and Religion, VII/2 (2006), pp. 139–54
(p. 148).

66 Ashkenazi, Handbook of Japanese Mythology, p. 150.

67 Norman Havens, 'The Changing Face of Japanese Folk Beliefs',
in Folk Beliefs in Modern Japan, ed. Nobutaka Inoue (Tokyo, 1994),
pp. 227–46.

68 Miyamoto, 'Possessed and Possessing', p. 139.

69 Ibid., pp. 139–40.

70 Akira Nomura, 'Fox Possession: The Functioning of Social
Prejudice Originating from Primitive Belief', Psychologia, III
(1960), pp. 234–42 (p. 237).

71 Miyamoto, 'Possessed and Possessing', p. 140.

72 Nomura, 'Fox Possession', pp. 235–6.

73 Naomichi Takehara, 'About Tofu Kozō and Smallpox', Journal
of Japanese Medical History, LV/2 (2009), p. 161.

74 'Tofu Kozō', Warner Bros, www.warnerbros.co.jp, accessed
9 August 2022.

75 Sin-wai, 'Cantonese Culture', p. 166.

76 Ibid., p. 150.

77 Herbert A. Giles, A Chinese–English Dictionary (Shanghai and
London, 1892), p. 931.

78 Ibid., p. 376.

79 Ibid., p. 1127.

80 Lee Yee-chong, 'The Unsettled Hearts and Souls: Aftershock of the Great Sichuan Earthquake', in *Natural Disaster and Reconstruction in Asian Economies: A Global Synthesis of Shared Experiences*, ed. Kinnia Yau Shuk-ting (New York and Basingstoke, 2013), pp. 147–8.

81 Eve Cary, 'China's Dangerous Tofu Projects', *The Diplomat*, www.thediplomat.com, 10 February 2012.

82 Eric Fish, 'The Forgotten Legacy of the Banqiao Dam Collapse', *Economic Observer*, www.eeo.com.cn, 8 February 2013.

83 Lee, 'Unsettled Hearts and Souls', p. 149.

84 Robert C. Thornett, 'Belt and Road Hazards, Coming to the Americas', *American Affairs Journal*, v/3 (2021), pp. 133–56.

85 Jovian Parry, 'Edible Subjectivities: Meat in Science Fiction', PhD thesis, York University, 2019, p. 139.

86 Helen Pidd, '"It's Not Woke": Braverman Dig Leaves Bitter Taste in Tory Tofu Capital', *The Guardian*, www.theguardian.com, 21 October 2022.

87 Jelisa Castrodale, 'A Brief History of Conservatives Using Tofu-Eating as an Insult', *Vice*, www.vice.com, 17 September 2018.

88 Iselin Gambert and Tobias Linne, 'From Rice Eaters to Soy Boys: Race, Gender, and Tropes of "Plant Food Masculinity"', *Animal Studies Journal*, vii/2 (2018), pp. 129–79 (pp. 133–4).

89 Vasile Stănescu, 'The Whopper Virgins: Hamburgers, Gender, and Xenophobia in Burger King's Hamburger Advertising', in *Meat Culture*, ed. Annie Potts (Leiden and Boston, MA, 2017), pp. 90–108 (p. 95).

90 Ibid.

91 e. melanie du puis, 'Angels and Vegetables: A Brief History of Food Advice in America', *Gastronomica*, vii/3 (2007), pp. 34–44 (p. 40).

92 Samuel Gompers and Herman Gudstadt, *Meat vs. Rice: American Manhood vs. Asiatic Coolieism, Which Shall Survive?* (San Francisco, CA, 1908), p. 13.

93 Gabriele Griffin, *Dictionary of Gender Studies* (Oxford, 2017).

94 Carol J. Adams and Matthew Calarco, 'Derrida and *The Sexual Politics of Meat*', in *Meat Culture*, ed. Potts, pp. 31–53 (p. 33).

95 Ibid., p. 35.

96 'The New Currency of Man – Lion Red's Man Points', *Business Scoop*, https://business.scoop.co.nz, 10 February 2011;

Sarah Harvey, 'Ad-Men Tell Us What It Means to Be a Good Bloke', *Stuff*, www.stuff.co.nz, 6 March 2011.

97 A. A. Gill, 'Steak Shows Its Muscle', *Vanity Fair*, www.vanityfair.com, May 2013.

98 Castrodale, 'Tofu-Eating as an Insult'.

99 Bill Hoffman, 'Docs: Soy Boys Shoot Blanks', *New York Post*, www.nypost.com, 26 February 2004.

100 Castrodale, 'Tofu-Eating as an Insult'.

101 Gambert and Linne, 'Rice Eaters to Soy Boys', pp. 131–2.

102 Ibid., pp. 137, 143.

103 Kristen Hartke, 'Tofu Sales Skyrocket during the Pandemic, as Consumers Search for Affordable Meat Alternatives', *Washington Post*, www.washingtonpost.com, 21 September 2020.

104 Larissa Zimberoff, 'Tofu Goes Mainstream in America Thanks to Big Meat's Covid Crisis', *Bloomberg*, www.bloomberg.com, 11 June 2020.

105 Pidd, 'It's Not Woke'.

SIX TOFU INC., THE BUSINESS OF BEAN CURD

1 Alys Key, 'How Tofu Makers The Tofoo Co Grew Sales by 89 Per Cent in 2020', *The i*, www.inews.co.uk, 1 February 2021.

2 George Steer and Madeleine Speed, 'Losses on Meat Alternatives Leave Investors with Sour Aftertaste', *Financial Times*, www.ft.com, 8 June 2023.

3 Kristen Hartke, 'Tofu Sales Skyrocket during the Pandemic, as Consumers Search for Affordable Meat Alternatives', *Washington Post*, www.washingtonpost.com, 21 September 2020.

4 Maria Chiorando, 'Sales of Tofu Skyrocketed by 81% amid COVID–19 Lockdown in UK', *Plant Based News*, www.plantbasednews.org, 11 August 2020.

5 'United Kingdom Tofu Market Size and Share Analysis', *Mordor Intelligence*, www.mordorintelligence.com, accessed 16 July 2022.

6 'Tofu Market Size and Share Analysis', *Mordor Intelligence*, www.mordorintelligence.com, accessed 2 June 2023.

7 'Plant-Based Foods Market to Hit $162 Billion in Next Decade, Projects Bloomberg Intelligence', *Bloomberg*, www.bloomberg.com, 11 August 2021.

8 'Tofu: Increasingly Appreciated by Italian Consumers', *Atlante*, www.atlantesrl.it, 2 March 2023.

9 Purity Wanjohi, 'Vegan Tofu: Mtofu Founders Make Soybean Food and Find a Ready Market', *Business Daily Africa*, www.businessdailyafrica.com, 11 November 2022.

10 Isabel Nepstad, 'The Dual Identity of Soybeans and Their Sustainability Opportunities', *Dialogo Chino*, www.dialogochino.net, 11 October 2021.

11 Morgan Smith, 'House Foods America Building New Tofu Plant', *Pro Food World*, www.profoodworld.com, 29 April 2021.

12 Key, 'Tofoo Co Grew Sales by 89 per cent'.

13 'The Tofoo Co. Continues to Skyrocket, Imports Soy Machinery from Japan to Keep Up with Production Demand', *Vegconomist*, www.vegconomist.com, 18 June 2020.

14 Michelle Perrett, 'The Tofoo Co Set for Further Expansion Despite "Tofu Phobia"', *Food Manufacture*, www.foodmanufacture.co.uk, 17 June 2020.

15 For Tofu King, see 'Independent Tofu Producer to Open UK's Largest Dedicated Tofu Facility by End 2020', *Vegconomist*, www.vegconomist.com, 20 July 2020.

16 'Performance Trend Survey of 591 Domestic Tofu Producers', *Tokyo Shoko Research*, www.tsr-net.co.jp, 14 August 2020.

17 Tatiana Sanchez, 'San Jose Tofu, Japantown Gem, Closes Its Doors after 71 Years', *Mercury News*, www.mercurynews.com, 30 December 2017.

18 'Young Employees Arbitrarily "Cut the Corporate Identity of a Cool Company"! No. 8: Otokomae Tofuten', *Concan*, www.concan.co.jp, 1 February 2021.

19 Iris Vermeir and Gudrun Roose, 'Visual Design Cues Impacting Food Choice: A Review and Future Research Agenda', *Foods*, IX/10 (2020), pp. 1–59.

20 See www.handsometofu.com, accessed 11 August 2022.

21 Rupert Sutton, 'The Just-Food Interview – Shingo Ito, Otokomae Tofuten', *Just Food*, www.just-food.com, 31 July 2007.

22 Florence Fabricant, 'Front Burner: Tofu That Can Make You Smile', *New York Times*, www.nytimes.com, 12 March 2018.

23 Satoshi Iizuka, 'FOCUS: Tofu Shops Facing Fight for Survival amid Rising Costs', *Kyodo News*, https://english.kyodonews.net, 14 August 2022.

24 Bee Wilson, 'Protein Mania: The Rich World's New Diet Obsession', *The Guardian*, www.theguardian.com, 4 January 2019.

25 '10 Gram Protein Tofu Bar', *Asahico*, www.asahico.co.jp, accessed 25 August 2022.

26 'History', *Sagamiya*, www.sagamiya-kk.co.jp, accessed 25 August 2022.

27 'American Soybeans Supporting Innovation in Tofu', U.S. Soy, www.ussoybean.jp, 4 October 2021.

28 'The 39th Food Hit Awards: No Grand Prize, 19 Excellent Hit Awards, 6 Long-Seller Awards', *Japan Food Journal*, http://news.nissyoku.co.jp, 23 December 2020.

29 'Tofu Is the Main Ingredient in Shōjin Ryōri Eaten by Monks', *Japan Tofu Association*, www.tofu-as.com, accessed 25 August 2022.

30 'Kiji-yaki', *Kotobank*, www.kotobank.jp, accessed 25 August 2022.

31 'Shigi-yaki', *Kotobank*, www.kotobank.jp, accessed 25 August 2022.

32 Preethi Ravi, 'How Traditional Tofu Brand Somenoya Is Evolving for the Plant-Based Era', *The Drum*, www.thedrum.com, 16 February 2023.

33 'About Tofoo', *Tofoo*, www.tofoo.co.uk, accessed 22 August 2022.

34 'Cauldron', *Protein Directory*, www.proteindirectory.com, accessed 22 August 2022.

35 'Hoisin Tofu Pieces', *Cauldron*, www.cauldronfoods.co.uk, accessed 22 August 2022.

36 'Quick and Tasty Tofu Block with Italian Herbs and Tomato', *Cauldron*, www.cauldronfoods.co.uk, accessed 22 August 2022.

37 Ligaya Mishan, 'Why Do American Diners Have Such a Limited Palate for Textures?', *New York Times*, www.nytimes.com, 8 May 2023.

38 Naoki Shino et al., 'A Framework to Collect Japanese Expression for Food Taste and Texture', *Procedia Computer Science*, XCVI (2016), pp. 1067–74 (p. 1068).

39 Anirban Dey et al., 'Tofu: Technological and Nutritional Potential', *Indian Food Industry Magazine*, LVI/5 (2017), p. 8.

40 Tegan Cruwys, Kirsten E. Bevelander and Roel C. J. Hermans, 'Social Modeling of Eating: A Review of When and Why Social

Influence Affects Food Intake and Choice', *Appetite*, LXXXVI (2015), pp. 3–18.

41 Vishwali Mhasawade et al., 'Role of the Built and Online Social Environments on Expression of Dining on Instagram', *International Journal of Environmental Research and Public Health*, XVII/3 (2020), p. 735.

42 Annur Khauirul, 'Fujiwara Tofu Shop: Initial D-Themed Cafe Has Arcade Racing, Black Tofu and a Toyota AE86 for Anime Fans', *The Smart Local Malaysia*, www.thesmartlocal.com, 13 May 2022.

43 Matthew Kang, 'Fans of Japanese Drift Car Series "Initial D" Are Blowing Up This San Gabriel Valley Tofu Cafe', *Eater Los Angeles*, http://la.eater.com, 2 February 2022.

44 Maggie Hiufu Wong, 'How "Bland" Tofu Became One of the World's Hottest Foods', CNN *Travel*, http://edition.cnn.com, 17 June 2022.

45 See www.an-soy.com, accessed 20 May 2023.

46 Sopida Rodsom, 'Mihara Tofuten', *Time Out Bangkok*, www.timeout.com/bangkok, 6 September 2018.

47 'Provoking Thai Taste Buds with Tofu', *Michelin Guide*, http://guide.michelin.com, 2 August 2018.

48 Eric C. Rath, 'The Invention of Local Food', in *The Globalization of Asian Cuisines*, ed. James Farrer (New York, 2015), pp. 145–64 (p. 158).

49 'Japanese Food Continues to Gain Popularity Overseas', *Japan Times*, www.japantimes.co.jp, 4 March 2022.

50 James Farrer, 'Introduction', in *The Globalization of Asian Cuisines*, ed. Farrer, pp. 1–19 (p. 10).

51 David L. Wank and James Farrer, 'Chinese Immigrants and Japanese Cuisine in the United States: A Case of Culinary Glocalization', in *The Globalization of Asian Cuisines*, ed. Farrer, pp. 79–99 (p. 82).

52 'Tofu Sorano', FOODGATE Co. Ltd., www.foodgate.net, accessed 12 August 2023.

53 See www.designandarchitecture.com, accessed 13 August 2022.

54 Catherine C. Ivanovich et al., 'Future Warming from Global Food Consumption', *Nature Climate Change*, XIII/3 (2023), pp. 297–302.

55 Gidon Eshel et al., 'Environmentally Optimal, Nutritionally
   Sound, Protein and Energy Conserving Plant Based Alternatives
   to U.S. Meat', *Scientific Reports*, IX/I (2019).

56 Gregory Meyer, Andres Schipani and Tom Hancock, 'Why
   Soyabeans Are the Crop of the Century', *Financial Times*,
   www.ft.com, 20 June 2017.

57 See 'Since Early 2000s, Growth in U.S. Soybean Planted Acreage
   Has Outpaced Corn and Wheat', *Economic Research Service, U.S.
   Department of Agriculture*, www.ers.usda.gov, accessed 1 May 2024.

58 Elin Röös et al., 'Less Meat, More Legumes: Prospects and
   Challenges in the Transition toward Sustainable Diets in Sweden',
   Renewable Agriculture and Food Systems, XXXII/2 (2020), pp. 192–205.

59 'Tofu Production: A Massive Opportunity for RE Biogas in
   Indonesia', REEEP, www.reeep.org, 18 May 2012.

60 Kevin Reilly and Lilian Manansala, 'Turning Tofu Waste into
   Natural Gas Is Helping to Clean Rivers in Indonesia', *Business
   Insider*, www.businessinsider.com, 28 November 2022.

61 Tao Li et al., 'Tofu Processing Wastewater as a Low-Cost
   Substrate for High Activity Nattokinase Production Using
   "*Bacillus subtilis*"', BMC *Biotechnology*, XXI/57 (2021), http://
   bmcbiotechnol.biomedcentral.com, accessed 16 June 2023.

62 'Tofu Production', REEEP.

63 Nick Perry, 'Clean Energy from Beans', *The Goan*,
   www.thegoan.net, 30 May 2016.

64 A. Gemardi et al., 'Use of Biogas from Tofu Industry for
   Domestic Use at Probolinggo City – Indonesia', IOP *Conference
   Series: Earth and Environmental Science*, CCLIX (2019), pp. 1–8 (p. 7).

65 'Tofu Production', REEEP; Reilly and Manansala, 'Turning Tofu
   Waste into Natural Gas'.

66 Fitria Febrianti, Khaswar Syamsu and Mulyorini Rahayuningsih,
   'Bioethanol Production from Tofu Waste by Simultaneous
   Saccharification and Fermentation (SSF) using Microbial
   Consortium', *International Journal of Technology*, VIII/5 (2017),
   pp. 898–908; 'What Is Bioethanol?', Energy Systems Research
   Unit, University of Strathclyde, www.esru.strath.ac.uk, accessed
   16 June 2023.

67 Gemilang Lara Utama et al., 'Electro-Stimulation of Tofu Wastewater for the Production of Single Cell Protein from Various

Microorganisms', *Saudi Journal of Biological Sciences*, xxx/7 (2023), pp. 1–10.

68 Ibid.

69 Tao Li et al., 'Tofu Processing Wastewater'.

70 Sladjana P. Stanojević et al., 'Composition of Proteins in Fresh Whey as Waste in Tofu Processing', *Journal of Environmental Science and Health, Part B*, LVIII/1 (2023), pp. 10–20.

71 Jethro Kang, 'Tofu Turns Tipsy: Meet the World's First Soy Wine', *Lifestyle Asia*, www.lifestyleasia.com, 1 November 2021.

72 Martina Colimoro et al., 'Environmental Impacts and Benefits of Tofu Production from Organic and Conventional Soybean Cropping: Improvement Potential from Renewable Energy Use and Circular Economy Patterns', *Environments*, x/5 (2023), www.mdpi.com, accessed 16 June 2023.

73 Mirjana B. Pešić et al., 'Okara-Enriched Gluten-Free Bread: Nutritional, Antioxidant and Sensory Properties', *Molecules*, XXVIII/10 (2023), www.mdpi.com, accessed 18 June 2023.

74 Ting Shien Teng, Jaslyn Jie Lin Lee and Wei Ning Chen, 'Ultrafiltrated Extracts of Fermented Okara as a Possible Serum Alternative for Cell Culturing: Potential in Cultivated Meat Production', ACS *Food Science and Technology*, III/4 (2023), pp. 699–709; Amy Woodyatt and Danielle Wiener-Bronner, 'Singapore Becomes First Country to Approve Lab-Grown Meat', CNN, http://edition.cnn.com, 2 December 2020.

75 Matt Reynolds, 'The Clean Meat Industry Is Racing to Ditch Its Reliance on Foetal Blood', *Wired*, www.wired.co.uk, 20 March 2018; Sally Ho, 'To Make Cell-Based Meat Cheaper and More Ethical, Researchers Use Tofu Waste', *Green Queen*, www.greenqueen.com.hk, 13 July 2021.

76 Wenjing Lu et al., 'Evaluation of the Quality of Whole Bean Tofu Prepared from High-Speed Homogenized Soy Flour', LWT – *Food Science and Technology*, CLXXII (2022), *Science Direct*, www.sciencedirect.com, accessed 20 July 2023.

77 Ibid.

78 See www.malnutritionmatters.org, accessed 2 July 2023.

79 Miranda Grizio, 'Soy Milk Solutions to Hunger', *Institute of Food Technologists*, www.ift.org, 1 July 2023.

80 Monika Sopov and Yared Sertse, *Setting Up Micro-Enterprises to Promote Soybean Utilization at Household Level in Ethiopia*, Centre for Development Innovation, Wageningen University and Research (2014), p. 4.

81 Ibid., p. 10.

82 Deresse Hunde Desissa, 'Soybean Research and Development in Ethiopia', ACTA *Scientific Agriculture*, III/10 (2019), pp. 192–4; Jane Byrne, 'Soybean Production on the Rise in Ethiopia', *FeedNavigator*, www.feednavigator.com, 12 July 2013.

83 'Ethiopia Production', *International Production Assessment Division, u.s. Department of Agriculture*, http://ipad.fas.usda.gov, accessed 20 July 2023.

84 Sopov and Sertse, 'Setting Up Micro-Enterprises', p. 10.

85 Monika Sopov, 'Soy – Promising Pulse in Ethiopia', *Wageningen University and Research*, www.wur.nl, accessed 20 July 2023.

86 Mengyu Li et al., 'Global Food-Miles Account for Nearly 20% of Total Food-Systems Emissions', *Nature Food*, III/6 (2022), pp. 445–53.

87 Arief Harsono et al., 'Soybean in Indonesia: Current Status, Challenges and Opportunities to Achieve Self-Sufficiency', in *Legumes Research*, vol. I, ed. Jose C. Jimenez-Lopez and Alfonso Clemente (2022), IntechOpen, www.intechopen.com, accessed 18 July 2023.

88 'Indonesia Tempe and Tofu Producers Hold Annual Meeting', *u.s. Soybean Export Council*, www.ussec.org, 25 February 2022; Etty Susilowati et al., 'The Evaluation of Cooperative's Role in Soybean Supply Chain: A Case Study on Tofu and Tempeh Cooperatives in Indonesia', *International Journal of Administrative Science and Organization*, XXI/2 (2014), pp. 121–7.

89 Harsono et al., 'Soybean in Indonesia'.

90 See 'Jakarta Tofu and Tempe Entrepreneurs Strike Production on January 1–3', *Suara*, www.suara.com, 1 January 2021.

91 See 'Indonesia Nightmare: No Tempe or Tofu for Your Meal', ASYX, www.asyx.com, 1 March 2022.

92 Kirk Maltais, 'Soybean Prices Hit Record as Inflation Stays Hot', *Wall Street Journal*, www.wsj.com, 13 June 2022; Joana Colussi, Gary Schnitkey and Carl Zulauf, 'Soybean Prices Rise as Drought in South America Reduces Harvest', *farmdoc daily*, XII/26 (2022), pp. 1–4.

93 Holly Demaree-Saddler, 'Indonesian Soybean Production Slips', *World Grain*, www.world-grain.com, 2 August 2021.

94 Christopher Bren d'Amour and Weston Anderson, 'International Trade and the Stability of Food Supplies in the Global South', *Environmental Research Letters*, xv/7 (2020), IOP Science, http://iopscience.iop.org, accessed 15 July 2023.

95 'The Soy Story', WWF, www.wwf.org.uk, accessed 22 August 2022.

96 Ibid.

97 Treena Hein, 'Soybeans Situation: 2021 and Beyond', *Dairy Global*, www.dairyglobal.net, 3 January 2021.

98 Rachel Moss, 'Is Tofu Really Worse than Meat for the Environment?', HuffPost, www.huffingtonpost.co.uk, 13 February 2020.

99 Kevin Coleman et al., 'The Potential for Soybean to Diversify the Production of Plant-Based Protein in the UK', *Science of The Total Environment*, DCCXVII (2021), www.sciencedirect.com, accessed 20 July 2023.

100 Amber Dance, 'Nitrogen-Fixing Bacteria Talk to Soybean Roots via Tiny RNAs, Suggesting New Avenue to Improve Yields', PNAS, www.pnas.org, 2 August 2019.

101 Ibid.

102 Angelika Hilbeck et al., 'No Scientific Consensus on GMO Safety', *Environmental Sciences Europe*, XXVII/4 (2015).

103 Marek Cuhra, 'Review of GMO Safety Assessment Studies: Glyphosate Residues in Roundup Ready Crops Is an Ignored Issue', *Environmental Sciences Europe*, XXVII/20 (2015).

104 Stephen R. Padgette et al., 'The Composition of Glyphosate-Tolerant Soybean Seeds Is Equivalent to That of Conventional Soybeans', *Journal of Nutrition*, CXXVI/3 (1996), pp. 702–16.

105 Carmen Costas-Ferreira, Rafael Durán and Lilian R. F. Faro, 'Toxic Effects of Glyphosate on the Nervous System: A Systematic Review', *International Journal of Molecular Sciences*, XXIII/9 (2022), www.ncbi.nlm.nih.gov, accessed 25 July 2023; Siriporn Thongprakaisang et al., 'Glyphosate Induces Human Breast Cancer Cells Growth via Estrogen Receptors', *Food and Chemical Toxicology*, LIX/9 (2013), pp. 129–36.

106 Thomas Bøhn and Erik Millstone, 'The Introduction of Thousands of Tonnes of Glyphosate in the Food Chain –

An Evaluation of Glyphosate Tolerant Soybeans', *Foods*, VIII/12 (2019), www.ncbi.nlm.nih.gov, accessed 25 July 2023.

107 Mary Taylor et al., 'Dicamba-Tolerant Soybeans (*Glycine max* L.) MON 87708 and MON 87708 × MON 89788 Are Compositionally Equivalent to Conventional Soybean', *Journal of Agricultural and Food Chemistry*, LXV/36 (2017), pp. 8037–45.

108 'Genetically Modified Oilseed Rape MON 94100 (MON -94100-2)', *European Parliament*, www.europarl.europa.eu, 14 March 2023.

109 Seth J. Wechsler et al., 'The Use of Genetically Engineered Dicamba-Tolerant Soybean Seeds Has Increased Quickly, Benefiting Adopters but Damaging Crops in Some Fields', *Amber Waves: The Economics of Food, Farming, Natural Resources, and Rural America*, IX/10 (2019), USDA, www.ers.usda.gov, accessed 25 July 2023.

110 Ibid.

111 Karoline Felisbino et al., 'Teratogenic Effects of the Dicamba Herbicide in Zebrafish (*Danio rerio*) Embryos', *Environmental Pollution*, CCCXXXIV/122187 (2023).

112 Ibid.

113 Chen Shen et al., 'Evaluation of Adverse Effects/Events of Genetically Modified Food Consumption: A Systematic Review of Animal and Human Studies', *Environmental Sciences Europe*, XXXIV/8 (2022), http://enveurope.springeropen.com, accessed 25 July 2023.

114 Rafael Fonseca Benevenuto et al., 'Integration of Omics Analyses into GMO Risk Assessment in Europe: A Case Study from Soybean Field Trials', *Environmental Sciences Europe*, XXXV/14 (2023).

115 Silvia Parrini et al., 'Soybean Replacement by Alternative Protein Sources in Pig Nutrition and Its Effect on Meat Quality', *Animals*, XIII/3 (2023), www.mdpi.com, accessed 25 July 2023; Patrycja Zawisza et al., 'Effects of Partial Replacement of Soybean Meal with Defatted *Hermetia illucens* Meal in the Diet of Laying Hens on Performance, Dietary Egg Quality, and Serum Biochemical and Redox Indices', *Animals*, XIII/3 (2023), www.mdpi.com, accessed 25 July 2023.

116 Arkadiusz Szpicer et al., 'The Optimization of a Gluten-Free and Soy-Free Plant-Based Meat Analogue Recipe Enriched with Anthocyanins Microcapsules', *LWT – Food Science and*

Technology, CLXVIII (2022), www.sciencedirect.com, accessed 25 July 2023.

117 J. A. Zee et al., 'Utilisation de la féverole dans la fabrication du tofu', Canadian Institute of Food Science and Technology Journal, XX/4 (1987), pp. 260–66.

118 John A. Zee et al., 'Chemical Composition and Nutritional Quality of Faba Bean (Vicia faba L. Minor) Based Tofu', Journal of Food Science, LIII/6 (1988), pp. 1772–4.

119 Ida Eriksen, 'Fava Beans Could Be the New Soy', Futurity, www.futurity.org, 15 April 2020.

120 Martin Vogelsang-O'Dwyer et al., 'Comparison of Faba Bean Protein Ingredients Produced Using Dry Fractionation and Isoelectric Precipitation: Techno-Functional, Nutritional and Environmental Performance', Foods, IX/3 (2020), www.mdpi.com, accessed 25 July 2023.

121 Eriksen, 'Fava Beans'.

122 Eva Wasney, 'Fava Beans Transformed into Tofu Thanks to Process Developed at Winnipeg's Prairie Research Kitchen', Winnipeg Free Press, www.winnipegfreepress.com, 7 May 2022.

123 'Big Mountain Foods Receives $1.4M from Canadian Gov't to Expand, Launch New Chickpea Tofu', Vegconomist, www.vegconomist.com, 13 July 2022.

124 Ibid.

125 Manisorn Silsin et al., 'Effect of Partial Replacement of Soybean with Chickpea to the Nutritional and Textural Properties of Tofu', Indonesian Food Science and Technology Journal, IV/2 (2021), pp. 27–31.

126 Julie Dixon, 'Beyond Tofu: Protein-Packed Soy Alternatives to Power Up Your Vegan Plate', One Green Planet, www.onegreenplanet.org, accessed 18 July 2023.

127 See www.livingharvest.com, accessed 21 July 2023.

128 'Peafu: Sustainable Tofu Alternative Made from Peas', Vegconomist, www.vegconomist.com, 26 April 2021.

129 Kate Williams, 'DIY Soy-Free Tofu: Yes, You Can Make Tofu from Any Bean You'd Like', KQED, www.kqed.org, 12 June 2017.

130 'Eighth Day Foods Pioneers Plant-Based Meat Substitute Lupreme for Asian Cuisines', Food Processing Technology, www.foodprocessing-technology.com, 4 May 2021.

131 Boguslav S. Kurlovick, 'The History of Lupin Domestication',
     in *Lupins: Geography, Classification, Genetic Resources and Breeding*,
     ed. Boguslav S. Kurlovich (St Petersburg and Pellosniemi, 2002),
     pp. 147–64 (p. 149).
132 Haldan Kirsch, 'Lupini: The Italian Beans That Pack a Protein
     Punch', *Tasting Table*, www.tastingtable.com, 2 February 2023.
133 Bruno Abreu, João Lima and Ada Rocha, 'Consumer Perception
     and Acceptability of Lupin-Derived Products: A Systematic
     Review', *Foods*, XII/6 (2023), www.mdpi.com, accessed 18 July 2023.
134 Smriti Shrestha et al., 'Lupin Proteins: Structure, Isolation
     and Application', *Trends in Food Science and Technology*, CXVI (2021),
     pp. 928–39.
135 Tomé Morrissy-Swan, 'Lupin Is the Latest Health-Food
     Craze – But What Is It and How Much of It Should You Eat?',
     The Telegraph, www.telegraph.co.uk, 2 July 2018.
136 V. Jayasena, W. S. Khu and S. M. Nasar-Abbas, 'The Development
     and Sensory Acceptability of Lupin-Based Tofu', *Journal of Food
     Quality*, XXXIII/1 (2010), pp. 85–97.
137 Sally Ho, 'What Are Lupin Beans? Meet the Superfood
     Transforming Vegan Food, from Milk to Meat', *Green Queen*,
     www.greenqueen.com.hk, 5 July 2022.
138 'Eighth Day Foods', *Food Processing Technology*.
139 See www.lufu.se, accessed 10 August 2022.
140 Daniel McDonald et al., 'American Gut: An Open Platform for
     Citizen Science Microbiome Research', *ASM Systems*, III/3 (2018),
     http://journals.asm.org, accessed 28 July 2023.
141 'Why Do Some People Live to Be 100? Intestinal Bacteria May
     Hold the Answer', University of Copenhagen, Faculty of Health
     and Medical Sciences, www.healthsciences.ku.dk, 31 May 2023.

RECIPES

1 Timothy Yun Hui Tsu, 'Who Cooked for Townsend Harris?
   Chinese and the Introduction of Western Foodways to *Bakumatsu*
   and Meiji Japan', *Journal of Japanese Studies*, XLVII/1 (2021),
   pp. 29–59 (pp. 55–7).
2 Randy K. Schwartz, 'Chicago, 1911: America's First Chinese
   Cookbook in English', *Repast*, XXIX/3 (2013), pp. 14–22 (p. 14).

3 Roberto A. Ferdman, 'Asian Food: The Fastest Growing Food in the World', *Washington Post*, www.washingtonpost.com, 3 February 2015.

4 TikTok Pte. Ltd. 2023. TikTok (30.5.3). [Mobile app], accessed 29 July 2023.

5 Louise Hagler, 'Layered Casserole', in *Tofu Cookery*, revd edn (Summertown, TN, 1991), p. 75.

SELECT BIBLIOGRAPHY

Aoyagi, Akiko, and William Shurtleff, *The Book of Tofu: Food for Mankind* (Brookline, MA, 1975)
Du Bois, Christine M., Chee-Beng Tan and Sidney Mintz, *The World of Soy* (Singapore, 2008)
Hagler, Louise, *The Farm Vegetarian Cookbook* (Summertown, TN, 1975)
Hall, Kenneth R., *A History of Early Southeast Asia: Maritime Trade and Societal Development, 100–1500* (Plymouth, 2011)
Nakayama, Osamu, and Sidi Osho, *Tofu Recipes: Introducing Tofu (Soy Cheese) into Traditional African Foods* (Ibadan, 1996)
Norberg, Matilda Baraibar, and Lisa Deutsch, *The Soybean through World History: Lessons for Sustainable Agrofood Systems* (Oxford and New York, 2023)

WEBSITES AND ASSOCIATIONS

Japan Tofu Association www.tofu-as.com
Plant Based Foods Association www.plantbasedfoods.org
SoyInfo Center www.soyinfocenter.com

ACKNOWLEDGEMENTS

There is a mascot in Japan created for promoting the udon noodles of Kagawa Prefecture. Called *Udon Nō*, which means 'Udon Brain', the character became a ghost with udon for brains after eating too much udon. I know how they feel. In writing this book, I think the same thing has happened with me, but with tofu. Nevertheless it would not have been possible without the help of various people along the way.

First, thank you to Eric Rath for his support and encouragement, and for introducing me to Reaktion Books in the first place. Thank you to Michael Leaman for believing I could do the job (and for his patience).

Thank you to Miranda Brown, Katarzyna Cwiertka and Hilario de Sousa for their respective linguistic and culinary correspondence with me; also Anny Gaul and Antonio Tahhan for their tenacious help in deciphering ancient Arabic and their knowledge of East-meets-West food history. Likewise, though in a more cannibalistic sense, thank you to Constance Cook, Keith Knapp and James Farrer for your advice and insight. For extra-crucial translation aid in medieval Chinese my thanks go to Xiuyuan Mi; I also have Jonathan Thacker to thank for casting his eye over my efforts in translating seventeenth-century Spanish. And thank you to Jolyon Thomas and Yuki Miyamoto for correspondence on all things *kitsune*.

Lastly, a thank you for Rebecca Saunders, without whose patience, editorial eye and support this book would not exist.

PHOTO ACKNOWLEDGEMENTS

The author and publishers wish to express their thanks to the sources listed below for illustrative material and/or permission to reproduce it. Some locations of artworks are also given below, in the interest of brevity:

Arthur M. Sackler Gallery, National Museum of Asian Art, Smithsonian Institution, Washington, DC: p. 51; Associated Press/Daisuke Urakami/ Alamy Stock Photo: p. 147; The British Museum, London: p. 150; photo Vernon Raineil Cenzon/Unsplash: p. 57; Chester Beatty, Dublin: p. 34; Harvard-Yenching Library, Harvard University, Cambridge, MA: p. 18; Hiram College Library, OH: p. 114; from Aimé Humbert, Cashel Hoey, trans., and H. W. Bates, ed., *Japan and the Japanese Illustrated* (New York, 1874), photo Robarts Library, University of Toronto: p. 153; iStock.com: p. 6 (patwallace05); Kotohiragū Shrine: p. 85; Kyoto University Museum: pp. 54–5; Library of Congress, Prints and Photographs Division, Washington, DC: p. 125; Museu Histórico da Imigração Japonesa no Brasil, São Paulo: p. 88; National Diet Library, Tokyo: pp. 110, 155; National Palace Museum, Taipei: p. 46; photo Yung-pin Pao/Pixabay: p. 59; courtesy Rudolf Pfister, Research Institute for the History of Afro-Eurasian Life Sciences, Basel (after Wenhua Chen, 'Dou fu qiyuan yu he shi 豆腐起源于何时?', *Nongye kaogu* 农业考古 (*Agricultural Archaeology*), 1991/1): p. 40; private collection: p. 82; Shanghai Museum: p. 26; Shinjo Digital Archive: p. 84; from Anna M. Stoddart, *The Life of Isabella Bird*

(London, 1906), photo Wellcome Library, London: p. 112; photos Russell Thomas: pp. 9, 11, 13, 14, 50, 53, 63, 64, 66, 67, 68, 70, 72, 86, 100, 104, 152, 166, 168, 169, 171, 172, 174, 175, 176; photo Gary Todd/Flickr (public domain): p. 39; courtesy Hiệp Trần: p. 31; The White House, Washington, DC: p. 121; Wikimedia Commons (public domain): pp. 21, 74, 126, 136 (photo Ocdp).

INDEX

Page numbers in *italic* indicate illustrations.